THE PROPER YACHT

ARTHUR BEISER

THE

PROPER

YACHT

THE MACMILLAN COMPANY

COLLIER-MACMILLAN LIMITED / LONDON

[FRONTISPIECE] *The phenomenal racing career of the Sparkman & Stephens-designed 39-foot yawl* FINISTERRE (*for example, three consecutive firsts in the Bermuda race*) *helped popularize the beamy, heavy-displacement centerboarder, which has many virtues as a cruising yacht.* (Rosenfeld)

Library of Congress Catalog Card Number: 66–18763

SECOND PRINTING 1 9 7 0

THE MACMILLAN COMPANY
866 Third Avenue, New York, N.Y. 10022
COLLIER-MACMILLAN CANADA LTD., *Toronto, Ontario*

Printed in the United States of America

TO GERMAINE

CONTENTS

DESIGNS

PREFACE

I BELIEVE THAT CRUISING UNDER SAIL is an essential part of the good life, that the best way to enjoy it is to possess a proper vessel of one's own, and that a certain amount of informed thought should be given to the choice of this vessel. The basic purpose of this book is to bring out and discuss those aspects of cruising-yacht design and construction that are relevant to someone seeking such a yacht, whether a small, handy gunkholer for coastwise cruising or a big, powerful craft for deep-sea passages to the ends of the earth.

A lot of the charm of sailing lies in the diversity of how and in what it can be done, but nobody can make an intelligent choice without being aware of the alternatives. Today the advent of mass-produced boats and the popularity of distance racing under handicaps set by arbitrary rules have given the majority of new sailboats a uniformity that may well lead a newcomer to feel that sailboat design has reached its natural limit, that the boat to get is the standard kind one now sees everywhere. To be sure, the latter is excellent in many respects, but it is also deficient in as many others, and the sensible way to go about seeking a proper cruiser is to begin by formulating one's own requirements and not by wandering through a boat show with checkbook in hand. I feel that a prospective owner should first decide how big a boat is right for him, what the best rig for it is, how it is to be laid out on deck and below, and so on. Armed with this design concept, he can then sally forth into the real world to see whether it is in principle possible of fulfillment and, if so, whether he can afford it. The actual designs should be left to the naval architect and the actual construction to the builder; if they are capable and conscientious, the result will be a thing of beauty, a companion in youth, and a comfort in age—at any rate, a proper cruising yacht, which is compliment enough.

Neither completeness nor infallibility will be found in the pages that follow, but I do claim to be honest in what I say. I am sure that I am horribly mistaken here and shamefully prejudiced there, but at least the mistakes are without motive and the prejudices have their roots in actual events. I have enjoyed messing about in boats, but I find it more fun in proper boats than in poor ones, and I hope that this book will help make it possible for the novice to find the proper boat for himself without unnecessary grief along the way. I do not want to seem discouraging, but the fact is that the proper yacht does not come into being by itself, and only by meticulous attention can one get exactly what one wants. There are just as many crooks and incompetents in the yacht business as in any other, and it is only realistic to be aware of this. Even honorable and skillful men can overlook things, and the best way to help them to do their best is to be skeptical of everything, to ask questions and investigate other approaches, to inquire constantly how easy it will be to get at this device for repairs (*everything* will need repairs eventually—and normally at the least convenient time) or whether that fitting will bear a man's weight hurled against it in a seaw_y.

In choosing the designs presented in the body of the book, I have tried to arrive at as wide a selection of types and sizes as might fit my definition of the proper cruiser: a fast, handsome, seaworthy sailboat capable of ocean passages, one that a man and his maid can live aboard indefinitely yet sail coastwise by themselves. Certainly sweet little *Coppelia* would not be everybody's first choice for crossing the Atlantic, nor sturdy *Angantyr* everybody's first choice for exploring Penobscot Bay; but among the boats illustrated, something to suit nearly every taste and appetite will be found. And I think every one of the boats is worth examining for the innovations and felicities it contains, which may well be of use in a different setting.

No attempt was made to be anything other than representative in assembling the various designs, and they are to be regarded as a kind of sampler and not as a complete catalog of what is possible. All the same, there are extremely light boats here and extremely heavy ones, overrigged boats and underrigged ones, overpowered boats and underpowered ones, 60-footers meant for two and 30-footers meant for six, motor sailers and ocean racers—and quite a number between these extremes. Every boat was picked by its designer as an example of his current thinking in cruising yachts; and I think that in the right hands, each is able to furnish more joy than a landlubber would imagine any mere object could. I make no apology for showing the work of only seventeen designers, for among them are the world's best, and their boats include examples of all major styles of sailing yacht architecture. But there are at least as many other designers of great distinction, and one of the latter might do a better job on a specific design concept.

For convenience in making comparisons, all dimensions are given in feet and inches, all weights in pounds, all capacities in U.S. gallons. Sail areas are based on 100 percent of each foretriangle. A quantity I have avoided is tonnage, because there are at least six methods of computing the tonnage of a yacht. My own Alden ketch, *Minots Light,* has a displacement fully loaded of 32 short tons, 29 metric tons, or 28.6 long tons; she has a Thames tonnage of 42, and her documents state that her gross tonnage is 26.5 and her net tonnage 24. I usually give the highest figure when I want to impress somebody and the lowest figure to toll collectors, so maybe there is point to having so many systems in use. While a fairly complete description of each boat is given, many items are usually optional, and another boat of the same design could well have a different engine, larger or smaller tankage, a different accommodation, and so on. Listed engines use gasoline unless otherwise noted.

I have learned a great deal from various books, both accounts of cruises and treatises on yachts as such. In fact, I came to sailing in the first place via the printed page, and I still find pleasure and instruction in the words of Joshua Slocum, William

Albert Robinson, Uffa Fox, Irving and Electa Johnson, George Millar, H. W. Tilman, Peter Pye, Ernle Bradford, and many others. Four books I have found unusually informative on matters of interest to anyone contemplating buying a new
yacht are *Offshore,* by John H. Illingworth; *Skene's Elements of Yacht Design,*
revised by Francis S. Kinney; *Sailing Theory and Practice,* by C. A. Marchaj; and
Practical Yacht Construction, by C. J. Watts and K. H. C. Jurd. A number of
significant topics are not treated in any of these books, and I disagree violently with
some statements in each, but I have no doubt that their respective authors will have
equal qualms about what appears in these pages.

One omission I regret is some sort of listing of reliable fittings and equipment.
The trouble is that such a listing is valueless unless it is reasonably comprehensive;
but my experience, even when combined with that of friends whose opinion I respect, is too limited. My General Motors diesel is satisfactory, but it is too large
for many boats, and for all I know, others of the same size may be still better. I am
happy with my Edson bilge pump, my Samson braided line, my Ideal windlass, and
my Danforth-White compass, but I might be happier yet with others. Equally useful,
and equally difficult to compile, would be a list of junk to avoid. When I read of a
mast going over the side because of a defective turnbuckle, I always wonder who
manufactured it. When I hear of a man's face being smashed in because a winch pawl
let go, I want to know what winch it was. The yachting press never says. Recently
the owner of a certain yawl received a splendid trophy for proceeding on to England
after his craft lost its rudder when it was two-thirds of the way across the Atlantic
(most of us lesser mortals would have said the hell with it at that point and taken a
cab home); it would be most interesting to know the origin of the defect involved.
Another desirable list would be of apparatus that can be repaired if it should fail. I
have had no trouble finding competent mechanics for my main engine, but my
Yanmar auxiliary generator had baffled mechanics in New York, Virginia, Florida,
Scotland, Holland, Sweden, and Denmark until I finally sold it for £2 as a dinghy
mooring in England. I have finally joined the legion of satisfied owners of Bendix
automatic pilots, but only because I myself finally found the trouble that, after four
years of "expert" servicing, had yielded only bills. I suspect I have been unlucky, but
I feel that luck should not be a consideration. All I can suggest is that nothing whatever be taken on faith and that one should take pains to seek actual users of gear
one has in mind and find out the score after a year or more of service. There are so
many really fine boats around, so much truly superb gear on the market, that to
have anything less is a pity; and I am sorry that I cannot give explicit advice on
what to get.

I have confined the book to single-hulled vessels. Where do catamarans (and
trimarans) fit into the picture? At their best, these exciting craft make possible long
passages under sail at speeds as high as 25 knots on stable platforms that are
relatively cheap for the space they provide. At their worst, they turn over—and
stay over. These two extremes summarize the arguments for and against big cruising
multihulls, but actually neither is quite fair. No large cat or tri has yet been quite as
successful as the propaganda from the West Coast would indicate. Even the best
cats are either fast enough but have hulls too narrow and too sensitive to weight to
make good cruisers or else roomy and able to carry the desired loads but disappointing under way. That is, even on their own terms, multihulls have not yet been

developed to the point that orthodox cruising sailboats have reached: the latter are today very close (except for cost) to what their proponents hope them to be. But if multihulls are not that wonderful for cruising, neither are they necessarily so dangerous; the danger of turning turtle is perhaps exaggerated and capable of being minimized to an acceptable point. To me, cruising catamarans and trimarans are still experimental craft whose development I watch with interest, but I cannot see them quite yet as fitting into the category of a proper cruising yacht.

Once upon a time I worried about whether my savings would not better be invested in a house than in a sailboat. Then I read certain magical words by Arthur Ransome, acquired the sailboat, and have lived happily ever after. The words are these, from *Racundra's First Cruise:* "Houses are but badly built boats so firmly aground that you cannot think of moving them. They are definitely inferior things, belonging to the vegetable not the animal world, rooted and stationary, incapable of gay transition. . . . The desire to build a house is the tired wish of a man content thenceforward with a single anchorage. The desire to build a boat is the desire of youth, unwilling yet to accept the idea of a final resting place. . . . When it comes, the desire to build a boat is one of those that cannot be resisted. It begins as a little cloud on a serene horizon. It ends by covering the whole sky, so that you can think of nothing else. You must build to regain your freedom." Precisely so.

A.B.

Palma, Mallorca
June, 1966

THE PROPER YACHT

CHAPTER ONE

The Proper Yacht

I START FROM THE PREMISE that no object created by man is as satisfying to his body and soul as a proper sailing yacht. The most splendid structure—building, bridge, statue—is still a static thing, immobile and unresponsive to nature and man alike, while even so perfect a vehicle as a rocket fulfills its destiny in only a single quick spurt. What other than a cruising sailboat is at once so lovely to look at, so exhilarating to travel on, and so comfortable to live aboard?

So varied and intense are the pleasures of cruising under sail that no summary is possible. But there are moments that stand out in the memory, moments that can be recaptured year after year until the end of one's days, each time as fresh as the first. I remember a hard day's sail on the coast of Maine under a gray and angry sky. At dusk we found a lonely cove with wooded shores, deserted and wholly apart from what has come to be called civilization. The anchor bit firmly in a mud bottom, and I took the riding light from its locker, plugged it in, turned it on, and secured it to the forestay. Alone on deck, nostrils filled with the mingled odors of the sea, pine trees, and dinner, I watched the fog roll in before descending to the food and drink, women and music that waited below.

Other moments leap to mind, many of them in which I recall myself streaming the log at the start of a passage. Over it goes, the line is paid out, and, after hesitating briefly, the flywheel begins to spin. A glance at the shore, a smile to my wife at the helm, and I go below to enter the departure. To me the laconic line "5/28; 1720 EDT; log 0; course 135°M; wind 10S; whistler R2 south of Martha's Vineyard" is far more vivid and full of emotion than the final line of the same record: "6/18; 0200 GMT; log 2996; course 90°M; wind 3SW; Dubh Artach light, Scotland, off port bow." And there are moments while under way that somehow stand out from the rest: in the Bahamas, watching my eldest daughter steer the boat for the first time; in Maine, every time I spied the mountains of Mount Desert Island from the west; in a November Atlantic gale off Virginia, my first experience of coping with serious weather; in Scotland, sailing down the Sound of Mull; in Finland, approaching Utö in a luminous afternoon fog. The list of such moments is long and grows longer each year, and for me they explain the lure of cruising far more than any chronicle of distances sailed or places visited.

A sailing yacht is but a thing, dead as a doornail, yet it is impossible to regard it as a mere lump of wood and metal. A proper yacht actually seems to respond to its master and crew, matching their ambitions and moods with its own behavior. On a sparkling sunny day it will leap forward in a shower of spray, a joyous steed eager to press forward; on a gray and dreary day it will advance more steadily, offering warmth and comfort within; on a stormy night it will look after itself and its crew, standing up to the wind and rising to meet the seas that rush upon it. A romantic conception? Certainly, but everything about cruising under sail is romantic and quite divorced from pragmatic reality. Bald truth is bracing, but shimmering illusion has its delights too, and each has its place in life.

There are many requirements a sailboat must fulfill to be really satisfactory: it must be seaworthy, fast, easily handled, and so on. But these are the barest minima. To my mind, unless one's spirit soars at the sight of a boat, unless one instantly sees oneself at its helm under a blue sky with porpoises leaping alongside, it just won't do. Some vessels have this quality under all circumstances, others are at their best only when meticulously kept, and still others require a certain disarray to bring out their charms. But without it, all is lost. As a matter of fact, this criterion turns out to be a pretty realistic one, because a vessel that is the result of enough care on the part of designer and builder to stir one's blood on first acquaintance is unlikely to be a total pig.

I believe that of all the elements that go into a proper yacht, the one that should never be compromised is beauty. No matter what the design concept, no matter what the list of specific requirements, the hand of an artist can produce a handsome boat, harmonious alike to the eye and the sea. The yacht architects I know are all careful men, anxious to do an honest job of work; but some of them are simply incapable of drawing an inelegant line, while others, under the delusion that beauty stems solely from function, create boats that make one want to weep. If one is in the fortunate position of looking around for a designer, I would say, first of all, be sure that the candidates being considered are men of sensitivity and spirit —the former quality to assure that whatever they do will show grace and the latter to assure that they will not permit the crotchets of owner or racing formula to distort their vision.

In recent years the drawing boards of the United States and Scandinavia have been perhaps more consistent in producing good-looking sailboats than those elsewhere. That is only one man's opinion, of course, but I note that George Millar, a distinguished English yachtsman, wrote recently: "Today in yacht design the French copy British uglinesses; the high uncouth silhouettes, often hump-backed, the parsimonious sail plans, the sawn-off counters, the grotesque farmyard railings right round the narrow decks. Meanwhile the Americans (of all peoples) continue to design, to buy, and to sail the world's beautiful new yachts. In this the cleverest Americans seem to be as conservative as the Dutch, who preserve the subtle lines of their cumbersome shoal-draft types. The glorious thing is that the Americans, sticking to sheer, to drawn-out elegance of bow and counter, to bowsprits, and to beam that gives even a racing hull the attraction of a brood mare, still achieve the pace and win the races."

I think this last comment deserves emphasis, because the standard justification for the ugly boat has been that beauty and speed are incompatible. (An echo perhaps of Leo Durocher's dictum that "nice guys finish last"?) Certainly no other designer has been more consistent at turning out prizewinners than Olin Stephens, yet whatever sacrifices have had to be made to achieve this record do not include that of beauty. The Royal Ocean Racing Club rating rule is customarily blamed for encouraging monstrosity, and this is partly true, but fine-looking boats designed by a variety of architects have nevertheless been able to clean up regularly in Europe. In Scandinavia, which uses the RORC rule, lovely craft are almost universal. My friend Aage Utzon, the dean of Danish yacht architects, has turned out scores of jewellike double-enders that do well in both American and European racing. So there is no excuse for an ugly sailboat, and every reason to insist that a vessel meeting almost any reasonable set of requirements, including racing ability, be a pleasure to the eye as well.

The word "almost" is a necessary qualification because there is one class of vessel that seems doomed to homeliness. This is the small (say, with an under 30-ft waterline) light-displacement boat. John Illingworth has nicely summarized the arguments in favor of such vessels: "For a given amount of material one gets more boat, and a faster boat, by going light. And the size of the rig needed is roughly in proportion to the displacement, so in this respect too the lighter boat is easier to work, costs less to build, and much less to maintain, since replacements of rigging and sail are smaller." True, it is much more difficult to design a light-displacement boat that is comfortable at sea and as easy to handle as a heavier one, but it *can* be done, so one cannot condemn the type out of hand. Still, my heart always sinks when I see a skinny, humpbacked, short-ended boat with a grotesquely small sail plan for its size bobbling around in rippled water that should hardly disturb a rowboat. I am unable to clear from my mind the feeling that such boats result from the putrefaction of more normal ones, the gases of decay having bloated shapely hulls into pitiful blobs.

In larger vessels, light displacement pays off better, both in less severe punishment to crews at sea and in appearance. *Outlaw,* for instance, is a very light cutter 39 ft on the waterline, that is, I would say, an almost melodramatically handsome boat. It is interesting that *Outlaw* was designed by Illingworth and Primrose, so one can be sure that no pains were spared to extract the maximum in racing efficiency and the minimum RORC rating compatible with it—indeed, *Outlaw* won the Class I points championship of the RORC in 1963. Despite this unpromising pedigree, *Outlaw* is both pleasing to the eye and exhilarating to the spirit. To be sure, there are things that would have to be changed to make *Outlaw* into a proper cruiser, but there is no reason why they could not be done without altering the distinctive flavor of the boat.

There is no single "perfect" yacht. Not only do different people have different tastes, but a number of very different craft may satisfy the same man. In essence, every sailboat design represents a compromise, and it is not always clear whether the best boat results from the most equal compromise, which might mean mediocrity

[OVERLEAF] *The all-aluminum yawl* ONDINE, *designed by William Tripp, is well able to face the most severe weather. Her dimensions are LOA 57 ft 6 in., LWL 38 ft, beam 14 ft, and draft 8 ft 1 in., and her sail area is 1521 ft². Inverted U-shaped rails on both sides of the mainmast are a valuable feature.* (Beken)

in all respects, or from a biased compromise in which one or two elements are given preference. It is easy to forgive a fast, responsive craft that is a thrill to sail its particular deficiencies, but it is hard to love a characterless one intended to offer something to everyone but not much to anyone. This latter fault is most common among stock boats meant to have the same wide appeal as, say, station wagons—and, like station wagons, they are all very well in their place, but their place is not in the heart.

Speed is not the only desirable attribute, of course. Ease of handling is another, a convenient label for a variety of requirements. An easily handled boat is more than just one whose sheets and halyards are so arranged that a small crew can sail her efficiently. Also desirable is a well-balanced hull that makes the boat manageable in all weathers and under all sail combinations: it is nice to be able to maneuver under main or jib alone and, in a divided rig, to be able simply to drop the main in deteriorating weather without having to alter course. Stability also enters here, since a boat that has to be reefed or has to have its headsails changed constantly is a pain in the neck, roller reefing or not. A boat that achieves speed only because it carries an oversized cloud of canvas aloft is a poor choice for anything but an afternoon sail on a nice day.

I would be the last to leave comfort out of any list of plus features. There are many things that contribute to comfort afloat: a sunken cockpit with a spray hood or an extended deckhouse roof at its forward end, a cabin heater that works in bad weather, berths of the proper width with high bunk boards, a galley that can be used under way, a roomy head, and so on. However, the most important single element in comfort at sea and in port is size—a big boat is more comfortable than a small one, period. Since a big boat is also faster than a small one and, up to a certain point, easier to handle, the odds favor a large vessel as the one to get. Two things alone should limit the size of one's boat: the minimum crew needed to handle it and the minimum bank account needed to purchase and maintain it. The latter is unquestionably the more potent factor. I think the feeblest and most decrepit couple able to sail a 30-footer will find a 40-footer of comparable pedigree to be easier to handle and easier on them. Do I hear mutterings about the area of the sails? If a 40-ft sloop is too much to cope with, surely the same size ketch cannot fail to present less of a problem than a 30-ft sloop. Might not the anchor be too heavy? While I hardly regard it as normally necessary in a 40-footer, an electric winch makes light work of anchor handling in any boat that can be managed under sail by two people—up to, say, 55 to 60 ft overall.

Choosing a yacht is by no means a simple or straightforward process if one seeks the perfect boat for oneself. Beauty, certainly; seaworthiness, of course; speed, naturally. But should it be the elegant beauty of the 12-meter sloop, whose breathtaking grace is apparent to everybody, or the complex beauty of the fat centerboarder, whose lines require an educated eye to appreciate? Should speed be obtained at the cost of tenderness, so that frequent reefing and sail changing will be called for, or are concessions to comfort and sloth worth the sacrifice of speed in light airs? Alas, these are not questions that can be decided in the abstract; and, as when one ponders marriage, they call for a degree of self-knowledge hard to summon up just when it is needed most.

An initial approach is to inquire into the role in one's inner life that the yacht is supposed to fulfill. Do I seek the sense of virility that comes from sailing a

(TEXT CONTINUED ON PAGE 17)

[I]

Two Minimum Sloops:
COPPELIA & LENE

THOUGH OPINIONS DIFFER ON JUST WHAT the lower limit of size for a proper cruising yacht is, these two sloops are surely very close to it. This does not mean that they are not fine boats, for in fact they are, but simply that while it is possible to squeeze a quart of accommodations into a pint pot of hull, the hull is still a pint pot and cannot offer the comfort and speed at sea plus the room and facilities in port that a larger one provides as a matter of course. The attraction of a capsule yacht lies in its price, but it is essential to keep in mind that for real cruising (not day sailing or racing), too small a vessel simply won't do. *Coppelia* and

Lene seem to me to be right on the border line —most people would find a long cruise or a sea passage in a smaller boat tolerable only by muttering a slight variation of Coué's famous formula ("Day by day, in every way, I am getting less and less miserable," repeated hourly), while they would be able to take more positive pleasure from a similar journey in a larger boat. So boats like these two—and apart from size, which is not their fault, they are handsome and able craft—are a natural starting point in any examination of yacht designs for proper cruising.

COPPELIA

Coppelia IS A YACHT with so much charm that even if her designer, Bruno Veronese, had not intended her for himself, the feeling that she was his little darling would surely have occurred to him sooner or later as he pondered her lines and worked out her plans. I cannot say exactly why a boat of the size and type of *Coppelia* should be so appealing, but I owned one very like her when I was young, and I have nothing but affectionate memories. Perhaps it is the honesty and directness of the concept behind her: a fast, well-mannered, seaworthy

boat of traditional appearance and wooden construction (though modern enough to make use of laminated frames and glued planking) that has accommodations for just two, the right number. True, *Coppelia* has a pipe cot up forward, but I prefer to think of it as meant for her owner's firstborn and not for some burly intruder.

Coppelia's sail plan shows the headstay terminating below the masthead, the only place where one might wish that her designer had compromised with tradition, since a full masthead rig would be a lot easier to handle. Her basic sail area seems on the scant side even though her hull is reasonably easy to drive, and in some parts of the world, more would be de-sirable. One of the nice things about a hull of this sort is that a small engine can push it right along, and the two yachts so far built from *Coppelia*'s design have been able to cruise at 6

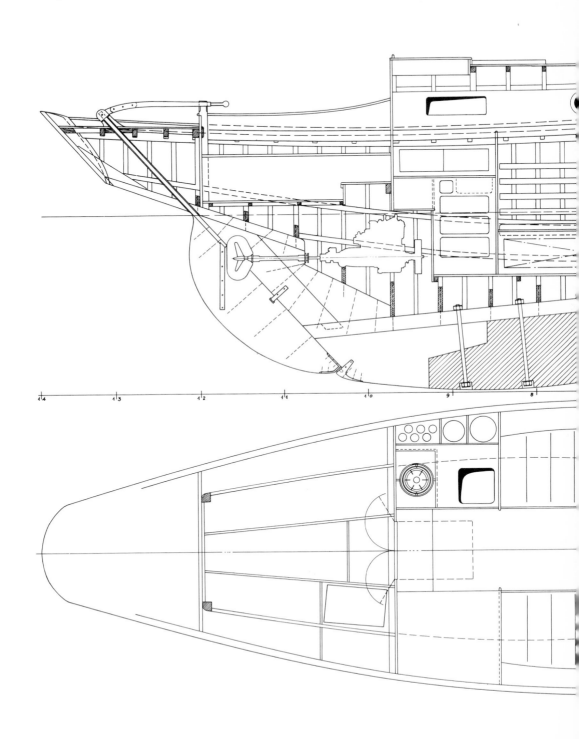

knots with, respectively, a 10-hp Albin gasoline engine and 12-hp D.M.V. diesel. A particularly noteworthy advantage of the straight cabin house is that a small pram can be carried on it without being too much in the way.

The accommodation is utterly simple and comfortable, the result of having a crew of only two in mind. There is a compact galley to port

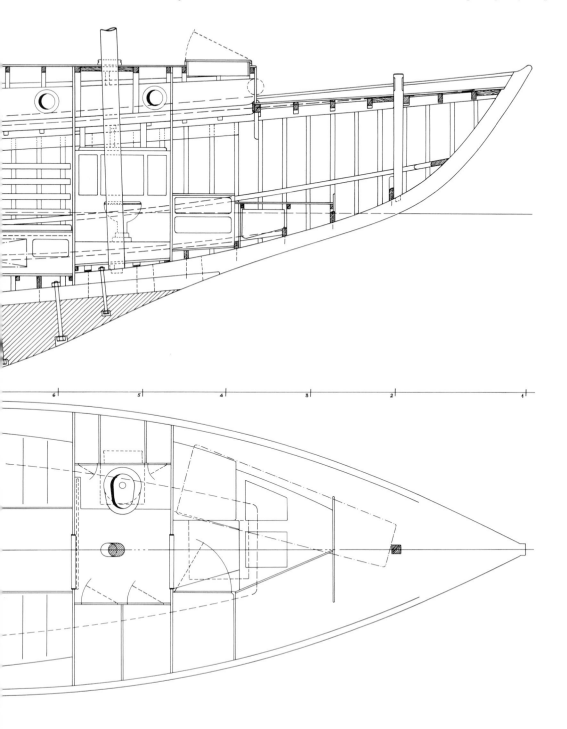

IBIS BIS *is a sister ship of* COPPELIA, *a 30-ft sloop designed by Bruno Veronese.*

and a chart table with an icebox under it to starboard. Then come two settee berths, and the head extends across the ship forward of a sliding door. The mast is in just the right spot to be of help in a seaway. Forward of the head is a fine storage compartment that will hold enough personal and boat gear for a long cruise. All in all, an attractive, wholesome little boat, but very close to rock bottom in size for its intended purpose.

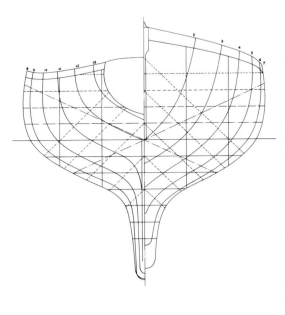

COPPELIA

DESIGNER *Bruno Veronese, Via Capo Santa Chiara, 25, Genoa, Italy*

LOA   30 ft 10 in.

LWL   23 ft

BEAM   8 ft 6 in.

DRAFT   4 ft 11 in.

DISPLACEMENT   10,300 lb

BALLAST   4,500 lb of iron

SAIL AREA   400 ft²

ENGINE   Albin (10 hp) or D.M.V. diesel (12 hp)

WATER   25 gal

CONSTRUCTION   Glued mahogany planking on locust frames, with oak and iroko centerline structure; canvas-covered plywood deck and mahogany deckworks; spruce spars

LENE

EVERY YACHT ARCHITECT OF TALENT EVOLVES a type of vessel that is the natural expression of his ideas and aesthetic feelings, and in time its proportions approach a kind of logical perfection, a refinement with no discordant notes or loose ends that no wholly new design can hope for. Aage Utzon has been fashioning beamy double-enders for many years, and his lovely boats are found all over the world even though their typically Scandinavian character, like aquavit and saunas, remains for the most part a special taste far from their Baltic home. *Lene* is one of the most recent Utzon creations, and it is sad that no two-dimensional representation can do justice to her elegant form. On the sail plan, for instance, the deckhouse may seem high, but in the flesh its shape and position are such that the structure fits in with the rest of the boat in an entirely natural manner.

The rig is tall, narrow, and efficient, and with the mainsheet leading from the boom end because of the roller reefing that is fitted, the vang tackle shown is a necessity. A tapered batten brings the mainsail track out from the mast some distance above the boom in order to make reefing easier. The stainless-steel tube on

the foredeck has three functions in all: it is a bitt for making fast dock and anchor lines, it is a ventilator for the forepeak (an adjustable cap can be used to close it off) and it has a tang for securing the tack of the spinnaker staysail. The deck is teak laid in narrow strakes for maximum strength and watertightness.

The cockpit is all the way aft, as is necessary with an outboard rudder controlled by a tiller, but *Lene*'s beautifully rounded stern is buoyant enough to support several people there without squatting. The full hull lines provide a good amount of space in the accommodation despite the over-all length of only 29 ft. Flanking the companionway are two quarter berths, while underneath the steps is the engine box. In back of the top step is the compass, which is visible from the cockpit through a small window, while not in the way on deck or below. To starboard is an adequate galley, and to port is a dinette that can be converted into a double berth. The table doubles as a chart table, and a drawer under it is large enough to hold a fair number of charts. Forward are an enclosed head to port and a locker to starboard; if the mast were stepped on the keel instead of on deck, the head door would not be wide enough, which shows how helpful stepping the mast on deck can be in small boats. There are two berths and a small hanging locker in the forepeak. Though *Lene* can "sleep six," two or three of them had better be children if all are to have adequate room once they leave their berths. But no law requires as many aboard as there are berths, and unoccupied forward or quarter berths in vessels of this size are always welcome for stowage.

Displacing only 9,260 lb on a waterline of 24 ft 1 in., *Lene* is not heavy, and her sail area of 430 ft² should be enough to give her satisfactory performance under sail. *Lene*'s beam of 9 ft is a big help in her layout below—a foot less beam and an altogether different arrange-ment would have been required—and gives her enough stability to cope with her tall rig despite the modest draft of 4 ft 9½ in. At the same time, she is not too fat to sail well, as anyone who has seen similar boats from Utzon's board can testify. Construction is first class, with laminated frames and stem and edge-glued mahogany planking. In hulls of this size and shape, Utzon prefers really substantial floors on every third frame instead of smaller ones more closely spaced, and this practice has worked out well. *Lene* is a little thoroughbred from a distinguished stable, and it is not surprising that a very successful fiberglass version of her, called *Sagitta,* is being manufactured in Denmark.

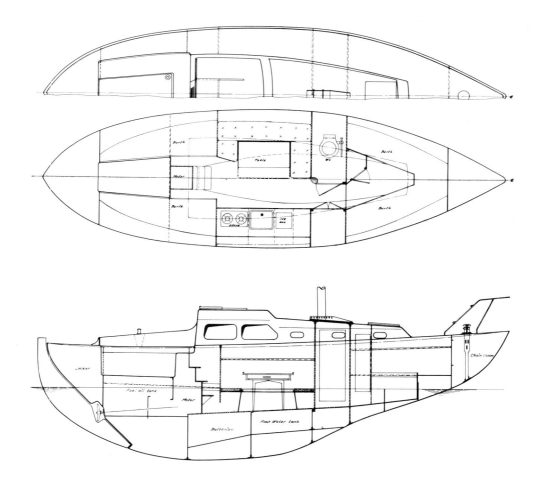

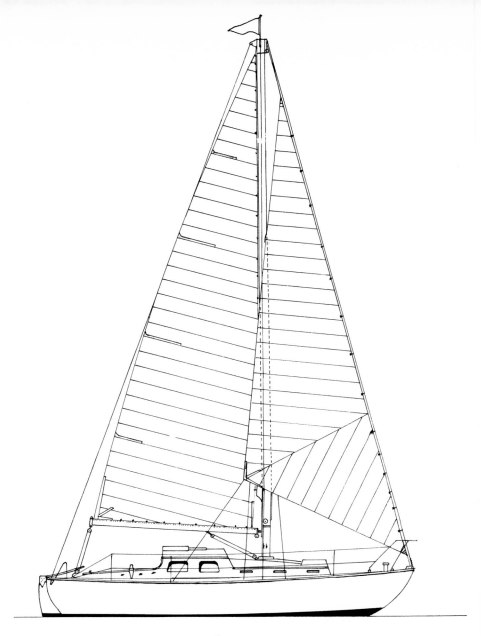

LENE

DESIGNER *Aage Utzon, Hellebaek, Denmark*

LOA 29 ft

LWL 24 ft 1 in.

BEAM 9 ft

DRAFT 4 ft 9½ in.

DISPLACEMENT 9,260 lb

BALLAST 4,160 lb of lead

SAIL AREA 430 ft^2

ENGINE 15-hp gasoline or diesel

CONSTRUCTION Glued mahogany planking on laminated oak frames, with laminated-oak center-line structure; teak deck and deck-works; spruce spars

(TEXT CONTINUED FROM PAGE 8)

swift, rapierlike vessel hard on the wind in a shower of spray? Or the feeling of adventure provided by the well-proportioned, well-found craft that is ready at a moment's notice to sail to Tahiti or Patagonia? Or the illusion of security and escape from the torments of the shore given by the plain, heavy, stolid lines of the "character" boat that derives from the vanished age of commercial sail? Or, perhaps, is my ego so frail that I must ride upon a monstrosity that proclaims my daring, my originality, my willingness to risk all in flamboyant experiment?

Finding the perfect yacht is well worth the effort. I can still summon up in my mind's eye the picture of a handsome black schooner reaching slowly toward Camden, Maine, late one August afternoon some years ago. Watching from the cockpit of my small cutter, *Nipinke,* I remember thinking how happy must be the man at the helm of the schooner to achieve such harmony with his surroundings, for surely the Camden hills at dusk call for a black schooner sailing before them. The boat was *Malabar II,* designed by John Alden and built in 1922, and I was not surprised to learn later that she had become so much a part of the life of her current owner that, in 1955, he replaced her aging hull with a new but otherwise identical one. An unusual thing to do, perhaps, but how often in life does one find perfection?

Having searched one's soul, the next step is to try to assess in a realistic way just how the yacht will be used. What will suit a weekend sailor on Long Island Sound or The Solent will hardly do for the man who has the time and yen for distant voyages, and vice versa. But here one must proceed cautiously, for a wonderful boat, like a wonderful woman, can open vistas not dreamt of on first meeting. I bought my ketch, *Minots Light,* to enjoy nothing more ambitious than living aboard during the summer while cruising casually along the New England coast; but I write these words in Spain, hardly five years later, after a transatlantic passage and thousands of miles of sailing in European waters. And all too common is the man who wants and buys a "pure cruising boat" and later curses himself for a fool and the designer for a knave when the boat turns out to have a Cruising Club of America or RORC rating a fraction too high for the boat to win the races that, mysteriously, now obsess the owner.

It is right here that self-knowledge pays off. Life is short, and there is no time to spare in making good use of its blessings, yet I have seen (and coveted) a perfectly grand ocean cruiser used exclusively for afternoon sailing by a man who constantly feels cheated and angry because Thistles sail circles around him at times, while in the same harbor is moored a converted 8-meter whose owner yearns to go offshore but has no stomach for it in that vessel. Each man is the captive of two visions, one of the kind of boat he must possess and one of the kind of sailing he wants to do, and it is unfortunate that in each case the visions are incompatible. Maybe psychoanalysis is the answer, or maybe there is no answer, but often some degree of psychic compromise can be attained without compromising the true nature of the yacht. And a really wonderful boat has the power to make its owner devote himself to getting the best out of it, whatever that best happens to be.

So it is poor advice to anybody to recommend that he seek out a boat that is exactly suited to the kind of sailing he thinks he is likely to do. A sailing yacht is not a truck, after all, and its primary purpose is dream fulfillment. If one yearns to sail to the South Seas, then, by God, one should have a boat that can take one there. After all, the fellow in the Thistle is the one who should be consumed with

SILVIO *going to windward in threatening weather during a race. Under the same conditions a proper cruising yacht would sail at least as fast but at a smaller angle of heel, and would not have to cope with so wretched a creation as a double-clewed genoa. This is not meant as a criticism of* SILVIO, *which after all is providing spectators with an exciting spectacle, but only to emphasize that the best cruiser and the best racer usually have very little indeed in common.* (Beken)

envy, not the man in a vessel capable of going around the world. It all depends upon whether one lives primarily in the present or in the future. A characteristic of all proper cruising boats is that they are so satisfying to the spirit that their faults are forgiven: if you love your wife, you will not be distraught at her inability to make cherry pie—though, of course, it is easier to love a woman skilled at cherry pies in the first place.

Not so many years ago, racing boats were racing boats, unfit for the sea and not adapted to living aboard, while cruising boats were ugly and slow, on the theory that beauty and sailing performance detract from seaworthiness. Then came the growth of offshore racing, surely the most glorious sport of all, calling as it does on one's every reserve of nerve, intelligence, skill, experience, endurance, and money. Combining the better features of the older boats of both kinds, the ocean racers developed from the 1930's on exploited the construction materials and methods of their times to the limit. Today the majority of sailboats more than, say, 30 ft in over-all length are in reality racing-cruising vessels, with the balance perhaps tipped a bit one way or the other in each case. In general, this has been a wholesome trend, making it possible for the racing man also to taste the pleasures of cruising, while assuring the cruising man that his vessel has the sheer strength and seaworthiness required for ocean racing built into it. However, racing considerations have become more and more important in recent years, largely because the intense competition permits no halfway approach. Design conflicts are now almost always resolved in favor of more efficient racing or lower CCA or RORC ratings. In 1934 Uffa Fox could write with perfect justice that "the best ocean racer is the best cruiser," but all one has to do is step aboard a typical contemporary flat-out ocean racer to see that this statement is nonsense these days. What this means is that the man in search of a proper cruising boat must keep a careful eye out to get what he wants, which is not always the same as what a racing skipper whose regular crew is equal in number and heft to the Green Bay Packers would choose.

While this book is solely concerned with yachts for cruising under sail, it is still impossible to avoid the influence of racing. Various rating formulas have been devised whose purpose is to handicap yachts of different sizes and types so that they can race against one another on an equitable basis. In theory, these formulas are not supposed to dominate design but are intended to serve merely as yardsticks for assessing the potential speed of the boat. Ha! Except where such patently nonracing craft as motor sailers and oversize vessels are concerned, I think it is fair to say that the CCA and RORC rules have influenced yacht architects quite as much as has Old Man Neptune himself. It is customary to pay tribute to the framers of these rules, for they are certainly honorable and conscientious men, but the results speak for themselves: by and large, American boats look almost identical, while the European fleet, which shows somewhat more diversity, contains a disproportionate number of freaks that are uncomfortable both at sea and in port. In America, really fast boats—for instance, that whole class of light boats with long waterlines and high, narrow rigs, offering excellent performance, easy handling, and relatively low costs—are given the compliment of such high ratings that they cannot hope to compete against their tubbier sisters. In Europe, at the other extreme, beam and shoal draft are looked upon with ill favor, though designers should be free to use their discretion regarding these factors. Despite the benevolent intentions of their framers, the rules are far from perfect, and it is particularly unfortunate that their inevitable biases appear to be accidental and not directed, as they could legitimately have been, toward greater comfort, convenience, and beauty.

In a way, the worst aspect of the racing influence has been the tendency to base designs on the assumption of a large, able crew. Today's ocean racer gives the helmsman a cockpit of his own so that he can concentrate on his task free from the hurly-burly of the tigers manning the winches. Splendid—but not much fun for cruising: the helmsman is trapped in his little hole and cannot help with the usual cockpit chores while under sail. (Moreover, two abbreviated cockpits make it rather difficult to stretch out in the sun.) I once owned a hot sloop that put the helmsman at the forward end of the cockpit with the sheet winches well behind him, which was fine for racing—we did nicely, thank you—but perfectly ridiculous for shorthanded cruising. I believe that all rating rules should incorporate a factor specifying a bonus or a penalty depending upon the size of the crew required relative to the size of the boat. A suitable basic number might be based upon sail area—so many men per 100 ft². Or maybe the number of men should depend upon the boat's displacement or waterline length or some combination of the two.

Rating formulas have the delightful habit of changing from time to time. On the whole, the trend has been toward fairer formulas, so that, for instance, the current CCA rule determines stability by actually measuring righting moment instead of by relying upon the ballast-displacement ratio (and so, suddenly, the construction of water tanks of ½-in. steel plate and 1,000-lb mast steps has ceased as if by magic), while the current RORC rule penalizes graceful overhangs less harshly than the old one. Among racing men who are in the habit of having boats designed and built solely to exploit weaknesses in a particular rule, any changes represent an affront, and their complaints about the unfairness of it all are most gratifying to those of us who regard the existence of slow, ugly, uncomfortable sailboats as a disgrace no matter how favorable their ratings. I think rating formulas should be changed annually to keep people from building rule beaters—unless, somehow, the formulas employ coefficients that favor beauty, comfort, economy of cost and crew, and other "irrelevancies." E. Farnham Butler has proposed an excellent idea in this regard. He thinks that there should be several formulas, each favoring a different style of boat, and that which formula is to govern the handicaps for a given race should be announced only at the start of the race. The likelihood of any of these sporting suggestions actually being adopted is, alas, very close to zero.

To be sure, the cruising man can often make good use of his racing counterpart's preoccupation with The Rule. For instance, I gather that the latest version of the CCA rule is a trifle kinder to sloops than to yawls and to keelboats than to centerboarders, both the reverse of the previous version; so if I were in the market for a secondhand boat, I would expect more chance of finding a bargain among centerboard yawls than among keel sloops.

But one must not be ungrateful for the influence of racing. Most of the improvements in racing boats have been brought about under the impetus of competition, and the unsuitability of the flat-out offshore racer of today for pleasant cruising does not mean that many of the design and constructional innovations it exploits cannot be adapted by the cruising boat with advantage. Certainly the modern racing rig, enormously strong and meant to get every last ounce of propulsive force out of modest sail area, is a good thing, and techniques for building staunch hulls of minimum weight are to the benefit of all sailors. What is done with these various

(TEXT CONTINUED ON PAGE 29)

[I I]

Two Small Fiberglass Sloops:

NICHOLSON 32 & SEABREEZE

MINIATURIZATION IS A MODERN ART THAT is hard to apply to yacht design owing to the unfortunate invariance of human dimensions. For all the prestidigitation that has gone into the designs of the *Nicholson 32* and *Seabreeze,* they are still only 24 ft on the waterline, and though entirely adequate for weekends on the water, an occasional passage, and an annual two-week coastwise jaunt, they are perhaps a hair too small for more ambitious cruising. The big advantage that these boats have over comparable ones of orthodox wooden construction is that the thoroughgoing use of fiberglass results in roomier interiors. In small wooden boats, the keel, deadwood, frames, stringers, deck beams, and so on take up in the aggregate proportionately more space than they do in larger boats. A fiberglass shell in a small boat has the effect of providing an accommodation a size beyond what one would normally expect, an effect that is marked when the waterline length is 24 ft but less significant when it is 30 ft or more. The *Nicholson 32* and *Seabreeze* offer a lot of excellent boat for the money and have had much favor for that reason, but it would be a mistake to regard them as more than superior little cruisers.

NICHOLSON 32

THE FIRM OF CAMPER & NICHOLSONS was established in 1782, but age need not mean lethargy, and the potentialities of fiberglass are exploited to the full in the *Nicholson 32.* The lead ballast, for instance, is molded inside the hull, "which has the advantage of tremendous strength as well as avoiding any chances of leaks occurring through the keel bolts. A metal shoe is let into the bottom of the keel to take chafe should the boat ground at any time." The deck, cockpit, and cabin house are molded in one piece for strength and watertightness, but it is disappointing to see that the companionway hatch does not slide into a closed housing to eliminate the last predictable source of water below. Such a housing, like a bead for a spray hood, is best molded in initially, even though, as on any boat, it can later be installed easily if not quite so elegantly. But this is a distinctly minor point, for it is difficult to find anything substantial to improve upon in the details with which the basic design has been carried out. And the latter is thoroughly sound, for there is no question that a fair amount of displacement (here 14,500 lb) is necessary if a small boat is to be tolerable in a seaway and is to be able to carry stores and gear without destroying performance. The sail plan seems small, and while it is probably just right for boisterous Channel weather, some enlargement might be desirable in other parts of the world. Further testimony that the designers had in mind more than afternoon sailing on nice days is the ground tackle that is provided as standard equipment—namely, 90 ft of galvanized chain and a 30-lb Danforth—and the sheet winches, which are geared for sufficient power. Such a

pleasant contrast to the paperweight anchors and watch-charm winches usually found on stock boats!

The accommodation of the *Nicholson 32* is meticulously arranged to permit eating, sleeping, and navigating under way, while still making it possible for the whole crew to enjoy a quiet drink in harbor afterward, if perhaps with a few contortions. The off-center companion ladder is a help, since the compact galley can be concentrated on one side (note the sideboard over the after end of the port settee to give a little more work space), with the chart table

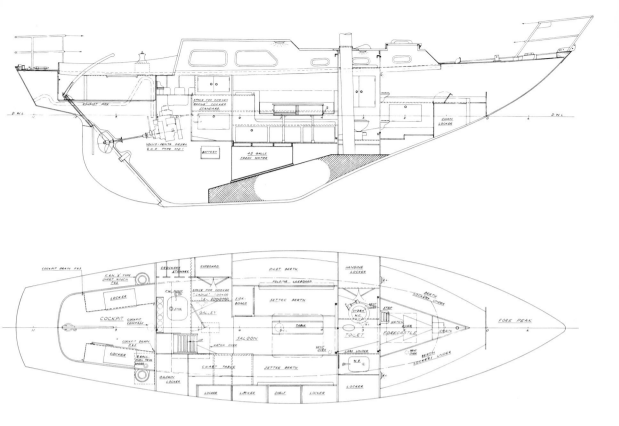

A proper folding spray hood on a Nicholson 32. (Beiser)

and oilskin locker on the other. The pilot berth to port is rather narrow, as might be expected, and the solid folding leeboard makes it narrower still; a large man would be better served by a canvas leeboard that could take on an outward curve. Still, not everyone needs a lot of space, and at sea a narrow berth is better than a wide one. Sliding doors close off the plastic-lined head, and a washbasin is built in to starboard facing the WC. Forward is the usual pair of V berths.

Two engine options are possible, a 6-hp Penta diesel and a 29-hp Watermota gasoline engine, both with reverse gears. The former is fitted with a reduction gear as well, so it can deliver ample power despite its unimpressive rating. A 55-gal water tank is molded into the hull under the cabin sole, and a 10-gal fuel tank is aft under the deck. I suspect that many owners of *Nicholson 32*'s will eventually fit supplementary fuel tanks or else will carry spare cans of fuel.

NICHOLSON 32

DESIGNER   *Camper & Nicholsons, Ltd., Southampton, England*

LOA   32 ft
LWL   24 ft
BEAM   9 ft 3 in.
DRAFT   5 ft 6 in.
DISPLACEMENT   14,500 lb
BALLAST   6,100 lb of lead
SAIL AREA   465 ft²

ENGINE   Penta M.D.1 diesel (6 hp) or Watermota Sea Wolf (29 hp)
FUEL   10 gal
WATER   55 gal
CONSTRUCTION   Molded fiberglass with teak trim; aluminum spars

SEABREEZE

Seabreeze IS ALSO A MOST IMPRESSIVE example of fiberglass design. A centerboarder, *Seabreeze* is longer and wider than the *Nicholson 32,* though the same on the waterline, and its draft with the board up is only 3 ft 10 in.—20 in. less than that of the *Nicholson 32. Seabreeze's* sloop rig is reasonable in size, and the aluminum mast is stepped on deck with its thrust taken by a plywood bulkhead that forms part of the head enclosure. The optional yawl rig would be hard to justify except for the large mizzen staysail it makes possible, together with the fact

that the centerboarders tend to have hard mouths when heeled, and a flexible sail plan helps in taming them. Even so, unless *Seabreeze* is exceptionally intractable (which is unlikely in view of the skill of her designers), I should think that the sloop rig wins the toss.

Owing to her hull form, *Seabreeze* is able to tuck away six berths, a separate head, an adequate galley, and a cockpit long enough to stretch out in, all on a waterline of 24 ft. Room has even been found for an oilskin locker, a hanging locker, a liquor locker, and a dinghy

FORERUNNER *is a* NICHOLSON 32 *sloop whose entire shell—hull, deck, cockpit, and cabin house—is of fiberglass-reinforced plastic.* (Beken)

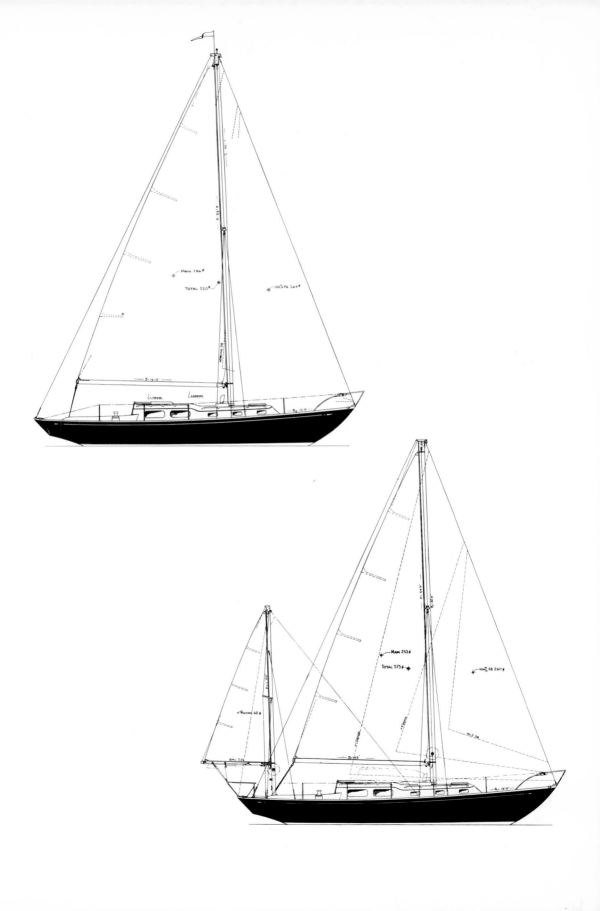

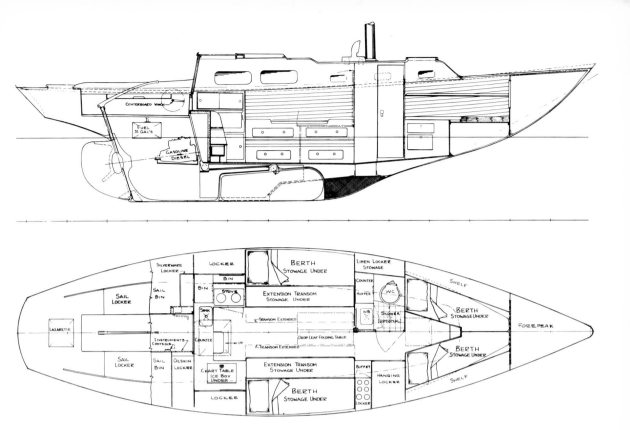

The 35-ft SEABREEZE *class of stock fiberglass sloops and yawls was designed by MacLear & Harris.* (Rosenfeld)

on the cabin trunk. *Seabreeze* is a veritable little giant, able to pack in an astonishing amount in what is, after all, a hull of no great size; but this hull is not made of rubber, as six adults trying to cruise together aboard her will soon find out. With fewer in the crew, of course, cruising on *Seabreeze* would be more enjoyable, and an advantage of such shoal draft in a small boat is that it facilitates getting to shore periodically to stretch one's legs without bumping into the other sardines.

There is enough room under the cockpit for the engine, a 25-hp Gray, and a 31-gal fuel tank. And 70 gal of water can be carried in integral bilge tanks on either side of the centerboard trunk. The 400-lb bronze centerboard is operated by a winch in the cockpit. The engine can be gotten at through the sail lockers, which in a boat of this size is probably more practical than having to tear the galley and companionway apart each time a filter needs cleaning or the spark plugs need wiping.

SEABREEZE

DESIGNER *MacLear & Harris, 366 Madison Avenue, New York City*

LOA 34 ft 6 in.

LWL 24 ft

BEAM 10 ft 3 in.

DRAFT 3 ft 10 in. board up, 6 ft 9 in. board down

DISPLACEMENT 13,400 lb

BALLAST 4,000 lb of lead

SAIL AREA 550 ft² as sloop, 575 ft² as yawl

ENGINE Gray (25 hp)

FUEL 31 gal

WATER 70 gal

CONSTRUCTION Molded fiberglass hull; aluminum spars

(TEXT CONTINUED FROM PAGE 20)

advances is the crux of the matter, and just because I feel that carried to its logical extreme in the current emphasis on racing efficiency and low rating above all else, the modern racing boat often makes an inferior cruising boat, it does not mean that I deplore in any way the pressures that have led to these advances. It is probably good in the long run for racers to become a species apart so that cruisers can develop in their own way—without the eyes of their owners on racing success in terms of an arbitrary and fallible formula.

Broadly speaking, a potential yacht owner has three options. First, he can commission a new design to his requirements, thereby exercising a good bit of control over both the planning and the actual construction of the boat. This can be an expensive procedure and carries with it the danger of catastrophe if everything does not work out as planned, especially since unconventional boats that are not quite successful are difficult to dispose of if one wants to try again. On the other hand, an experienced man with a clear idea of what he wants may find that having a boat built to his specifications is the only way to materialize his vision—and it *is* great fun to be closely involved with the creation of anything as magical as a sailboat. The cost, too, may not be astronomical if the builder is carefully chosen. There are yards in Denmark, Holland, Italy, Spain, Finland, Japan, Hong Kong, and elsewhere that can do perfectly acceptable work at reasonable expense provided that the type of construction is what they are accustomed to. Dutch yards, for instance, are very experienced in constructing steel yachts, while Danish and Italian yards do gorgeous work in wood. American, Swedish, and German craftsmen are excellent but far from cheap, so they are unlikely to be competitive except for small boats for their own countrymen or when special techniques are involved. Most designers know of competent yards all over the world from whom they can solicit bids for a new design, and arrangements for checking on the quality of the work can be made in various ways.

It may seem risky to go in for a new design. After all, while it is no great feat to design a fast hull, a stiff hull, a well-balanced hull, a roomy hull, or a beautiful hull, to combine all these desirable features into a single shape takes a good deal of doing. However, every yacht architect has several basic sets of lines in his files that have turned out well in the past, and each "new" design he turns out is actually a modification of one of these models—a bit wider here, perhaps, a slightly sharper turn of the bilge, a somewhat deeper draft. Each alteration has an effect, sometimes small and sometimes major, which the architect, if he is a good one, takes pains to find out and remember for future reference. The cumulative result is that on the basis of both direct experience and an intuition that he develops, the architect is able to estimate pretty well how each of his new creations is likely to perform, and he will be able to make a good guess as to how well a given set of preliminary design specifications will turn out. So it would seem most intelligent to go to the architect with the most eminence, the one with the most successful boats behind him. The other side of the coin is that such an architect may well be the prisoner of his own prowess and may be able to design in only one idiom, so to speak. Perhaps a particular concept will just not fit into his way of thinking, while being exactly what the fellow down the street has been actively developing. And the grand panjandrums of the profession might either be unsympathetic to one's ideas or find them too exorbitant a claim on their time to work them out in detail. This is where the younger men have their place: anxious to make their marks with something novel, unfettered by habit, with no reputation to fear losing, and able to devote time and enthusiasm to a new project, one of them might be the best choice.

The second option is a so-called stock boat, a standard model built in batches for economy and featuring a proven design. Here the buyer knows just what he is getting and, in principle, can get it at a more reasonable price. I say "in principle" because I am by no means convinced that stock boats invariably represent a saving over custom construction. The price quoted often covers little besides hull and rig, and as much as 50 percent more must be spent in order to provide lifelines, pulpit, adequate winches, genoa and spinnaker fittings, anchors, cabin table, stove, dinghy, compass, bilge pumps, and other features that normally are included in the contract price of a custom boat. I doubt that a purchaser of even the best-equipped stock boat on the market can get away without spending at least 20 percent more for various necessary items—exclusive of sails, of course, which are almost always "optional extras." Actually, one must not think that the builders of stock boats are a bunch of crooks because nobody in his right mind would think of sailing their products (which are invariably described as being sold in "sail-away condition") as they are actually delivered, since individual preferences vary so widely on the kind of ancillary gear required. I personally know of no "completely equipped" stock boat with what I would consider adequate ground tackle, to give just one example, and certainly a random dozen sailors will have four or five different choices in the matter of a proper stove. (But I hardly think there is much difference of opinion in regard to a compass or spreader lights, say, yet these are usually spoken of as "optional extras.") So in looking at stock boats, it is necessary to start with a complete list of what one wants and to tote up costs on the basis of this list, not on the basis of meaningless advertised prices.

My own opinion is that only fiberglass stock boats really pay off, for the cost of the molds needed can be amortized over a number of boats. Aesthetic considerations apart, fiberglass-reinforced plastic is a fine material, strong, monolithic, durable, and not subject to rot, electrolysis, or galvanic action, and one can defend its use in sailboat hulls without much difficulty. If a design being produced in fiberglass is just what one wants and the price is right, fine; but most fiberglass boats either are primarily racing craft and no fun at all to cruise in or are meant to provide the maximum possible accommodations at the minimum price and hence are indifferent sailers and comfortable only for midgets. There are exceptions to these melancholy classifications, and it is usually possible to have an otherwise suitable fiberglass shell completed to one's own specifications—at a price.

A new boat, custom or stock, invariably turns out to be more expensive than one thinks it will be. For this reason, the standard advice is to choose a type and size that is just right for the pocketbook and then actually order one 10 to 20 percent

[OPPOSITE] *Designed for extensive cruising,* BLACK WATCH *has little in common with most contemporary sailing yachts. To some, her splendid appearance makes up for her lack of windward ability, a deficiency that her diesel engine compensates for in any case. Since the photograph was taken,* BLACK WATCH's *topsides have been painted white.* (Beken)

smaller. I think this is a terrible idea. I would say instead that one should find a design one can afford and then order a boat that is *larger* by the same 10 to 20 percent. Where will the extra money come from? It is very simple: omit all frills and nonessential equipment that can be added later. All else equal, the bigger boat will be prettier, faster, more comfortable, and more able and thus will give a bonus in pleasure out of proportion to the percentage increase in size. The basic structure and rig of a cruising sailboat are relatively cheap, but the hand labor involved in building the interior and fancy deck structures and the extraordinary cost of much modern mechanical gear send the total soaring. A simple cabin with a minimum of intricate joinery need be no less comfortable or pleasing to the eye than its rococo cousin, and it may well be more satisfactory in the long run. Interior paint makes for a brighter cabin and easier maintenance than varnish and permits a lower level of craftsmanship and less expensive materials at no sacrifice in strength or utility. Lockers instead of drawers are another example of a worthwhile saving that may even turn out to be a positive blessing, since they provide a gain in usable stowage space and a reduction in unnecessary weight. And, of course, major economies can be made if the basic design calls for a flush deck instead of a trunk cabin, fiberglassed plywood decks instead of teak, and so on.

Many expensive optional features can be put in subsequent to the construction of the yacht at little or no penalty in cost owing to the delay. If one definitely wants them later, provision for their ultimate installation can usually be made at the start. Postponing the installation of a steering wheel in favor of a tiller, a mechanical refrigerator in favor of an icebox, pressure water in favor of hand pumps, a radio-telephone in favor of a good flare pistol, for example, adds up to big money saved. To begin with a simple sail outfit is also perfectly acceptable if one can restrain oneself from racing as soon as the boat is delivered. A genoa, working jib, storm jib, main, and, if appropriate, a mizzen and mizzen staysail will do very nicely for quite a while; though, of course, tangs for a spinnaker halyard block and a spinnaker-pole lift block should be provided initially. The cost of the various fittings, poles, lines, and shackles needed for a spinnaker and of the sail itself totals a pretty penny. Without the spinnaker, only two cockpit sheet winches are needed instead of four; though, again, these two should be sited so as to leave room for the other two in due course.

Not everything can be ruthlessly put aside. I personally would not compromise safety by leaving out a pulpit and lifelines and an inflatable life raft, though others may be less fuddy-duddy about their lives and those of their guests. I would certainly accept a modest plywood pram instead of a plastic dinghy with a price tag three or four times greater, though. An intelligently mounted first-class compass is a must in any boat, but an anchor windlass might or might not be worth installing initially, depending upon the kind of boat and the kind of cruising to be done. The necessity of sail covers, cockpit awnings, and similar items also varies, but generally their purchase can be left for later without serious consequences.

It takes a certain amount of imagination and strength of character to put off perfecting one's dream vessel, but I feel that the dividends paid by the larger craft are worth so modest an expedient. A hummingbird is a lovely little creature, perfect in every detail, but how compare it with the eagle soaring overhead?

The third possibility is a secondhand boat. Like a woman, a vessel with five to fifteen years' experience is old enough to represent a worthwhile saving yet young enough to have kept its shape and its looks. Typically such a boat comes on the market because, though perfectly sound, it is about to require major expenditures to keep it at top of its form: new sails and running rigging, engine rebuilding or replacement, taking hull and brightwork down to bare wood, and so on. Instead of making the required investment, which he may regard as putting new wine in an old bottle, the owner may well decide to try another boat—presenting a fine opportunity for the discerning buyer who may not be able to afford a craft of such breeding in mint condition.

What to do? I believe the best course is first to formulate one's requirements in as complete detail as possible. The very process of doing so may make the choice inevitable given the funds in hand: it may become quite clear that only a second-hand boat will be possible. It is worth keeping in mind that major changes in an older boat or in a stock boat can be expensive; so if one is not happy with what is offered, a custom vessel may turn out to be cheaper in the end. Hopefully a new boat will make sense, in which case one can start on an adventure whose beginning is a sketch on the back of an envelope and whose end (itself another beginning) comes when one sets out on the first cruise, no doubt with mixed feelings but nevertheless wholly and completely alive—which is the point of it all.

CHAPTER TWO

Hull Design

WIND AND SEA like everything else must obey the laws of nature, but the range of their behavior seems hardly inhibited on this account. In point of fact, the ocean of air and the ocean of water that envelop the earth are not by themselves especially disorderly, at least as the scientist sees them, but it is their joint dominion, the boundary between air and water, that is perhaps uniquely irregular and unstable. The statistics of winds and waves, tides and currents, temperatures and pressures all fit together into a comprehensible pattern, but at sea one is exposed to the raw, disheveled data and not to neat, tidy averages. For this reason there can never be a truly perfect yacht, one that excels on every point of sailing in all weathers; but a yacht should be able to make a fair showing in general, while reserving its best behavior for a certain specific set of circumstances. It is up to the prospective owner to specify these circumstances and up to the designer to plan a craft that can achieve what is wanted. A vessel at home in an Atlantic gale will hardly shine in a Force 2 breeze in protected waters, and vice versa—though a good boat should not be at a total loss in either situation. It is unfair to all concerned not to have clear from the start in what sector a planned boat should be most at home—unfair to the would-be owner, who may not get what he really wants; unfair to the designer, who is, after all, not clairvoyant; and unfair to the boat itself, which may turn out to be a lovely creature, eager to please but not given a chance to do so.

The most important factor in the performance of a yacht is its hull, and the first requirement for any hull is that it float. According to Archimedes' principle, the buoyant force on an immersed object is equal to the weight of the fluid it displaces. This means that a boat is in equilibrium when the hole it makes in the water, so to speak, is the same in volume as a weight of water equal to the entire weight of the boat. For this reason, the weight of a boat is called its displacement. Since 1 ft³ of seawater weighs 64 lb, a boat weighing 64 lb floats in such a way that its immersed volume is exactly 1 ft³. Were the boat hewn from solid lead, whose density is about 700 lb/ft³, its total volume would be less than 0.1 ft³; and even if submerged, the resulting buoyant force of 6 lb or so would not be enough to balance the downward force of its 64-lb weight, and it would sink. However, if the boat were instead fashioned from thin sheet lead with a total enclosed volume of 1 ft³, it might weigh perhaps 16 lb and would float with three-quarters of its volume above water.

A seagoing vessel other than a balsa raft invariably takes the form of a hollow shell whose total volume exceeds the volume of an equal weight of water. As long as its shell remains intact, the vessel cannot sink. In practical terms, the hull must be strong enough to take whatever stresses may be put upon it at sea without opening up, an imperative that applies with equal force to the deck and cabin structure and to any fittings, ports, and hatches that pierce them as well.

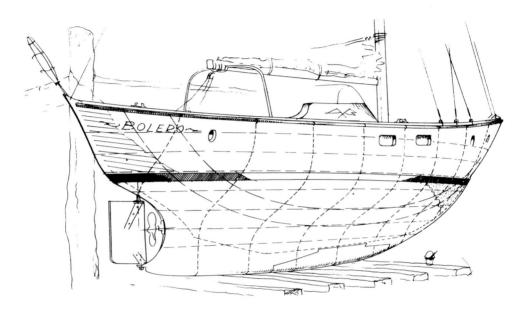

This sketch by William Garden of the double-ended sloop BOLERO, *which he designed, shows what the various sets of lines in the plans of a hull signify. The* waterlines *are essentially the outlines of horizontal slices taken from the hull; the* sections *are outlines of vertical slices perpendicular to the centerline; the* buttocks *are outlines of vertical slices parallel to the centerline; and the* diagonals *(not shown here) are outlines of oblique slices parallel to the centerline.*

Fair enough, one might say, but right here is the first of an almost endless series of conflicts that make yacht design so fascinating—if sometimes frustrating —a profession. For a given type of construction, more strength involves more weight, while the heavier the boat, the stronger it must be in turn to withstand the extra stresses imposed, directly or indirectly, by the additional weight. A craft light for its size rides over the waves; its more massive cousin plows through them. And there are still other considerations involved here in the case of a sailboat, which must be able to bear the pressure of the wind in its sails without either turning over or sliding off to leeward. Any increase in the structural weight of the hull or deck means a corresponding increase in the ballast if stability is to be kept the same, so that adding another $\frac{1}{4}$ in. in thickness to the hull and deck may lead to a greater increase in displacement than the weight of the additional wood alone. And more displacement calls for more sail area, which may mean yet more ballast. It is the original vicious circle, and where to terminate it without jeopardizing strength, comfort, and speed is the problem.

Experience has shown that there is a certain range of displacement for a given waterline length within which a sailing yacht capable of good performance in safety will fall. That is, all acceptably seaworthy combinations of hull form, ballast, and construction turn out to have displacements that lie between certain limits that depend upon the waterline length of the vessel. Even within these limits, not all displacements for a given length are necessarily desirable for cruising: boats at the light end of the scale are likely to be ugly and uncomfortable, and those at the heavy end tend to be sluggish. Generally speaking, satisfactory cruising yachts tend to have displacements in pounds in the neighborhood of $(0.8LWL + 4)^3$, where LWL is the waterline length in feet. In round numbers, for a waterline of 25 ft, this means a displacement of 14,000 lb; for a waterline of 30 ft, 22,000 lb; for a waterline of 35 ft; 33,000 lb; for a waterline of 40 ft, 47,000 lb. A vessel with a displacement within perhaps 10 percent of these figures either way is a "normal" one; if its displacement is between 10 and 25 percent greater, it is heavy for its size but may still be a nice boat; while if its displacement is more than about 25 percent greater, it will almost certainly be a clunker. On the other side, a cruising boat between 65 and 90 percent of the formula figure needs careful planning if the virtues of the light displacement are to outweigh its disadvantages, a task all but hopeless when the displacement is below 65 percent.

In my opinion, yachts of moderate displacement are best for cruising. A light boat of the same size as a normal one will be cheaper, since costs are very nearly proportional to weight, and will have a smaller engine, smaller sails, smaller anchors, and so on. But unless it is a large boat, it will have an unpleasantly quick motion and be more sensitive to the exact area and trim of the sails, the presence of stores for a long trip, inattention at the helm, and so forth—in other words, a good deal of effort and some sacrifice will be needed to get the most from it. A really heavy boat has a more docile and forgiving nature: another thousand pounds of stores makes little difference, nor does it usually matter much just where it is stowed, and rarely is there any hurry about reefing or changing sails. And heavy boats are apt to be steady, so that the larger size of their gear relative to light boats is compensated for by the ability of their crews to stand up and get their backs into their work without having to cling precariously to a lurching deck. But hares *are* faster than tortoises and more nimble besides, and not everybody can be happy with a tub, however comfortable it may be. Given a skilled designer, a vessel whose displacement fits the above formula will possess to some degree the good features of both lighter and heavier ones, while avoiding the penalties each extreme exacts.

[OVERLEAF] *One of the few really handsome yachts built to the Royal Ocean Racing Club measurement rule,* STARFIRE OF KENT *is also unusually well-constructed with teak planking and every fourth frame in stainless steel.* STARFIRE *was designed by Alan Buchanan, and her dimensions are LOA 53 ft, LWL 36 ft, beam 12 ft 5 in., draft 7 ft 9 in., and sail area 1284 ft². Her sweet lines, moderately high freeboard, clear deck, and divided rig are what every cruiser should have, and her concessions to racing— open, dormitory-style interior and puny engine—can be remedied without detracting from her virtues.* (Beken)

The desirability of moderate displacement does not preclude the fact that under special circumstances, a heavy or a light boat may be more suitable. At first glance, *Mischief*—an immensely heavy Bristol Channel pilot cutter built in 1906, converted to a yacht thirty years later, and since having passed through nine owners—seems an unlikely prospect for ocean cruising, yet H. W. Tilman, a formidable mountaineer newly turned sailor, has happily logged tens of thousands of miles in her. To be sure, Tilman, an old Himalayan hand, is a remarkable man, but even the greatest resources of intelligence and pluck can be canceled out by the wrong boat. *Mischief* is not the wrong boat, although her displacement of about 55 tons on a waterline of 41 ft is well over twice what is considered normal, and it is hard to say how much more successful Tilman's voyages might have been in a more modern vessel of similar cost. The latter would have been smaller, though doubtless as fast or faster, and it would not have been as comfortable or as able to hold up on the kind of long, hard expeditions Tilman has set out upon.

When cruising of a less ambitious kind is in prospect, some people may find a quite light boat to their taste. For a number of years I have admired the *Controversy* series of light-displacement yachts designed by E. Farnham Butler and Cy Hamlin. *Constellation,* Butler's own boat, weighs hardly more than half as much as a normal boat 30 ft on the waterline, yet for family cruising in the sheltered waters of the Maine coast it has worked out well, and it can be taken offshore with confidence. However, I would not care to beat through Deer Isle Thoroughfare in *Mischief* or to voyage to Patagonia in *Constellation,* while a yacht of moderate displacement might well be able to do both with equal facility and felicity.

The lower limit of the size of a proper cruising boat, in my definition of the term, is set by the requirements that two people be able to live aboard it for a few weeks at a time and that it be capable of an ocean crossing on its own bottom, both without serious discomfort. To my mind, the lowest displacement that can meet these requirements is 15,000 lb. The upper limit is set by the requirement that a man and his maid be able to manage the boat by themselves on a coastwise cruise, which points to a maximum displacement somewhere in the vicinity of 45,000 lb. To be sure, comfort is relative and people vary in robustness and competence, so perhaps it would be more precise to say that my wife and I would not especially care to live aboard or sail offshore in a vessel lighter than about 15,000 lb, nor would we especially look forward to a passage by ourselves in a vessel heavier than about 45,000 lb. I think the lower limit is a sharper one than the upper limit, since comfort and displacement are much more closely related than ease of handling and displacement.

Much fine cruising can be done in boats outside the above range, but such boats seldom possess the versatility required of the proper yacht.

A displacement between 15,000 and 45,000 lb means roughly a waterline length between 26 and 40 ft by the above formula, or, still more roughly, an over-all length between 36 and 56 ft. This spread is a substantial one, and depending upon one's needs, the most suitable range can be narrowed further without prejudicing an ability to voyage upon the high seas or to potter about shorthanded. A lot depends upon whether one normally goes off with a total complement of just two or three or whether a gang of children and/or friends are usually aboard. Another consideration is how many of the amenities of life ashore are wanted: refrigerators, heaters, showers, bidets, washing machines, and (God save us!) television sets all

(TEXT CONTINUED ON PAGE 50)

Bigger and Better in Fiberglass:
EXCALIBUR & CHALLENGER

Two further examples of the best in current fiberglass construction are *Excalibur* and *Challenger*. They are especially interesting because they are safely past the bottom of the size range for proper cruising, and each uses the freedom the extra space affords in a somewhat different way. But though *Excalibur* is a very fine boat indeed, I think it fair to say that she shows the strains of trying to combine sailing ability and extensive accommodations in a modest hull. *Challenger*, benefiting from a relatively minor increment in size, is just able to combine performance and comfort without a struggle. *Challenger* is, to my mind, a wholly satisfactory yacht and not just a "big little boat"; in *Excalibur*, compromises have had to be made that take a little of the edge from her many outstanding qualities. Of course, one cannot expect something for nothing, and *Challenger* is substantially the more expensive of the two; but the owner of *Challenger* can enjoy the heady feeling that his cup is filled to the brim (for it to runneth over, a still larger boat is needed), while the owner of *Excalibur* will, after a few years, no doubt begin to look around covetously at his neighbor's loved ones.

EXCALIBUR

E. G. VAN DE STADT IS A DUTCH NAVAL ARCHI-tect of great ability and originality, and both these qualities are reflected in *Excalibur*. The displacement of 14,500 lb is light, though not extremely so, for a waterline length of 26 ft 3 in., and advantage has been taken of this to cut away the underwater profile to reduce wetted surface. An independent balanced rudder is not common practice—most light-displacement boats with rudders aft of a fin keel have them hinged to skegs—but *Excalibur*'s speed and handling qualities do not seem to have suffered because of it. Certainly the propeller benefits from being in clear water instead of in an aperture, which means that a smaller one with less resistance can be used. The tiller is set aft of the rudderstock for convenience and is joined to it by a chain drive.

A prominent feature of *Excalibur*'s appearance is the conical bulge in the cabin house over the companionway that constitutes a kind of built-in spray hood. The companionway itself is an oval opening in a plywood bulkhead that joins cockpit and accommodation without a bridge deck; the opening is reasonably high above the cockpit sole. With a fixed boom, the

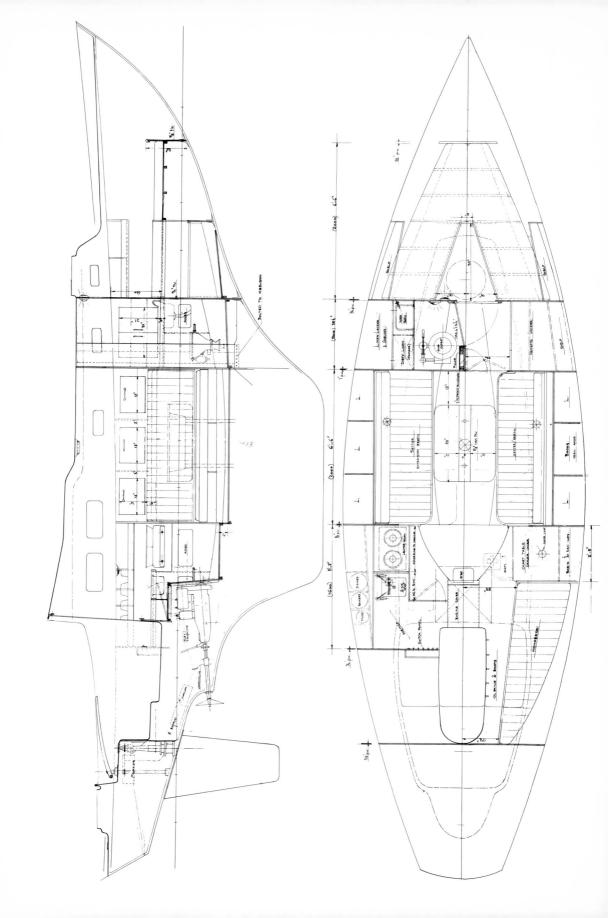

mainsheet can be led through a block atop the bulge (I don't know the correct term for this sensible innovation) to help distribute the load on the boom; but when roller reefing is fitted, a longer boom is used and the mainsheet leads directly from the boom end to the cockpit. A toe rail of good height runs around the ship, which helps keep both sea and crew where they respectively belong. It is remarkable how welcome are a few more inches in a toe rail. The

One of the EXCALIBUR *class of all-fiberglass sloops designed by E. G. van de Stadt.* (Ramsay)

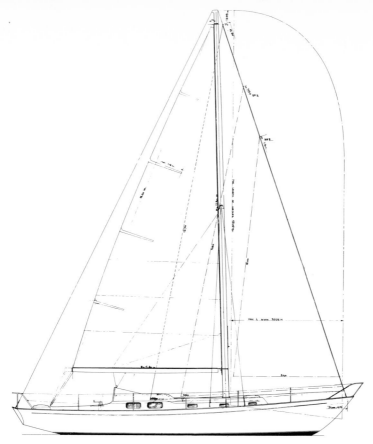

forward hatch is circular, a sporty note, and just large enough to wriggle through. Though off the beaten track in looks, *Excalibur*'s exterior is eminently practical.

The moderate beam means a fairly cramped accommodation, but with his usual care, E. G. van de Stadt has made use of every available cubic inch. Thus the pillar that supports the deck-stepped mast is a narrow hollow box against which two doors fold, thereby closing off the head from the main cabin to form a sizable compartment. The galley is adequate and well placed, there is a separate chart table, and a quarter berth is squeezed in alongside the cockpit well. The small engine is in a box under the companionway and should be easy enough to get at.

Excalibur

DESIGNER   *E. G. van de Stadt, Zuiddijk 412, Zaandam, Holland*

LOA   36 ft
LWL   26 ft 3 in.
BEAM   9 ft 10 in.
DRAFT   5 ft 11 in.
DISPLACEMENT   14,500 lb
SAIL AREA   600 ft²

ENGINE   Färe-Göta 15-18 P.K., Universal Atomic Four, Albin or Arona two-cylinder diesels
CONSTRUCTION   Molded fiberglass hull; aluminum spars

CHALLENGER

FEW BOATS ARE AS WELL CONCEIVED and well executed as *Challenger*. With a basic displacement of 15,000 lb (it is more in practice) on a waterline of 27 ft, *Challenger* is just large enough to be a proper cruising yacht, but she is much more than a minimum boat in every respect other than size. With adequate sail area in a masthead yawl rig and a tank-tested centerboard hull, she performs well under sail, and a large engine, optionally gasoline or diesel, and 80 gal of fuel tankage assure both speed and range under power. *Challenger*'s hull and deck

are in fiberglass but she is otherwise built of wood, and no raw fiberglass shows anywhere in the interior, so she makes use of the advantages of fiberglass where they mean most while retaining the looks and livability of wood. Because the cabin house is of wood, there is a certain flexibility in its exact shape, and some sailors will no doubt prefer a straight trunk to the low deckhouse that is standard. A capacious deck box is fitted on a number of boats of this design just aft of the mizzenmast, where it provides welcome additional stowage for lines

Building a sailing yacht requires craftsmanship of the highest order. Here under construction at Poul Molich's yard in Hundested, Denmark, are an Alden CHALLENGER *(at left) and a near-sister to Sparkman & Stephens'* GIRALDA *(in the background). The* CHALLENGER *fiberglass hull is molded by Halmatic in England and completed at Hundested. (Beiser)*

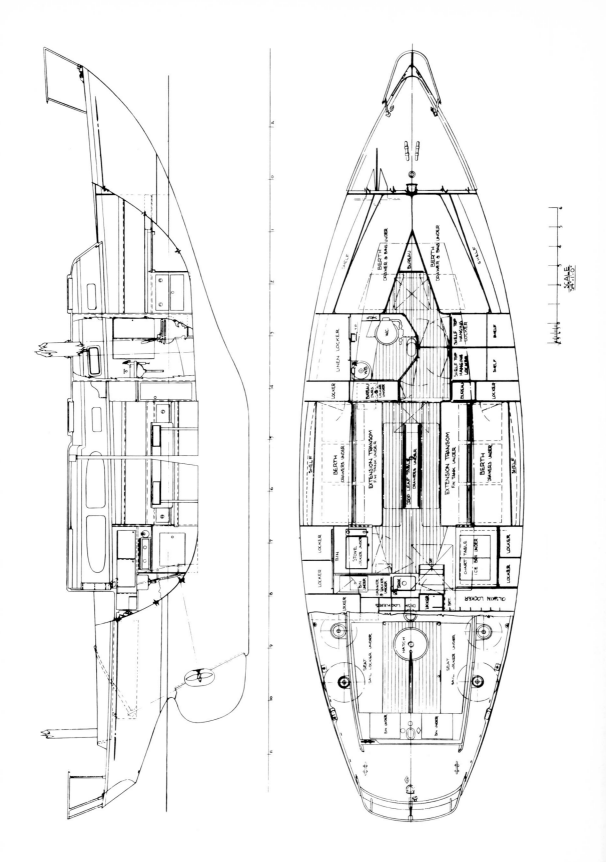

SCALE
3/4"=1'-0"

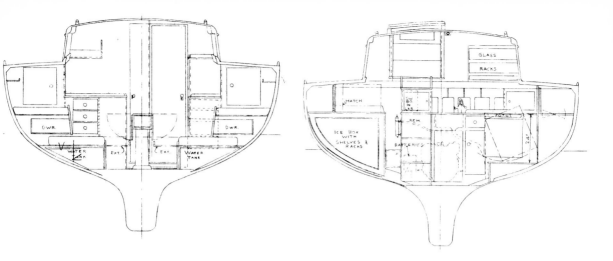

HIGHLIGHT *is a* CHALLENGER-*class yawl designed by Alden. Note the two rows of eyelets in the roller-reefing main for lacings to give the reefed sail the proper shape. In a boat of this size (38 ft overall), a spinnaker is relatively easy to handle and can be great fun, and mizzen staysails of all sizes are docile and effective on a reach.* (Fortier)

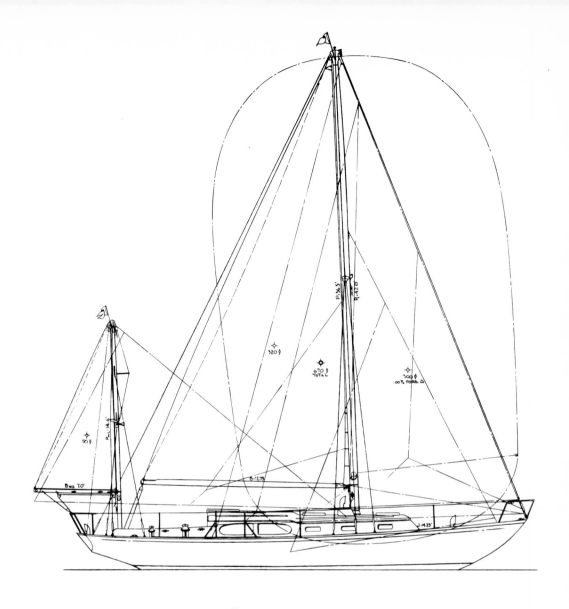

Challenger

DESIGNER   *John G. Alden & Co., Inc., 131 State Street, Boston, Massachusetts*

LOA   38 ft 6 in.

LWL   27 ft

BEAM   11 ft

DRAFT   4 ft centerboard up

DISPLACEMENT   15,000 lb

SAIL AREA   670 ft²

ENGINE   Gray 4-112 (35 hp) or Perkins 4-107 diesel (47 hp)

FUEL   80 gal

WATER   80 gal

CONSTRUCTION   Molded fiberglass hull and deck; teak and mahogany deckworks; spruce or aluminum spars

and blocks and miscellaneous gear plus some protection to the helmsman without detracting from the boat's appearance.

The accommodation has been worked out with both quantity of contents and quality of spaciousness in mind. Another berth—even another locker—and the interior would be crowded; but everything necessary is already

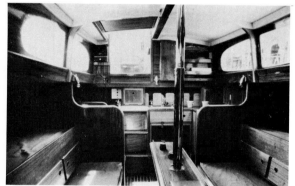

Four views of WIND SONG, *another* CHALLENGER. *These fine stock boats combine a fiberglass hull and deck with a wooden cabin house, cockpit, and accommodation in a pleasing and practical way. The central pillar in the main cabin carries the centerboard pennant to the cockpit and is handy as a grab rail as well; the fireplace and the deck box on the counter are valuable out of proportion to their cost.*

there, and no major additions are required. In most boats of the *Challenger* series, a small fireplace is installed on the port side just aft of the head to provide a source of warmth and cheer on cold nights. The only possible criticism of the design is the difficulty of engine access, a problem very hard to avoid in vessels of this size but on occasion a serious matter. It is not surprising that a great many *Challenger*-class boats have been built and are giving pleasure in all kinds of cruising.

(TEXT CONTINUED FROM PAGE 40)

take up space. But a big boat means big sails and big anchors, and how big is too big is an individual matter. Given a size range that seems to make sense, every experienced sailor I know would say to have the largest in that range that one can afford to buy and keep up, advice I agree with wholeheartedly.

There is no general relationship between over-all length and waterline comparable to that between waterline length and displacement. The performance of a sailboat hull is primarily determined by its underwater shape, so that the character of the upper part of the hull, though not without significance, is more at the mercy of whim and fashion. The most important effect of overhangs fore and aft is to increase the effective waterline length of a boat when it is heeled. At low speeds the chief source of resistance is friction between the bottom surface and the water, while at higher speeds the chief source of resistance is the effect of the waves generated by the boat's motion. Both of these influences will be examined later in this chapter, but for the moment the important thing is that the wave resistance varies according to the square root of the waterline length, or $\sqrt{LWL}$. When there is plenty of wind, a boat will heel; and if it can thereby increase its waterline length, it will travel faster than if the waterline length remains unchanged.

In addition to increasing the sailing length of a boat when it is heeled, overhangs provide reserve buoyancy without compromising hull shape. That is, overhangs permit a vessel to have as fine lines fore and aft as the designer thinks best without danger of green water over the bow or stern at every wave. This is especially important in heavy boats, since the reserve buoyancy needed is in proportion to displacement; and if freeboard and above-water hull form are to be kept within reason, there is no other place for additional above-water volume than overhangs. Boats light for their size can get away with limited overhangs and, in fact, usually are the better for them if the motion at sea is not to be too violent.

Another valuable attribute of overhangs is that they make possible an all-inboard rig without a bowsprit forward or a main boom protruding astern. An all-inboard rig is safer and easier to manage, since it means that all sail handling can be done from the deck and a permanent backstay can run to the mainmast head. Further, there is more deck space available for the cockpit and for various items of gear such as anchors, not to mention room for sunbathing. And nothing is lovelier than a boat whose lines terminate gradually in overhanging ends instead of being chopped off bluntly. It has been said that a transom stern is more practical because it makes it easier to get at the rudder in case the latter is damaged, but I should think it more sensible to have a strong rudder in the first place; indeed, I should imagine an outboard rudder to be more vulnerable. Modern rudders are adequately robust, and a reserve tiller is insurance against the occasional troubles that arise in steering-wheel linkages. The other objection to a counter stern is expense, but I think, on the contrary, that the outlay for the extra amount of boat that one gets from an overhang aft is cheap compared with the cost of working in a similarly useful volume and deck area elsewhere. Overhangs totaling one-third to one-half the waterline length seem to work out best in practice, and naturally the exact ratio should be at the discretion of the designer. However, it is wise to insist on overhangs adequate to permit an inboard rig; and when there is any choice, generosity in respect to overhangs is better than penuriousness.

A question that often comes up where overhangs are concerned is whether they must be left empty or can be filled up with spare sails, potatoes, and so on. It seems to me that there are really two questions here: first, whether the motion of the boat is affected by the manner in which a certain amount of weight is distributed and, second, whether the buoyancy of an overhang is affected by its contents if the total displacement of the boat remains the same. These questions are easy to deal with: the answer to the first is yes; the answer to the second, no. A boat whose weight is concentrated more or less at its center has a low moment of inertia about a transverse axis and accordingly will pitch rapidly, rearing back to meet a sea and then falling forward, behavior that is safe enough but uncomfortable if carried too far. If the weight is spread out along its length, the moment of inertia (which for each parcel of weight is proportional to the square of its distance from the axis) is higher about a transverse axis and the boat will be steadier and its pitching motion will be slower. Carried to an extreme, a high moment of inertia is bad, since it means that the boat will recover slowly and, if the seas are close together, the craft may stick its nose into green water unnecessarily often. Full overhangs have so much reserve buoyancy that really large excursions are rare; and if that is the case, one may as well spread out the weight to a certain extent to make the ordinary pitching bearable. Rocking horses belong in the nursery, not at sea. By Archimedes' principle, the buoyancy of an object is equal to the weight of the water it displaces, with no reference to whether the object is hollow or filled. Therefore, how much stuff to put in forepeak and lazaret lockers depends entirely upon the dynamic response of the vessel—if it is quick and bouncy in fore-and-aft motion, a few coils of line away forward and a few sacks of onions away aft may help to a surprising extent; while if it takes forever for the bow to rise, maybe it would be a good idea to shift the spare anchor and those cases of beer elsewhere.

The most important factor in the performance of a yacht of a given size is the shape of its hull, and the objective is a hull that will go in any desired direction at the greatest possible speed. But a hull form that excels at reaching and running will not be as close-winded as a hull form developed for maximum windward ability, and a relatively small difference in how near a boat can sail to the wind means a big difference in the speed made good to windward. A compromise is therefore necessary between those hull characteristics that promote speed through the water and those that permit a boat to travel efficiently whither its crew wants, and as in any compromise, some sacrifices must be made for the good of the whole. In some boats, stability and docility on the helm are favored at the expense of speed; in others, windward ability is primary; in still others, performance off the wind is the goal. A further complication is the wide range of wind and sea conditions that a cruising boat must face, since a hull that is at its best in calm waters and light airs will not be much fun on a wild night at sea, and vice versa.

The faster a boat moves, the greater the resistance to its forward motion. At low speeds, the bulk of the resistance arises from frictional forces between the hull and the water, so that what counts is the area of the hull's wetted surface. A lot of skin means a lot of skin friction. In conflict with the desirability of the least possible wetted surface are two other requirements—adequate lateral plane and stability. Lateral plane refers to the underwater profile of a boat as seen from the side: the larger this profile, the less the tendency of the boat to move sideways. And a deep profile enhances the stabilizing effect of the ballast keel. The problem is to have enough lateral plane so that the leeway made when beating is not excessive, enough beam and draft so that stability is adequate, and yet the least possible wetted area. If these were the only factors involved, the answer would be simple: a hull with circular underwater sections and a fin keel with a bulb of ballast on its lower end. But a hull form of this kind is practical only in a light-displacement vessel, because the immersed volume is small and because of strength problems, and exactly how to accommodate greater displacement without compromising speed or stability is a major design headache.

Clearly it is most important that the shape of the lateral plane be the most efficient possible in order to be able to reduce its area and hence the wetted surface. Square foot for square foot, the farther down the lateral plane, the better, because the deeper water does not drift to leeward as much as the surface water. It was once thought necessary for a boat to have a long, straight keel in order to handle well, but there are so many easily managed boats with cutaway underwater profiles that while the former requirement may still hold for certain hulls, it is certainly not true in general. Different designers prefer different profiles, with Olin Stephens, for instance, holding to a triangular shape, while Laurent Giles usually draws a more rectangular one with a definite corner at its forward end; but other aspects of their typical hulls are also different, and it is the effectiveness of the design as a whole that counts. Whatever the character of the hull shape, however, wetted surface must be the smallest possible one consistent with the various basic functions of the hull.

At high speeds, skin friction is less important than what is usually called the wave-making resistance. As a boat moves, the forward part of its hull pushes water out of the way to form a wave on each side. To produce this wave takes energy, which must be supplied by whatever forces are propelling the boat. At low speeds, the length of the wave is less than the length of the boat, the second crest is alongside, and part of the energy that went into the wave is returned to the boat. As Philippe Harlé has aptly described it, the second wave "pushes the boat through the water somewhat in the manner that a cherry stone will fly out when pressed between finger and thumb." But the faster the boat goes, the longer the length of the waves; and when the wavelength begins to exceed the boat's waterline length, the proportion of energy that is returned decreases sharply. The thumb and finger are now behind the cherrystone and hardly affect it. At the same time, the rate at which energy must be supplied to the waves increases, since more speed means more water to be pushed out of the way per second, so both factors coincide to make the force required to propel the boat larger and larger. This situation is described by saying that the wave-making resistance rises rapidly with the boat's speed once the second wave's crest is astern of the after end of the hull at the waterline.

The wave-making resistance of a boat depends upon its speed-length ratio, which is the ratio between its speed V and $\sqrt{LWL}$, the square root of its waterline length. It is convenient to express V in knots and LWL in feet when working with the speed-length ratio. When $V/\sqrt{LWL}$ is less than 1, that is, when V is less than $\sqrt{LWL}$, the frictional resistance exceeds the wave-making resistance, and the sum of the two is relatively small. When $V/\sqrt{LWL} = 1$, the two kinds of resistance are approximately the same in magnitude, but their total is still not beyond the driving force that a moderate wind can produce in the sails of nearly any yacht. At a speed about 20 percent greater than $\sqrt{LWL}$, in other words when $V/\sqrt{LWL} = 1.2$, the second wave is at the after end of the waterline and the wave-making resistance has begun to go up sharply. When the ratio is 1.3, the second wave is behind the hull and the boat is, in effect, climbing up the back of its bow wave: now the wave-making resistance is by far the more significant element, and the force needed to overcome it is several times greater than it was when $V = \sqrt{LWL}$. In a typical moderate-displacement boat, the total resistance might double between speed-length ratios of 0.6 and 1.2, double again between 1.2 and 1.3, and continue doubling at every further increment of 0.1 in the speed-length ratio. Thus a gradual increase in resistance with speed, which is characteristic of skin friction, is replaced by a resistance that increases very rapidly with speed once past a certain critical speed.

A boat 36 ft on the waterline will have a speed-length ratio of 1.0 when its speed is 6 knots, since the square root of 36 is 6; and at this speed, the resistance to its motion through the water, which is the force that is needed to propel it, might be only 250 lb. But nearly this much force again must be furnished to increase its speed to 7 knots, and more than 1,000 lb of force is necessary to get its speed up to 8 knots—about as much as its sails (or engine, for that matter) are ever capable of developing. Because the resistance is already so large and is growing still larger at a rapid rate when $V/\sqrt{LWL}$ is about 1.4, this figure is often referred to as the hull speed. Actually there is no sharp limit, and under exceptional circumstances (for instance, running downwind under spinnaker in a young gale at sea when the boat surfs down wave fronts—the most intensely exciting experience sailing offers), a speed-length ratio of 1.4 can be exceeded. More often than not, it will be found that a ratio between 1.3 and 1.4 is the practical limit for boats with normal hull forms; the ratio may go as high as 1.6 for boats whose hull forms are such that their overhangs contribute to their effective LWL's to an unusual extent.

A heeled hull offers more resistance than an upright one despite the increase in the effective waterline length produced by the overhangs; of course, without overhangs, the resistance would be still greater. In a well-designed hull, the added resistance due to heeling is relatively small, only a few percent up to angles of 20 to 25°. Leeway is much more serious because the hull is dragged crabwise through the water instead of moving straight ahead. In a boat heeled to 25° but making no leeway, the resistance at a moderate speed-length ratio might be merely 5 percent greater than for the same boat upright, but if it is also making 5° of leeway—not an exceptional figure for a close-hauled boat—the resistance might be 50 percent greater. What this means is that the lateral plane, which is primary in controlling leeway, must be adequate, and skimping on it to reduce skin friction and so improve light-weather performance may mean a serious reduction in windward ability in moderate and strong winds.

While the purpose of these remarks is to help in the interpretation of a set of plans rather than to advocate any specific style of yacht architecture, I do feel that a remarkable amount of utter nonsense has been said in advocacy of the "cod's head and mackerel's tail" hull shape. No codfish or mackerel of my acquaintance swims around half in and half out of the water, and a totally submerged vessel interacts with the water through which it moves in a way very different from that characteristic of a surface vessel. It is an empirical fact that a surface vessel with sharp bows, perhaps even slightly hollow, that part the water surface neatly experiences less resistance than a similar vessel with blunt bows that shove water in front of them. Submarines are round and fat forward, and they travel much faster when submerged than when on the surface because of this; if they had fine lines forward, they would go faster on the surface but more slowly submerged. So a sailboat hull with a very full forebody should be looked upon with suspicion unless it is meant to be sailed underwater.

What is surprising is that the codfish theory should have persisted as long as it has. Back in 1851 the schooner *America* surprised orthodox thinkers by having a fine entry with her maximum beam well aft, simplified rigging, and sails cut flat instead of in the baggy fashion of the day. Her designer, George Steers, had had no formal training in naval architecture and relied upon observation and intuition instead of dogma in developing his vessels. *America* turned out to be spectacularly fast, stable, and close-winded, and she had no trouble in cleaning up the entire Royal Yacht Squadron fleet at Cowes that summer to win a grotesque silver object now known as the *America*'s Cup. (Ah, the good old days! *America* was 94 ft overall, displaced 170 tons, and had a sail area of about 5,300 ft^2. She cost $20,000 complete—and her career spanned nearly a century before she was finally burned in 1944 to make possible the salvage of her fastenings.) Yet even today one sees bulbous forebodies on sailboats and hears boats praised because of their resemblance to codfish, though the inadequacy of the design concept embodied in the codfish as a basis for sailboat hulls has been known since the first race of the *America*.

Stability in a sailboat refers to the resistance it offers to being heeled. The more stable a hull, the more upright it is under sail and, all else equal, the faster it is, since less force is then needed to propel it and its rig is at the same time more effective. Another virtue of a boat that sails on its bottom is that its lateral plane is more nearly vertical and thus better retards leeway. And, of course, a stable boat is more comfortable and, being less sensitive to changes in wind strength, easier to manage as well.

Part of the stability of a hull arises from its shape and part from its weight. When the hull is heeled, its immersed shape is asymmetrical and the buoyant upward force on it acts through a point (the center of buoyancy) that is to leeward of its center of gravity. The result is a moment that tends to restore the hull to an upright position. The greater the beam, the farther to leeward the center of buoyancy for a given angle of heel and the greater the righting moment. But too much beam is undesirable for a number of reasons, one of which is *not,* in general, that the boat will be slower than otherwise: a skillful designer can produce a fat boat that is just as fast on and off the wind as a narrow one, or even faster. Excessive beam in a light-displacement boat means that the hull is lifted upward bodily when it is heeled, which, by reducing the effective lateral plane, increases the amount of leeway and in turn the resistance of the hull to forward motion. Further, such a boat almost always requires considerable helm when it is heeled, which also slows it down. While the initial stability of a light, beamy hull is great, it drops when the hull is heeled past 30° or so, so that a sudden squall can really put the boat over on its ear. To add to the disadvantages of this type of boat, its motion is so quick as to be acutely uncomfortable in almost any sea. I speak from experience, having owned a boat of this kind—a wonderful vessel in moderate winds in protected waters, but impossible under other circumstances.

(TEXT CONTINUED ON PAGE 67)

[IV]

Three Stock Sloops:

LE QUARANTE PIEDS,

K-43, & RELIANT

I N PLANNING A STOCK BOAT, THE TEMPTA-
tion is always to be conventional and compromise in everything so as to offend nobody's
taste. The trouble with this approach is that
mediocrity is the usual result, and a boat needs

character in order to be a yacht. *Le Quarante
Pieds, K-43,* and *Reliant* are all standardized
designs, but none of them lacks distinction or
individuality.

LE QUARANTE PIEDS

FEW DESIGNERS HAVE HAD AS MUCH ACTUAL
sailing experience as Captain John H. Illingworth, and the partnership of Illingworth and
Angus Primrose has produced yachts that have
been phenomenally successful in offshore racing. Most (though not all) of these yachts have
had markedly light displacements, which keeps
costs low but makes it harder to achieve comfort. At first glance, the combination of light
displacement and a racing objective does not
seem promising, but so artfully are the lines
drawn and so solicitous are the designers for
the comfort of the crews that much happy
cruising has been done in Illingworth & Primrose boats. A case in point is their stock
Quarante Pieds design, which the designers feel
has "an extremely fast and very sea kindly hull
admirably suited to cruising." A yawl-rigged

version of this design, *Primivere,* crossed the
Atlantic after a respectable showing in the 1963
Fastnet and was unfortunately sunk in an
accident in the West Indies.

The sloop rig is small in area but very efficient, with a high aspect ratio and a main boom
well off the deck. A baby forestay replaces the
forward pair of lower shrouds and is a big help
in keeping the mast straight, but it is too small
for a sail to be set on it. In *Primivere* a true
double-headsail rig is fitted, with a big forestaysail and a high-cut Yankee (as the British call
it) on top for an aggregate area exceeding that
of a masthead genoa of the same overlap. One
argument for a genoa staysail is that, since it
normally is sheeted inside the rail when on the
wind, it can be cut so as just barely to clear the
deck. Such a low foot means that the flow of air

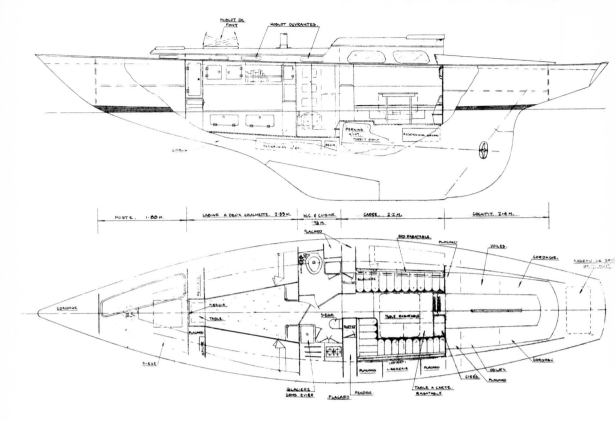

off the sail is all horizontally aft, with no downward component, thereby enhancing the propulsion obtained. Most of the flow along the lower part of a genoa cut to clear the lifelines, and so several feet off the deck, is downward, which is a complete waste. A proper low-cut genoa needs a break in the lifelines just aft of the pulpit, which now not only is outlawed by many racing rules but also is a poor idea from the point of the foredeck hands, and such a sail outboard may also get into trouble by scooping up a wave when the boat is heeled. For cruising, a rig like this is more trouble than it is worth, and the masthead sloop rig of the standard

Quarante Pieds may be a better idea—or, better still, a yawl rig with only a single head stay.

Instead of a sliding hatch, *Primivere* has a hinged cover over the companionway. This is cheaper and lighter and does not require a protective housing to be made reasonably watertight. However, it makes a spray hood impossible, and the deckhouse is too low to offer any real protection to the cockpit. A pair of sheet winches on the cabin house is also in the way of a spray hood; only a single pair can be installed outboard of the coaming because of the mainsheet traveler that bisects the cockpit. A purely cruising version of *Primivere* might be

PRIMIVERE *is a modified version of the stock* LE QUARANTE PIEDS *design of Illingworth & Primrose. Note the folding companionway hatch, the mainsheet traveler, the shock-cord control line from the running backstay to the base of the lower spreader, and the jib-topsail sheet-block mounted on the after pulpit.* (Beken)

1941

Primavera.

Beken & Son
Cowes

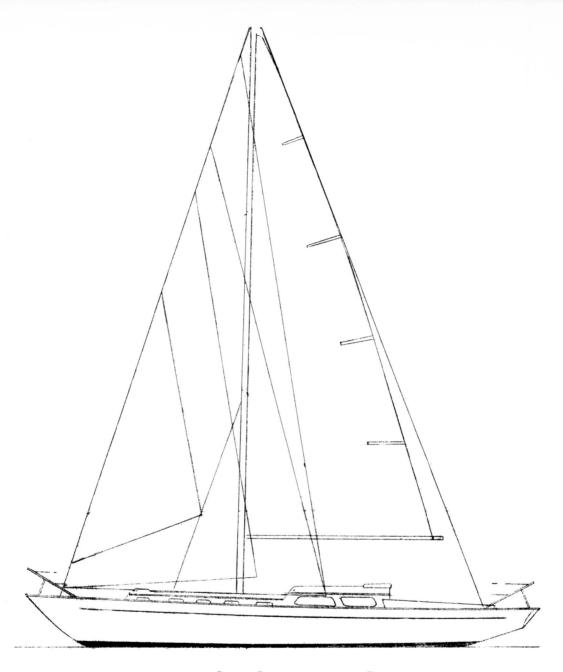

LE QUARANTE PIEDS

DESIGNER   *Illingworth & Primrose, 36 North Street, Emsworth, England*

LOA   40 ft

LWL   30 ft

BEAM   10 ft 4 in.

DRAFT   6 ft 6 in.

DISPLACEMENT   17,600 lb

SAIL AREA   612 ft^2

ENGINE   Perkins 4-107 (47 hp)

better off with an undivided cockpit that has some shelter over its forward end. Two nice details are a transparent insert in the companionway cover—which, together with the large windows, makes the deckhouse a cheerful place rain or shine—and a large enough lazaret hatch to permit stowing an inflatable life raft in the counter.

The accommodation of the stock *Quarante Pieds* features a respectable double cabin not too far forward to be unusable under way. Forward of a solid bulkhead is a small compartment with its own head and a single pipe berth, presumably for a paid hand. If a paid hand is not carried (and it should not be necessary in so small a boat as this), another pipe berth could be squeezed in to hold two guests in harbor.

The main head is adequate, and the galley, though small, is sensibly arranged, with a seat for the cook and everything within reach. The deckhouse needs a hump to clear the Perkins diesel, since light displacement means limited room in the bilge; and at 17,600 lb, *Le Quarante Pieds* is light indeed. To starboard is a narrow pilot berth that will be prized at sea, and to port are a folding chart table and an oilskin locker adjacent to the companionway.

In performance and accommodation, *Le Quarante Pieds* has a lot to offer a man and his maid: real speed with a compact rig, a comfortable stateroom, an airy deckhouse just right for dining tête-à-tête, and, best of all, enough money left over with which to enjoy it all.

K - 4 3

THE *K-43* IS THE LATEST CREATION OF THE California designer and builder Paul Kettenburg, whose previous boats have been most successful in cruising and racing on the West Coast. To be built in wood at first, it is expected that the *K-43* will eventually also be available with an aluminum hull. The aluminum hull will be about 1,200 lb lighter, permitting this much more weight in the keel and therefore greater stability. With a cutaway underwater profile to reduce wetted area and enough beam and ballast to enable her to stand up to her ample sail area, the *K-43* should be a swift boat indeed. The sail plan has a number of points of interest that show the *K-43* to be no ordinary stock boat: the narrow, almost rectangular rudder for maximum effectiveness with least resistance; the angled braces on the pulpits; the large but good-looking deckhouse; roller reefing on the main, desirable in a masthead rig of this size; and finally a "storm jib" 283 ft² in area,

planned no doubt in collaboration with the California Chamber of Commerce as part of its campaign to promote the local climate.

The accommodation shows the same clear thinking and direct approach apparent in the sail plan. By the simple but infrequently used expedient of setting the forward bulkhead of the head compartment at a sharp angle, adequate standing and sitting room is provided in the forward cabin, and a door leads to the head from this cabin as well as from the main cabin. The main cabin has a single transom to starboard and a U-shaped settee to port inboard of a pilot berth. Aft to starboard are a hanging locker and a quarter berth; it should be easy to arrange a chart table in this region. To port is a practical galley, with a double sink, a gimbaled two-burner stove with oven, and a handy icebox. The engine and fuel tank are housed under the cabin sole, which is unusual in a vessel of this size and made possible by the

combination of a small engine and an elongated deckhouse.

There is no bridge deck, making it easy for people to go up and down, and the cockpit sole slants downward aft to help keep water out of the accommodation. In a climate that permits a storm jib in a sloop of three-quarters the area of the main, such an open companionway is plausible. The cockpit itself has a sunken thwartship seat aft and two short fore-and-aft benches forward, an arrangement that some prefer to the usual one of a pair of fore-and-aft seats only. The jib-sheet winches are aft of the helmsman, so the thwartship seat makes the crew's job easier when the boat is under sail; in port, a cockpit of this kind is also very convenient. An optional wheel could be located to place the helmsman on the after seat, which would have to be raised to enable him to see over the deckhouse.

The construction of the *K-43* is orthodox except for the substitution of some woods more readily available on the West Coast for the customary ones for particular purposes. Thus the keel, deadwood, and horn timber are Douglas fir, the stem and some of the floors are apitong, and the hull is planked in Philippine mahogany.

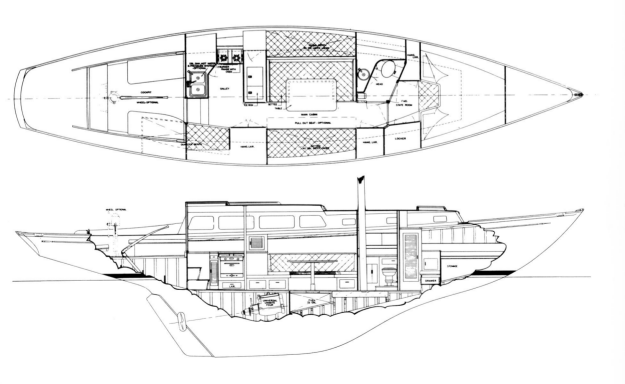

K - 4 3

DESIGNER *Paul A. Kettenburg, 2810 Carleton Street, San Diego, California*

LOA 43 ft

LWL 29 ft

BEAM 11 ft

DRAFT 6 ft 2 in.

DISPLACEMENT 19,000 lb

BALLAST 7,750 lb of lead

SAIL AREA 791 ft²

ENGINE Universal Unimite Four

FUEL 55 gal

WATER 100 gal

CONSTRUCTION Philippine-mahogany planking on white-oak frames, with Douglas-fir and apitong center-line structure; fiberglass-covered plywood deck and Honduras-mahogany deckworks; spruce spars

RELIANT

FOR THREE DECADES, Philip Rhodes has been designing superior cruising yachts, though his greatest fame has perhaps come from such racing craft as *Carina* and *Weatherly*. He has shown a sure hand with a varied output—big or little, heavy or light, conventional or imaginative, a Rhodes boat is sure to be able, handsome, and comfortable. But there *are* other architects of comparable skill, and what seems to me to be Rhodes's unique talent is his way of infusing a special, distinctive, pleasing character into each of his creations. I have seen and admired a score of different cruising vessels of Rhodes design, and all of them draw the eye

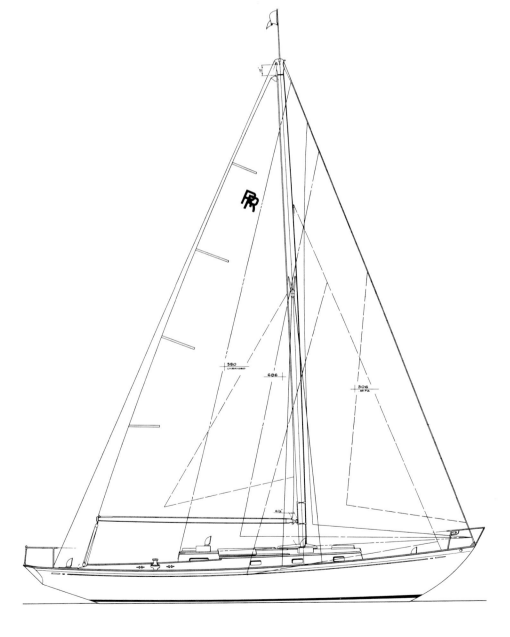

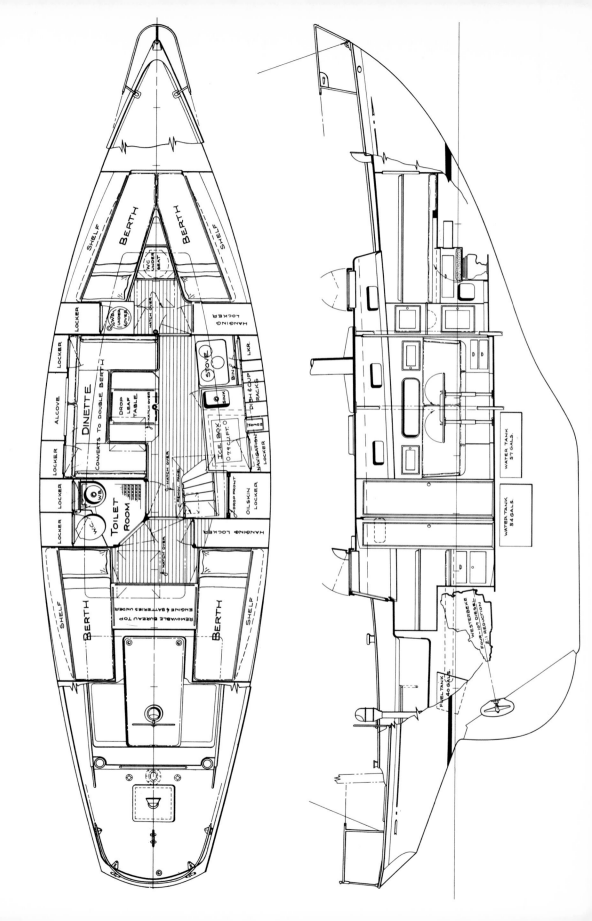

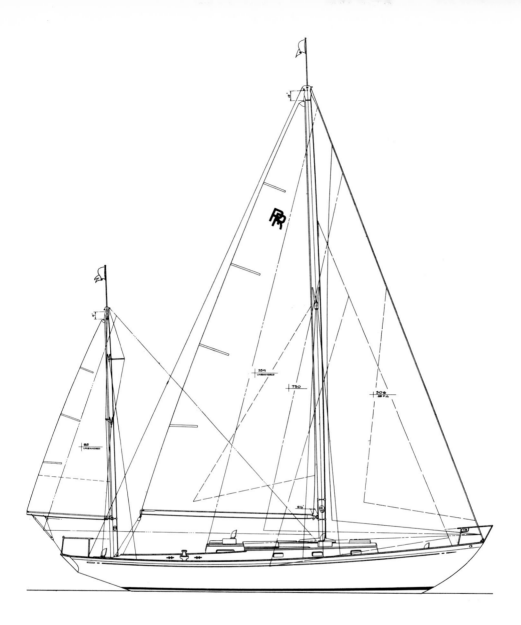

at once for the exact rightness of their looks.

In view of this kind of parentage, then, it is not surprising that *Reliant* should be a fine-looking masthead sloop (or, alternatively, yawl) of obvious ability under sail. However, what really distinguishes *Reliant* from the hundreds of other auxiliaries of similar size and external appearance is the three-compartment accommodation, a triumph of meticulous planning. To sleep six on a boat with a 28-ft waterline is no trick at all, but to do this with two double cabins, both small but not impossibly cramped, and without any serious sacrifice in the main cabin, galley, head, or stowage space counts as a real achievement.

Reliant's mast is stepped on deck and supported by two pipes, one at the forward end of the main cabin and the other at its center; the latter makes a splendid grab rail—indeed, it would be useful for this purpose alone. The off-center companion ladder is curved to permit easy passage, and the seat across from its foot is just the place to cope with the oilies and sea-boots that stow outboard of the ladder. The icebox top is the chart table, and its location below the companionway makes communication between navigator and cockpit reasonably convenient and also facilitates the loading of ice if a refrigerator is not fitted. For most cruising, the convertible dinette is acceptable, especially if supplemented by a folding stool to permit someone to sit to starboard of the table. For offshore passages with a large crew, a Root berth could probably be fitted over the dinette, since a double berth at sea in so relatively narrow a boat is a dubious proposition and the forward berths would be untenable much of the time. The after cabin, however, redeems whatever disadvantages the main cabin may have, since it makes it possible for two people to sack out properly at any time in a good part of the ship. In port, of course, the forward cabin comes into its own as an independent unit, with its own sink and head and enough standing room to dress in.

RELIANT

DESIGNER   *Philip L. Rhodes, 369 Lexington Avenue, New York City*

LOA   40 ft 9 in.
LWL   28 ft
BEAM   10 ft 9 in.
DRAFT   5 ft 9 in.
SAIL AREA   686 ft² (sloop), 750 ft² (yawl)

ENGINE   Universal Atomic Four
FUEL   40 gal
WATER   65 gal
CONSTRUCTION   Wood or fiberglass

(TEXT CONTINUED FROM PAGE 54)

Excessive beam in a heavy boat is not quite so bad, though it may not always contribute proportionately to stability. As the American yacht designer Francis S. Kinney has put it: "What happens as a boat moves is that its bow wave builds up in front, and the stern wave rises aft, leaving a large trough or hollow in the water at the middle of the boat. The boat literally digs a hole for herself in the water and sinks into it. There is then less water amidships to buoy up those wide midship sections. Thus, when she moves she is not as stiff as she would be if heeled over at anchor." Past a certain point, then, additional beam does not help stability in proportion, and there is more to be said for putting the displacement it represents elsewhere. In a keelboat, a beam of about 35 percent of the waterline length seems to give good results—perhaps 1 or 2 percent less for a large boat, 2 or 3 percent more for a small one.

Beam aids stability as a boat heels by increasing the distance between the upward force that acts at the center of buoyancy and the downward force that acts at the center of gravity. Weight aids stability by increasing the magnitude of these forces (they are equal, as the buoyant force is the same as the displacement in any hull that floats), since the righting moment is the product of either force and the horizontal distance between them. A heavy boat is more stable than a similar light one. Ballast helps stability by lowering the center of gravity, which automatically increases the distance between the centers of buoyancy and gravity when the boat heels by a given amount. The greater the proportion of ballast and the lower it is, the lower the center of gravity and the more stable the boat. Stability due to form is more effective at small angles of heel, stability due to ballast at large angles; so the two complement each other, and a satisfactory hull must combine them in the right proportions. Excess ballast is just that much extra deadweight to be dragged along: every pound of unneeded ballast means a book of verses, a jug of wine, or a loaf of bread less—and if there is really too much ballast, thou also must be left behind. The best modern cruising yachts seem to have 30 to 40 percent of their displacement as ballast, though the proportion in racing machines may go beyond 50 percent.

The lower the ballast, the more effective it is, but too much draft leads to excessive wetted surface as well as general inconvenience in cruising. And draft, like beam, has a point of diminishing returns, since a deep lateral plane tends to heel a boat more in the course of impeding leeway than a shallower plane of the same effectiveness. The more beam a boat has, within reason, the more form stability and the less draft it needs, which is a good argument for a moderately large beam. Though it is possible to give rule-of-thumb figures for the beam of a proper keel cruising boat, no such figure can be given in the case of draft, because different hull forms and keel shapes have different requirements. However, so many fine yachts up to 30 ft on the water have had drafts of 6 ft or less, so many between 30 and 35 ft on the water have had drafts between 6 and 7 ft, and so many between 35 and 42 ft on the water have had drafts between 7 and 8 ft that it would seem appropriate to avoid exceeding these figures by very much unless one lives only for RORC racing or has no desire to visit shallow harbors or travel through inland waterways.

British yachts have always been narrower and deeper than those designed elsewhere. The British yachtsman often must cope with steep seas and high winds, and the reason often given for the small beam and large draft of his boats is that these factors make for better windward going under such conditions. While this assertion may be true when the comparison is with a fat tub of poor design, the fact is that a properly shaped hull can have a great deal of beam and relatively shallow draft and still perform very well to windward even in bad weather. After all, American boats, which to an Englishman are just "bloody saucers," have regularly crossed the Atlantic and done well in European racing; and when the ex-Colonials have been put in their place, it has been for the most part with vessels just as broad as theirs. John Illingworth lays the blame for excessive narrowness on fashion set by "chance and local work boats," but there seem to have been two other influences that are equally irrelevant to the actual sailing of a yacht. The first is the manner in which boats were handicapped for racing in the last century: beam was heavily taxed, while draft, displacement, and sail area were unlimited. The result was a spectacular style of yacht design: a 5-ft beam on a 30-ft waterline was accepted as normal in those days, and to get a really large spread of canvas, great bowsprits and topmasts were employed. It took splendid seamen to handle such boats, but they would have been still more splendid had they taken the rule makers by their throats and insisted on an intelligent rating rule, an idea not totally devoid of merit in more than one country even today.

The other potent factor encouraging narrow, deep boats in England is the formula adopted by the Royal Thames Yacht Club in 1854 and, with only very minor changes, still used today to compute the Thames tonnage of a yacht. The formula is $\frac{1}{2}B^2(L-B)/94$, where B is beam and L the length from the stem to the sternpost at deck level or, if there is no sternpost, to the rudderstock (or its extension) at deck level. While a simple means of comparing the bulks of different yachts in a rough-and-ready way is desirable, it is hard to see how any such formula that does not consider the depth of the hull as well can mean much. However, the point at issue is beam, and it is clear that since the square of the beam appears in the above formula, a not very great increase in this measurement sends the TM (Thames measurement) shooting upward. A boat with a length of 30 ft according to the above definition, which might be 33 ft overall, would have a TM of $7\frac{1}{2}$ tons if its beam were 8 ft and a TM of 11 tons if its beam were 10 ft; but the latter boat would be far from being half again larger than the former. Since British yards even today follow the absurd practice of quoting for new construction on the basis of so much per Thames ton, skinny craft are favored on the basis of pounds, shillings, and pence as well as rating.

A retractable centerboard provides an efficient lateral plane when it is required, while minimizing skin friction and draft at other times. Centerboard cruisers are given extra beam to compensate for the reduced effectiveness of their shallow ballast keels, and the beam of a small centerboarder often exceeds 40 percent of its waterline length. A centerboard with just the right cross-sectional shape acts as a hydrofoil owing to the dynamic action of water flowing past it, and the result is a positive "lift" to windward in addition to the static resistance to leeway its area provides. A centerboard is more efficient as a hydrofoil than a fixed keel is (except for the fin keel of an ultralight-displacement hull), and a shallow bilge offers less resistance than a deep one. While a fat boat can hardly be said to knife its way to windward, it may still get to the weather mark ahead of its narrower-keel cousins. Off the wind, the reduced wetted surface that is obtained by cranking up the centerboard is a help, and the cranking process itself will be found useful for keeping un-skilled guests occupied and out of the way—it may be hours before they recover.

But the advantages of a centerboard must be paid for in the form of an expensive installation that may be a serious source of weakness unless carefully engineered and built. And for all the benefit of a broad hull to the accommodation, it has its bad aspects there as well. For one thing, it is difficult to provide adequate tankage, since there is little room beneath the cabin sole, and it is almost impossible to have the engine under a cabin or deckhouse sole unless it is unduly raised. For another, bilge water sloshes around relatively high up when the boat is heeled, making it hard to keep lockers and berths dry. In hard weather, some water always finds its way below even if the hull and deck are tight, and a gallon or two of it, which would never be noticed in a keelboat, can make the watch below in a centerboarder more uncomfortable than it should be. I personally feel that the primary justification for a centerboard is the shoal draft it permits, which in many parts of the world may double or triple the number of possible harbors while reducing the danger of grounding almost everywhere. And a large centerboarder can traverse the French canals, for instance, while a keelboat of the same size cannot. But at sea I much prefer a solid keel under me, and while a draft of 6 to 8 ft cannot be carried to as many places as one of 4 to 6 ft, there is still plenty of splendid cruising available for long-legged vessels.

A word on the elusive quality of balance is in order, for a well-balanced yacht is a delight to sail while a badly balanced one is fit only for the knacker. Balance refers to the ability of a yacht under sail to stay on any desired course without requiring more than a trifle of weather helm. A small weather helm helps retard leeway by the hydrofoil action of the rudder and makes steering easier by providing a "feel" to the tiller or wheel. A proper hull retains a good degree of balance whether heeled or not, whether on or off the wind, and under a variety of sail combinations. As C. A. Satterthwaite has said: "The happy vessel that possesses good balance . . . floats, as it were, on the worship of her lucky owner, and enjoys immortality in the memories of her crew." Many factors affect balance, and their interrelationships are so subtle that only experience can really establish whether a given design will be balanced or not. Theories of balance abound, and every designer has pet formulas he has found helpful; but for all that, any new hull shape is always a gamble. The modification of a hull known to be satisfactory is less risky, and, of course, this is the route most designers follow in evolving new boats.

Beamy hulls seem harder to balance than narrower ones, and few centerboarders are much fun when rail down, fortunately a rare thing with them. This is an argument in favor of fixed keels on the one hand and in favor of twin centerboards on the other. By adjusting the relative drafts of the centerboards, balance can be achieved under almost any circumstances and the boat made self-steering in a steady wind on any heading. Such an installation makes sense principally in large steel or aluminum boats, where the associated construction problems are smaller and where, in any case, a single centerboard might present difficulties because of its size and weight.

The testing of model hulls is sometimes looked upon as an infallible way to arrive at a good hull shape, fast and balanced. In reality, the chief function of the tank is to help refine a specific basic design concept, and no tank can help a poor concept. What it *can* do is help the designer to maximize those aspects of performance that he wants to stress—windward ability, perhaps, or speed in light airs or steadiness downwind in heavy seas or whatever. If all-round good performance is required, tank testing can help by uncovering any specific vices a hull may have. But if tank testing is good insurance, it is also expensive insurance; and when the designer is a talented man, it is really necessary only if a departure from his accustomed style is involved. The tank can give answers to specific questions, but it cannot design a boat, and the best advice, as always, is to find a good designer who is in sympathy with your goals and rely on his advice.

[V]

A Trio by Sparkman & Stephens:
ALNAIR, SIMBA, &
CLARION OF WIGHT

Alnair, Simba, AND *Clarion* ALL WERE designed by Olin Stephens with almost identical waterline lengths and displacements, and all are similar in appearance, yet each is quite distinct from the others in a number of significant ways. What this emphasizes is the need to have a clear idea of what one wants even though one has already chosen the size and general type of a prospective yacht and its designer. So talented a man as Olin Stephens has many strings to his bow, all superb, and which one he selects depends upon the specific requirements he must resolve.

ALNAIR

PERHAPS THE MOST CONVENTIONAL OF THE three, *Alnair* is a keel yawl of pleasing but unremarkable proportions. There is little in *Alnair*'s stated dimensions or outline to suggest that she is actually so far out of the ordinary that her architect, who is responsible for many thousands of fine yachts, should be able to write that "I think she is one of the best behaved all-around boats that we have designed. Her balance under sail seems to be maintained under all conditions of weather and most combinations of canvas. She is also a notably dry and comfortable sea boat." The great advantage of experience is that it permits refining a basic design concept to about as close to perfection as that concept can be brought, and *Alnair* is the result of an evolutionary process of this kind. It is easy to pick out an isolated item and criticize it, for instance by asserting grumpily that her short keel means that she will be unsteady on the helm and that, as compared with a longer, straighter keel of the same depth, the higher center of gravity of her ballast will make her tender; but other factors also influence these aspects of performance, and what counts is the combined effect of all of them—an effect that is highly satisfactory in the case of *Alnair*. The cutaway underwater profile means a low wetted surface and hence speed in light weather with only a moderate sail area, which in turn reduces the demand on the keel for righting moment, and the shape of the hull as a whole

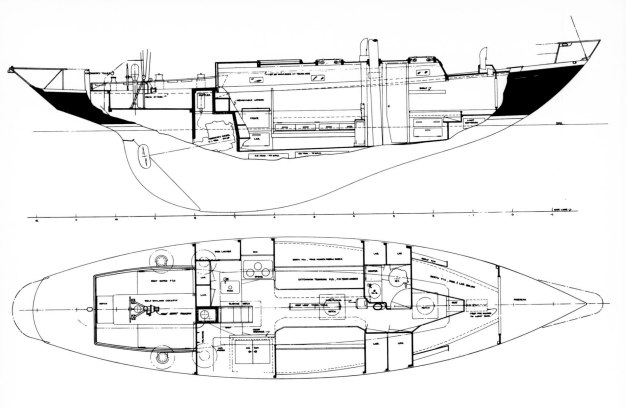

has more to do with docile steering than does the area of the lateral plane by itself. So all in all, it would have to be a rash man who would find fault with *Alnair*'s lines.

Alnair uses conventional reefing, which permits the mainsheet to lead conveniently to a pedestal in the cockpit just forward of the wheel. The foot block for the mizzen sheet is mounted on a suitably reinforced after pulpit, also a neat scheme.

A Mercedes-Benz 34-hp diesel engine with 2:1 reduction gear is shown on the plans, assuring good performance under power, and there is reasonable access to the engine from the cabin through removable panels in the front and sides of the engine box. A 600-watt auxiliary generator is belted to the engine for the lighting batteries, in addition to a smaller one for the starting battery; the lighting batteries are under the forward end of the berths in the forward cabin, which helps with the distribu-

tion of weights and makes good use of a normally wasted space. The 45-gal fuel tank and the largest water tank fit in the bilge, where their weight does the most good, and two smaller water tanks go under the main-cabin transoms for a total water capacity of 100 gal.

By limiting the number of berths to six, there is enough room for a really adequate galley, chart table (the icebox top), and head, and there is a substantial amount of stowage space throughout the entire boat. A gimbaled three-burner stove with oven, a cabin heater, and an oilskin locker near the companionway all add to the good life below without being in the way. The only improvement I can think of is based on my own experience in trying to cook in a similar boat when going to windward: the moderate beam means a certain amount of heel, and something for the cook to brace himself against—for instance, a vertical post or a short rail at bottom height—can be most helpful.

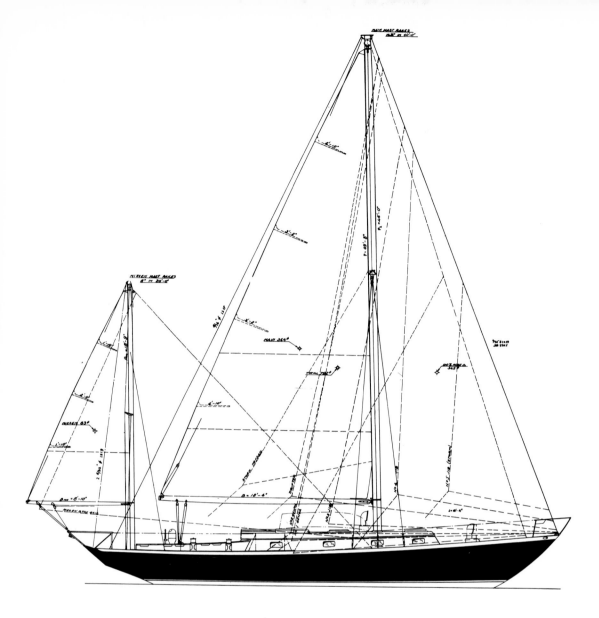

ALNAIR

DESIGNER *Sparkman & Stephens, Inc., 79 Madison Avenue, New York City*

LOA 41 ft 6 in.

LWL 29 ft 6 in.

BEAM 10 ft 9 in.

DRAFT 6 ft 3 in.

DISPLACEMENT 22,900 lb

BALLAST 7,500 lb of lead

SAIL AREA 800 ft²

ENGINE Mercedes-Benz OM636 diesel (34 hp)

FUEL 35 gal

WATER 100 gal

CONSTRUCTION Mahogany planking; fiberglass-covered plywood deck; spruce spars

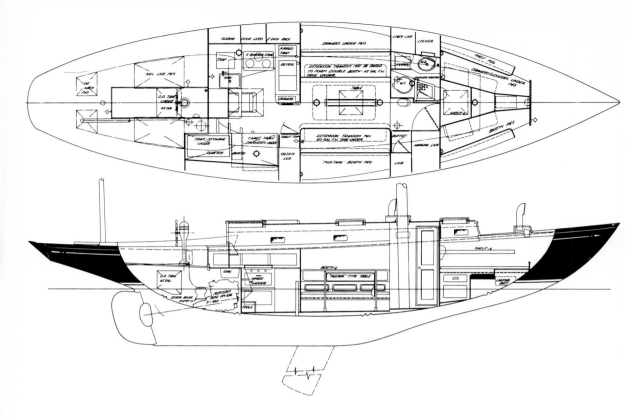

SIMBA

Simba, THOUGH HAVING THE SAME WATERLINE length and about the same displacement as *Alnair,* is 1 ft ½ in. broader in beam and 2 ft 3 in. less in draft, the result of having a centerboard in place of a deep keel. Her rig is larger by about 10 percent to furnish the additional drive this hull form requires, an increase that is obtained by extending the mainmast 4 ft and the mizzenmast 3 ft. A removable forestay and running backstay to support it are indicated on the sail plan to permit switching to double headsails whenever desirable. Both main and mizzen are fitted for roller reefing, which means

that the mainsheet leads to the after end of the cockpit and the mizzen sheet to a boomkin. *Simba*'s spray hood is actually a grander affair than that shown on the sail plan, being a segment of a sphere and extending across the entire cabin trunk with transparent plastic windows. Because the centerboard is narrow, it stows below the cabin sole, but it is long enough to be effective.

Simba is about a foot longer and a foot wider than *Alnair,* which does not seem like much, but the additional volume available for the accommodation is considerable. There is room

SIMBA *is a centerboard yawl designed by Sparkman & Stephens. Note the manner of sheeting the mizzen, the tackle on the main boom to help the mainsail set properly (a mainsheet track would make the tackle unnecessary), the large hatches for access to the lazaret, and the standard compass in its own binnacle on the stern.* SIMBA's *large and effective spray hood is folded down out of the way.* (Rosenfeld)

for a quarter berth to starboard in *Simba*, with a chart table over its forward end and an oilskin locker between it and the main cabin. To port is a U-shaped galley that includes a refrigerator. Both main and forward cabins are less cramped because of the added beam, and the feeling of spaciousness is probably as important as the extra elbowroom itself.

On the plus side for cruising, then, the major items are *Simba*'s draft of 4 ft (which in some parts of the world means twice as many possible harbors as those accessible to a boat having a 6-ft draft), her large accommodation for her length, and her pronounced initial stiffness. On the minus side are the centerboard, an expensive installation that provides something else to go wrong, the need for an enlarged rig, and the poorer handling characteristics of centerboarders as compared with keelboats. Of course, with roller reefing on main and mizzen, an optional double-head rig, and the ability to adjust the centerboard, *Simba* can be made happy at all times, but there is more to it than in the case of *Alnair*.

It is more difficult to design a centerboarder than a keelboat of the same length if the result is to be handsome and without unsightly bulges when looked at from certain angles. The counter in particular must be drawn with great care. Olin Stephens has done his usual fine job with *Simba*, which is a lovely boat indeed; her appearance is enhanced by varnished mahogany topsides and aluminum spars painted white.

CLARION OF WIGHT

IN PLANNING *Clarion*, THE DESIGNER'S PRIMARY consideration was racing ability under the RORC rule. Thus the basic sail area is small, and most of it is in the broad-based foretriangle, which permits large overlapping headsails: the biggest genoa has an area of 626 ft², nearly double the area of the mainsail. The main itself terminates several feet below the masthead, which is consistent with its inferior status in racing. The purpose of the forestay and running backstays is more to help the mast withstand the stresses imposed by large genoas than to exploit double headsails. The backstay turnbuckle shown on the plans has folding handles that permit the rake of the mast to be adjusted conveniently while the boat is under way. The twin goal in *Clarion* is speed and a low RORC rating, and a different formula for assessing sail area would mean a different rig. *Alnair*'s rig, while not without racing potency, has a sounder basis and is more suited to cruising.

The accommodation too shows the influence of racing, though it has some interesting features. The theme everywhere is lightness, since every pound saved by eliminating excess weight can go into the keel and so enhance the windward ability that wins races. *Clarion*'s keel contains 10,000 lb of lead, while *Alnair*'s contains only 7,500 lb, yet *Alnair* is the heavier boat by 700 lb. In *Clarion* there are few drawers, lockers are mostly open caves, the fixed berths have canvas bottoms, and so on—measures that add up to a lot of omitted lumber. The only extravagance is in the 6½ ft headroom, which *Clarion*'s owners deplore as much as they do the high freeboard at the ends that makes possible the fine sweep of her sheer. If The Rule favors low freeboard and drooping ends, however ugly and unseamanlike they may be, then low freeboard and drooping ends it must be. But *Clarion* won the 1963 Fastnet, so perhaps the penalty for good looks is not so severe after all.

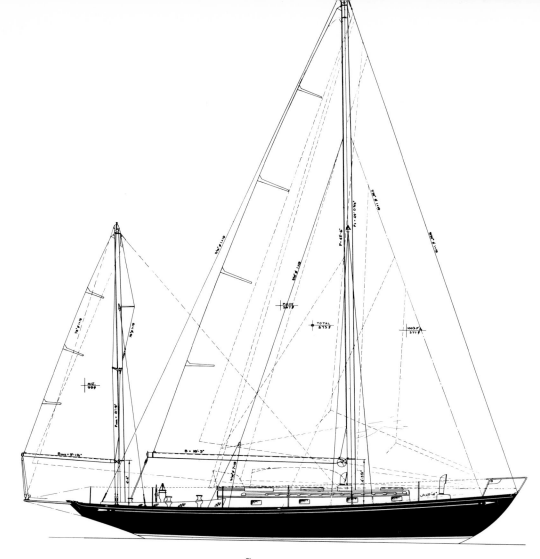

SIMBA

DESIGNER   *Sparkman & Stephens, Inc., 79 Madison Avenue, New York City*

LOA   42 ft 7 in.

LWL   29 ft 6 in.

BEAM   11 ft 9½ in.

DRAFT   4 ft board up

DISPLACEMENT   22,000 lb

BALLAST   7,000 lb of lead

SAIL AREA   873 ft²

ENGINE   Mercedes-Benz OM636 diesel (34 hp)

FUEL   45 gal

WATER   90 gal

CONSTRUCTION   Mahogany-over-cedar double planking with garboard strakes of teak on white-oak frames, with oak and teak centerline structure; teak-over-plywood deck and mahogany deckworks; aluminum spars

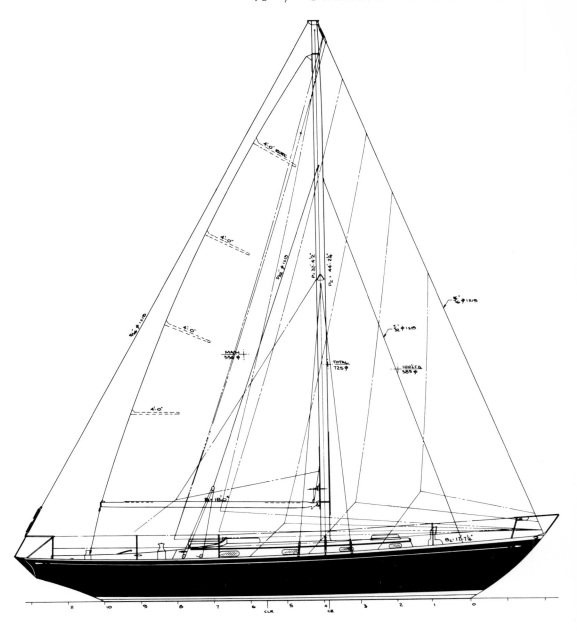

CLARION OF WIGHT, *designed by Sparkman & Stephens for ocean racing, nevertheless has many of the qualities that a good cruising yacht requires.* (Beken)

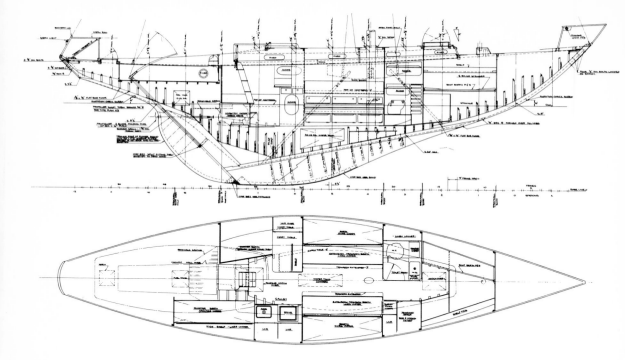

Clarion's plans show eight berths, of which four can be occupied at sea without using the main-cabin settees. However, since stowage space is scant, the galley is minute, and there is only one head, cruising with eight people aboard would not be very pleasant. But this criticism is valid only for the original layout, which could readily be altered in another boat built to the same lines, as could the rig shown for that matter. It is entirely possible that with a proper accommodation and rig, *Clarion* would make a superlative cruiser. Olin Stephens has written: "With respect to suitability for cruising, I am very partial to two of our small boat designs [*Alnair* and *Clarion*] which although not worked out specifically for long distance cruising, but actually with a view to long distance racing, I am sure are good sea boats and may be adapted to extended cruising." It would be most interesting to see how a cruising version of *Clarion* actually works out.

C L A R I O N   O F   W I G H T

DESIGNER   *Sparkman & Stephens, Inc., 79 Madison Avenue, New York City*

LOA   43 ft 6 in.
LWL   30 ft
BEAM   10 ft 11 in.
DRAFT   6 ft 9 in.
DISPLACEMENT   22,200 lb
BALLAST   10,000 lb of lead
SAIL AREA   725 ft²

ENGINE   Coventry Victor (16 hp)
FUEL   12½ gal
WATER   36 gal
CONSTRUCTION   Mahogany planking above waterline, teak below; canvas-covered plywood deck; aluminum mast; spruce boom

CHAPTER THREE

Hull Construction

W HEN THE FORM of the hull has been arrived at, it must then be transformed from a series of curved lines on a sheet of paper to a three-dimensional object about the size of a whale. If the transformation is done well, the result will be a yacht that can give pleasure for perhaps a half century despite such indignities as grounding, storage ashore, and occasional lapses in maintenance. If it is done badly . . . well, in that unhappy event, the yacht will at least have the grace to fall to pieces before many years of misery have passed.

Normally the stresses a sailboat hull is called upon to withstand are surprisingly small—some remarkably flimsy craft have remained afloat despite all the laws of God and man. But there is a vast difference between an afternoon sail in sheltered waters and a real offshore passage and between taking the ground when the tide falls and striking a submerged rock full tilt. Improvements in masts, rigging, and sails have made it necessary for hulls to be tougher than in the past. Aluminum masts, stainless-steel rigging, and synthetic-fiber sails can take almost anything the sea and sky can dish out, which means that boats are being driven harder than before. Skippers no longer worry about sails blowing out or masts going over the side (though poor design or flawed construction still lead to such happenings), and the twin results are remarkable sailing performances and enormous stresses on hulls. Scantlings that seemed adequate a decade or two ago may not be able to yield yachts capable of carrying on cheerfully to windward in a moderate gale at full bore, and only modern materials and techniques can produce the required strength without sacrificing lightness.

By "hull" I refer, of course, to all parts of a boat that contribute to its structural strength and watertight integrity, not just to its frames and planking. Considerable inward forces are developed at the chain plates, for instance, which must be supported by adequate deck beams and cabin-house reinforcing. At one moment the sea is a glorious rippled expanse of green or blue, at another a wild mass of matter gone mad, and a wave crest breaking upon even a small vessel may hurl many tons of water upon her. Deck, cockpit, cabin house, hatches, and companionways must be able to take such a battering.

Boats have been built of wood for thousands of years, and even today, despite competition from fiberglass-reinforced plastic, aluminum, and steel, wood still remains an excellent material for the purpose. However, this remark needs qualification, since modern methods of constructing a wooden boat are different from the traditional ones. The best contemporary practice makes extensive use of glues as well as metal fastenings to join the various structural elements of a boat into what becomes a virtually monolithic shell, so that the result is both stronger and lighter than it would otherwise be.

Not long ago the backbone of a hull was bolted together from solid wood, the frames were steam-bent from solid wood, and the planking consisted of separate strakes between which caulking was driven to achieve watertightness. Individual fastenings do all the work of holding such a boat together, which means that each member has to be large enough to accept fastenings adequate in size and number without thereby having its own strength cut down too much. Such a vessel must fight itself as well as the elements, because its solid frames are always trying to straighten themselves out; in addition, the annual swelling and shrinking of the planking when the boat is stored ashore tend to loosen the hold of the fastenings. Without question, many fine boats have been built in this manner and have stood up well over the years, but the point is that still stronger boats can today be built from the same amount of building material, or for the same strength, less material is needed.

Three basic options are available today in building first-class wooden boats. The first and most widely used represents the orthodox technique carried to its logical conclusion. The backbone is laminated from thin strips glued together, keel and stem as a single unit, which provides an enormous gain in strength since the grain of the wood always runs the right way and there are no joints at which stresses are localized. Frames are laminated in advance, and since they are made from thin strips bent into shape before being glued together, they are stable, with no inclination to straighten out. Metal floors with straps that run up the frames are used in the way of the mast step and are welded to it, which spreads out both the immense thrust of a highly loaded mast and the equally great racking stresses of the ballast keel when the boat is heeled. The planks are planed to a perfect fit and are glued together as well as to the frames, so that each plank helps the one next to it instead

[OPPOSITE] WANDERER III *was designed by Laurent Giles for Eric Hiscock, who, with his wife, has sailed her twice around the world. Her dimensions are LOA 30 ft 4in., LWL 26 ft 4 in., beam 8 ft 5 in., draft 5 ft, and sail area about 450 ft². The comments of* WANDERER's *owner are most valuable in view of his great experience: "She is a fine small cruiser, but I am of the opinion that greater beam and more spread-out ballast would tend to ease her rather violent motion; also she could do with an increased sail area and an engine of greater power." The original engine was a 4-hp Stuart-Turner, and an 8-hp engine was subsequently installed. Hiscock states in his book* Voyaging Under Sail *that he would much rather have cruised in a larger vessel—say, 15 tons TM—which would be perhaps 40 to 42 ft overall, but that the increased expense deterred him. (Beken)*

of merely pressing against it via the caulking. One might think this method of construction is terribly expensive, but I have been assured that it is cheaper than the traditional method provided the builders are experienced. For one thing, less wood is wasted and smaller pieces are needed initially, since the laminated members are made from strips instead of being hewn from solid wood. For another, no molds are needed; the laminated frames themselves are set up on the backbone and the planking is attached to them directly. Nor is it extravagant of labor. I have seen a man and a boy turn out eight pairs of laminated frames for a 52-ft yawl in a single day working to templates made in the loft.

Another construction method that depends upon glue for its success is strip planking. Here the hull is built from narrow wooden strips, often square in cross section, that are glued and edge-nailed to one another. No frames are needed, though such interior structures as bulkheads help stiffen the shell. A strip-planked hull is enormously strong for its weight because it is so thoroughly joined together. This very robustness is sometimes held against the method, since repairs are impeded by the interlocking of the hull members—an odd argument, since repairs are less likely to be required in the first place. A further advantage is the ease of maintenance of a strip-planked hull, whose smooth interior has few pockets to collect water and promote rot.

Strip planking is perhaps most easily carried out with the help of sawed outside molds, since the strips are then held in place automatically when they are being fastened together, though inside molds are often used. No special skills or machinery are required, but a good deal of time must be spent in merely applying glue and nailing the strips. An amateur can do as good a job on a strip-planked hull as a professional, but the latter will need less time to build a hull by a more conventional method. Time is money, and as a result few boats other than light-displacement ones are strip-planked—a shame, since the method has very real merits.

The third relatively new procedure for building wooden boats involves laminating the hull itself. Thin sheets of wood or plywood are glued together with the help of a mold to form a one-piece shell with multiple skins. The resulting structure is exceptionally strong for its weight, and because of this, laminated hulls are most often found in light-displacement vessels. The ancestor of lamination is double planking. In orthodox double planking, two thin layers of strakes are used, one on top of the other, with cloth laid in shellac or linseed oil between them. Each layer of planking is separately attached to the frames. One criticism of this method is that the need to countersink the screws holding the outer planking means that since this planking is thin in the first place, the actual amount of wood under the screwheads is precariously small. In practice, carefully built double-planked boats have proven themselves quite sturdy, but no more so than boats built by either of the modern techniques mentioned earlier, while being more expensive. The advantage of going the whole hog and laminating the hull with multiple skins glued together is that the result is far lighter for the same strength than in double planking. An intermediate procedure that has been used on occasion with success is a triple skin on light framing; the inner layers have their grain running diagonally, and the outer one has its grain fore and aft as usual. Lightness and strength are again the result, while the expense of building a mold is avoided.

While timber is customarily divided into softwoods and hardwoods, the distinctions between them actually have little to do with the actual hardness of the

(TEXT CONTINUED ON PAGE 92)

[V I]

Two 30-Ft-Waterline Ketches:
ATLANTIC & DANDY

I<small>N THESE TWO INTERESTING KETCHES, THE</small> emphasis is on minimizing the burden on the crew while still permitting reasonable performance under sail. Each is beamy, which in combination with a low rig means great stability. While not "young men's boats," they are not "old men's boats" either, and what they may not always be able to provide in the way of exciting sailing, they make up for by being able to furnish far-ranging adventures without discomfort or heroics.

ATLANTIC

D<small>ESCRIBED BY THEIR DESIGNER</small>, Walter F. Rayner, as "power ketches," the *Atlantic* class of yachts "can easily be sailed by a man and wife on long cruises and in fact several of them have been, including voyages from England by sea to Toulon and other Mediterranean ports. One of the vessels is at present on her way to Tenerife." That they should be such able cruisers is no surprise, for the boat fairly radiates sturdy competence. The displacement of 21,000 lb is moderate for a waterline length of 30 ft, and there is plenty of power in the 56-hp Parsons diesel to push the boat along in weather too light for her snug rig. The top speed under engine power is 8¼ knots, which is very good for a sailboat of this size, and good fuel economy can be had with the throttle backed down to the still considerable cruising speed of 7½ knots. There are two steering positions, one at the forward end of the self-draining cockpit, where the helmsman has excellent visibility and is protected from the weather, and another, less comfortable one at its after end, where the sails can be watched more conveniently.

The draft of *Atlantic* is only 5 ft, which opens to her many canals and inland waterways that few fixed-keel vessels of her seagoing capabilities can negotiate. Thus she can avoid an upstream passage in the mighty Rhone by taking the shoal Canal du Midi to Bordeaux, an excursion I should love to make, if only to listen for the nightingales of Castelnaudary.

The midships cockpit, with engine and lighting plant beneath, separates the accommodation into two parts. Aft is a compact double cabin with one wide berth and one narrow one, together with a washbasin and limited stowage.

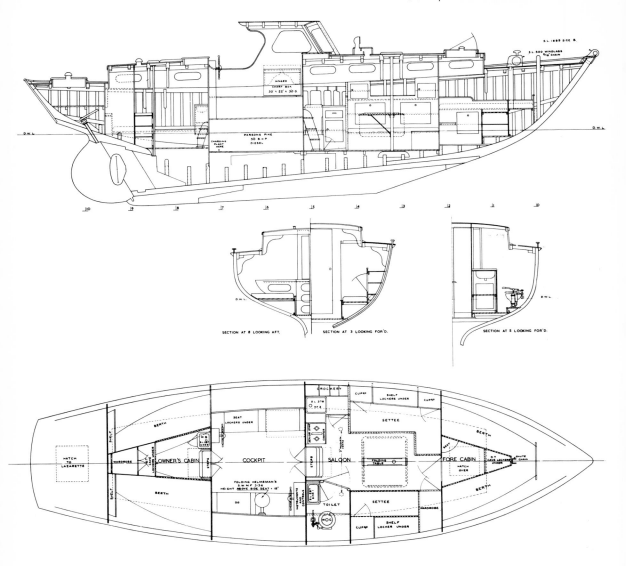

ATLANTIC

DESIGNER *Walter F. Rayner, Ltd., 22 Parkstone Road, Poole, England*

LOA 38 ft

LWL 30 ft

BEAM 11 ft 6 in.

DRAFT 5 ft

DISPLACEMENT 21,000 lb

BALLAST 7,800 lb of iron

SAIL AREA 583 ft^2

ENGINE Parsons Pike diesel (56 hp)

FUEL 82 gal

WATER 82 gal

CONSTRUCTION Mahogany planking on oak or rock-elm frames, with oak and elm centerline structure; canvas-covered plywood deck; spruce spars

Forward are an enclosed head to starboard and the galley to port, a well-thought-out main cabin, and a just-adequate forecabin. To get an accommodation this extensive yet still efficient into so modest a hull is an accomplishment, and what is especially commendable is that a full-length settee in the main cabin has been sacrificed in favor of more locker space—a commodity that is seldom in excess in a cruising boat.

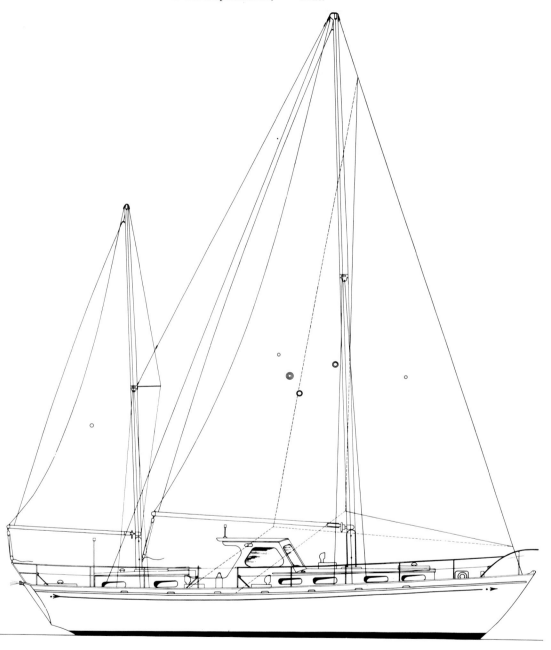

DANDY

LIKE ALL OF AAGE UTZON'S YACHTS, *Dandy* shows the influence of his Viking ancestors. I cannot watch one of *Dandy*'s many near-sisters sailing in from Øresund without expecting her to have bloody decks and treasure in the hold —though these days, it is more likely that any liquid spilled will be beer and any gold aboard will be in the form of blond tresses. *Dandy* herself is a flush-decked double-ender so nicely shaped that, despite a displacement of 23,000 lb in an over-all length of only a little more than 36 ft, there is a certain grace to her as well as an air of sober purpose. More than 40 percent of *Dandy*'s displacement is in her iron ballast keel, which, with her beam of 11 ft 5 in. and draft of 6 ft 1 in., will keep her on her feet no matter what the weather. The rig is tall and narrow, a necessity if enough sail area is to be packed into an inboard ketch with such small overhangs. To get the most from such sails, it is essential to keep them from twisting, and the main accordingly has both a permanent vang leading to the foot of the mast and a mainsheet foot block near the middle of the boom, and the mizzen sheet is secured to the mizzen boom well in from its end. A small forestaysail is drawn as a working sail, and a much larger genoa can be set on the topmast stay—perhaps an unnecessary complication in so small a vessel, but one that some prefer because the effectiveness of the smaller sail is enhanced by being closer to the main. A noteworthy detail on deck is the bow hawsehole, which is built into the stem with a curvature 5 in. in radius to reduce the friction of chain without the complication of a roller.

Dandy has a snug cockpit well aft to facilitate steering by tiller, but the designer also had in mind a supplementary steering position in the deckhouse using a wheel. *Dandy*'s navigator is well treated, with a nook of his own to starboard in the deckhouse that includes a large table and extensive stowage space for charts and instruments. The deckhouse also includes a quarter berth to port, which looks as though it might be a wet one, and an oilskin locker. The galley is two steps down and includes a large refrigerator operated from kerosene or bottled gas; there is no provision for enough generating and battery capacity to run more than a miniature electric refrigerator, and whether one seeks Danegeld or Danish girls, iced Pilsner and smørrebrød are indispensable. The main cabin has an unusual arrangement made possible by the high flush deck, namely, built-in upper and lower berths on each side with narrow seats inboard of them. Four people can sleep securely here at sea without getting in anybody's way. Overhead is a large plastic-topped hatch that admits light and, when open, air in copious amounts to relieve what might otherwise be something of the atmosphere of *The Lower Depths*. Forward are a head to port and large lockers to starboard, and the forward cabin contains two berths.

The construction indicated is interesting. Every fourth frame is laminated and heavier than the others, with a heavy oak floor; additional laminated frames are used in the vicinity of the mast and deckhouse. The frames at the ends are set perpendicular to the hull rather than to the centerline, which helps strengthen the structure there. Plywood is used liberally in the accommodation and is tied into the basic structure. With her simple construction, "*Dandy* can be built relatively cheaply at any average yard, and be economical in maintenance," according to her designer. Continuing the theme of robust simplicity, the engine contemplated is a small air-cooled Lister diesel, which, with a 2:1 reduction gear, should be capable of driving *Dandy* at somewhat more than 6 knots with modest fuel consumption.

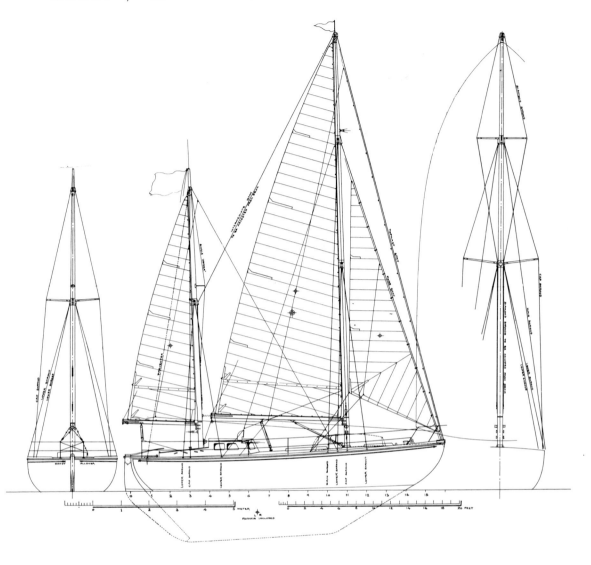

D A N D Y

DESIGNER *Aage Utzon, Hellebaek, Denmark*

LOA   36 ft 4 in.
LWL   30 ft
BEAM   11 ft 5 in.
DRAFT 6 ft 1 in.
DISPLACEMENT   23,000 lb
BALLAST   9,600 lb of iron

SAIL AREA   800 ft^2
ENGINE   Lister S.L.3 (12¾ hp)
WATER   60 gal
CONSTRUCTION Wooden hull on laminated
  frames; spruce spars

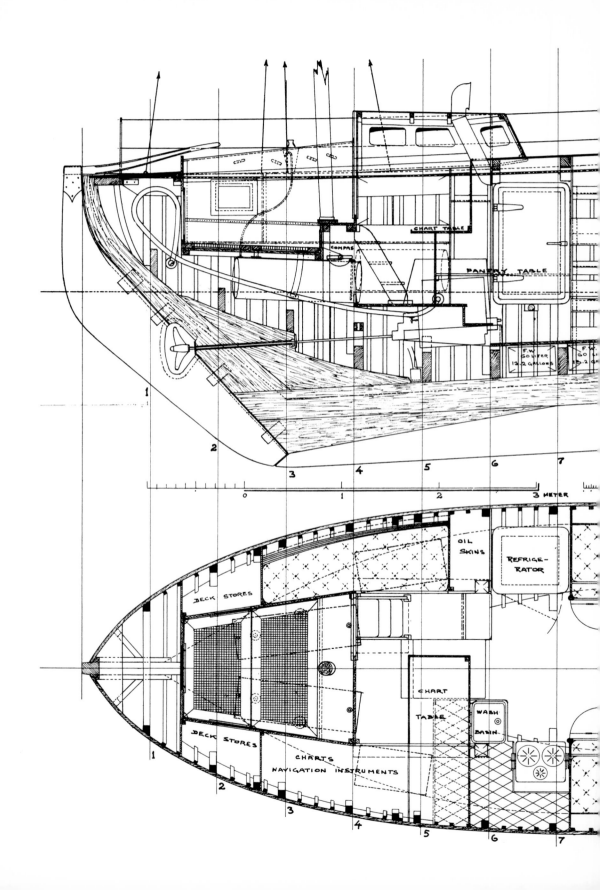

CHART TABLE

COMPAS

PANTRY TABLE

F.W.
SO...FER
12.2 GALLONS

F.W.
GO...
...2 G...

1

1

2

3   4   5   6   7

0   1   2   3 METER

OIL
SKINS

REFRIGE-
RATOR

DECK STORES

CHART

TABLE

WASH
BASIN

DECK STORES

CHARTS
NAVIGATION INSTRUMENTS

1

2

3

4

5

6   7

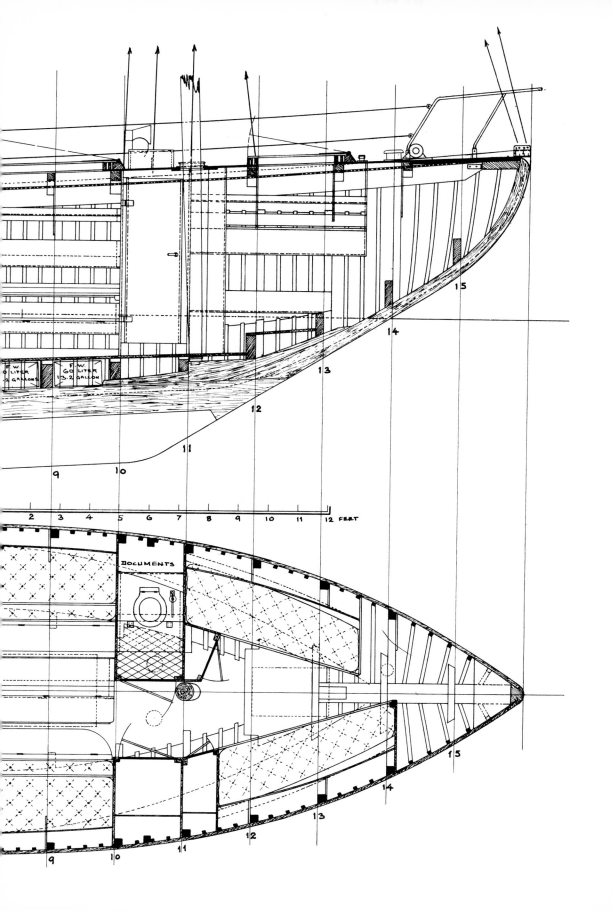

F.W.
O LITER
2 GALLON

F.W.
GO LITER
13.2 GALLON

15

14

13

12

11

9   10

2   3   4   5   6   7   8   9   10   11   12 FEET

DOCUMENTS

15

14

13

12

11

9   10

(TEXT CONTINUED FROM PAGE 84)

material. Softwood trees have needlelike leaves, while hardwood trees have broad leaves, and the chemical composition and physical structure of the wood from each differ in certain respects. Each category contains both excellent and poor boat-building woods, and to further complicate matters, wood from a particular species varies from tree to tree depending upon the soil and climate conditions in which the growth took place. Still, much of the appeal of wood lies in this very variability: however much the engineer may admire the predictability and uniformity of metal and plastic, even he cannot fail to respond to the contrasting charms of oak, teak, mahogany, and spruce on display on the deck of a traditional boat.

Different functions aboard ship call for different materials, and it is, in fact, quite remarkable that such a broad range of properties exists in wood that a proper combination can take care of nearly all the requirements. The stem, keel, and frames require great strength and durability, together with an ability to hold fastenings securely, which makes white oak the best choice. Planking needs a stable wood, not too heavy, that can be given a smooth finish and that is available in long, defect-free lengths, specifications that eliminate oak but lead directly to mahogany. Clamps and bilge stringers require a strong, fairly light, straight-grained wood, making fir the logical candidate. A wooden deck must be very stable and durable—in fact, capable of being left bare for the life of the boat—and no better wood than teak has been found for this purpose. A tiller must be strong yet limber enough to take up some of the shocks that the rudder produces, and ash is good on this score. A light but durable wood is needed for ceilings, for which cedar is excellent. Wooden spars must be both light and strong, and the wood they are made from must be available in long lengths and have a straight grain, with hardness unnecessary, and spruce invariably is the selection. Cabin soles of teak are best constructed with thin raised alternating strips of a hard wood to improve slip resistance, and now the finger points to holly. Eight different woods, yet this is so far from being unusual that a competent surveyor would look askance at a wooden boat with more than one or two fewer.

While the above woods are perhaps most widely used in top-quality construction for their special purposes, substitutions may well be desirable owing to some special circumstance such as the availability of rarer but equivalent timber. For instance, iroko is a strong, hard wood from Africa that is a perfectly acceptable alternative to teak provided that pieces with irregular grain are avoided. Another not uncommon alternative to teak for decking is afromosia. In the case of planking, although mahogany is a good all-around choice, it is not the strongest or most durable wood, and teak and iroko are often preferred despite greater weight and cost. A boat planked in teak is heavier than one planked in mahogany; all else equal, the boat is less stable, since its center of gravity is raised; and certainly mahogany planking finished bright is one of the happier creations of man, yet the virtues of teak are enough to tip the scales in the judgment of some experienced cruising men whose exchequers are in good shape. Sometimes a different wood is used below the waterline—for instance, pitch pine or makore—but this is seldom done these days.

A point to be mentioned here is that not all wood with the same generic name is the same. White oak, a first-class timber for boatbuilding, is not at all the same thing as red oak, a most inferior timber for this purpose owing to its tendency to rot. Mahogany, too, comes in different varieties, though all of them are successfully used in boats. The strongest, hardest, and least absorbent of water is Honduras mahogany, whose expense keeps it from wide use. African mahogany is a bit weaker and softer, but it is still a fine wood that does a good job. Philippine mahogany is actually a type of cedar and, while acceptable, is perhaps least preferred of the three.

Preservatives have been developed for wood that, if properly applied, reduce the likelihood of dry rot to a minimum. A good preservative should be applied to the inside of a hull when it is planked out, and enough should be used for it to penetrate to the outside of the planking. A simple measure and usually an effective one, but it is still necessary to have properly selected and seasoned wood in the first place.

Wood must also be suitably protected on the outside. Here synthetic coatings, notably those in the polyurethane family, seem to have many advantages over conventional paints and varnishes, though not everybody is happy with them. The most significant are their greater durability and resistance to abrasion, which, since the primary function of a surface coating is to protect what lies beneath it, constitute sufficient recommendation by themselves. Their hardness, too, is useful in that a really smooth, polished finish can be obtained. But all is not perfect with these new materials. They are more expensive than ordinary paint and varnish, and once the two components are mixed, the pot life is limited. Synthetic coatings harden rapidly and therefore must be applied very quickly, with a technique somewhat different from that used with conventional coatings. In the case of clear coatings, it is more difficult to obtain a perfect mirrorlike sheen than it is with good varnishes because the former dry too quickly to be adequately self-leveling. For these reasons, it is sometimes hard to convince a yard to use synthetic finishes; possibly their greater durability is also a factor in this reluctance. I can see no reason not to insist upon a suitable synthetic coating on all new work and on all surfaces that have been stripped down to the bare material, whether wood, fiberglass, or metal. What to do when there is an existing conventional finish in good condition is less clear-cut, since the newer coating may not stick or, worse, may impair the adhesion of the original one. Probably the risk is not worth taking in the case of paint, but where brightwork on deck is concerned, it might be acceptable. Personally, I became so fed up with the inability of standard varnishes to stand up to hard usage that I put a clear polyurethane lacquer allegedly compatible with ordinary varnish on the exterior brightwork of my yacht—and it neatly peeled off in three months.

From the point of view of ultimate safety, steel and aluminum hulls win on every count. A welded hull of either material is absolutely watertight, enormously strong, and fireproof. Apart from their strength, these metals have the further advantage over wood and fiberglass of the engineering quality of toughness: the strength of a material refers to the force needed to break a sample of it, while its toughness refers instead to the amount of energy that must be expended in so doing. The latter is equal to the applied force multiplied by the amount by which the sample stretches under load before rupture, so that a ductile material may be many times tougher than a completely rigid material of the same breaking strength. For instance, a sharp blow of sufficient force against a submerged rock will open up a fiberglass or wooden hull, while it will merely dent a metal hull of identical ultimate strength according to handbook tables. Applied for long enough, of course, an excessive force will have the same destructive effect on any material, but this is emphatically not true for shocks of brief duration. By itself, therefore, tensile strength is an ambiguous criterion in comparing hull materials, and when all the relevant factors are considered, steel and aluminum come out well on top.

Steel hulls are much cheaper than aluminum ones, partly because aluminum is more expensive in itself and partly because it is more difficult to work with. The two disadvantages of steel are its weight and its liability to corrosion. Thin sheet metal—say, less than $\frac{1}{8}$-in. thick—may be adequately strong for a certain hull but may not be stiff enough to withstand pounding to windward in a seaway or bumping against a dock without being deformed. The results are wavy topsides, with ridges where the frames have provided local support and hollows in between. Such a hull may be perfectly seaworthy, but it looks terrible and is probably a bit slower than it otherwise would be. Even heavy shell plating is not immune to some deformation; but in a properly built boat, merely cutting down the gloss of the topsides paint is enough to make it inconspicuous, and it is unlikely to be severe enough to affect speed at all. The result is that the smallest boat that really makes sense in steel is perhaps 45 to 50 ft in over-all length if the hull is not to be excessively heavy. The weight of steel is a meaningful objection only in smaller yachts.

Some large steel vessels have irregular shell plating due to an incorrect welding sequence. Unless the various parts of the hull are welded together in proper order, the thermal expansion and contraction of the steel make a smooth skin impossible, and stresses may well be set up that can distort the entire structure. However, the art of building steel ships of all sizes is hardly a mystery, and a competent yard accustomed to steel construction can normally be trusted to do the right thing.

The other stock objection to steel boats is the possibility of corrosion. Certainly there is nothing quite as dreadful looking as rust stains on a yacht's topsides or as discouraging as a hull eaten away by electrolysis or galvanic action. These three sources of trouble are quite distinct from one another, though they often join forces in an alarmingly sinister way: rusting is much more rapid if either of the other sources of corrosion is also active. To the chemist, rust is a hydrated ferric oxide that is formed on iron or steel in the presence of both water (either liquid water or atmospheric moisture) and oxygen. Interestingly enough, rusting is promoted by a moderate restriction in the supply of oxygen. The process occurs in a definite sequence of steps, beginning with the formation of ferrous ions from the metal and ending with the formation of the hydrated ferric oxide. If the sequence takes place fast enough, the rust acts to some extent as a protective coating and impedes further corrosion. However, if it is slow, the ferrous ions diffuse away from where they were formed and turn into rust nearby, leaving behind a pit in the metal that continues to be eaten away. Thus rusting is actually accelerated by a poor paint job, and it may be better to leave a rusty surface exposed than merely to slap some paint on it without first scraping it clean and doing the job properly. All in all, a depressing picture; but in point of fact, a rusty steel boat is no more inevitable than a rotten wooden one or a delaminated fiberglass one.

One approach to dealing with the problem of rust is to use special steels (such as Corten) that are both stronger and less susceptible to corrosion than ordinary steel. This was done in the case of Irving Johnson's new *Yankee,* a Sparkman & Stephens-designed ketch that has seen thousands of miles of cruising in European canals and waterways where wear and tear on a hull is considerable. The improved steels are more expensive, but the additional cost as a percentage of the entire cost of a boat may not be excessive.

(TEXT CONTINUED ON PAGE 103)

[VII]

Two Classic Cutters:
CARDHU & CLIO

LARGE ENOUGH FOR SPEED AND COMFORT, *Cardhu* and *Clio* are also large enough for idiosyncrasy to find scope in their accommodations. Both have cutter rigs of enough area to be effective without overlapping headsails except in the lightest airs, and both have shapely hulls, but there the resemblance ceases. The problems of wind and sea are always the same, but the dreams of sailors are not, and in this lies the fascination of studying yacht designs.

CARDHU

Cardhu's PROFILE INSTANTLY IDENTIFIES HER AS a product of the Giles drawing board. The wide gap between jibstay and forestay means a small forestaysail, which must be set against the ease in getting the jib topsail through when coming about—perhaps a fair trade, perhaps not, depending upon the conditions under which the boat will be sailed. The staysail boom secures directly to the forestay and not to a pedestal, which means that it can be high enough to clear an inverted dinghy forward of the mast. The dinghy shown is 9 ft long, big for a vessel of this size but most welcome when cruising, and nothing so large could fit between deckhouse and mast. If *Cardhu* were a ketch, the mainmast would be several feet farther forward and the dinghy could be stowed aft of the mast; but the cutter rig is better suited to the boat, and it is an unexpected bonus that it permits a capacious dinghy to be carried as well. The sunken cockpit is smallish and is well protected by the deckhouse and high sides—*Cardhu* is not just a fair-weather friend. In fact, there is a bold, dauntless look about the entire design, with its sweeping sheer forward, honest deckhouse, and tall rig. Somehow I see *Cardhu* beating up the Sound of Mull on a clear fall day on its way to Tobermory or Loch Sunart, perhaps to anchor between Oronsay and the Morven shore, where a wee dram will add its glow to that of the setting sun.

The handling of line and bulk in *Cardhu* is masterful. The high deckhouse is made necessary by the presence of the engine, and it could have turned out to be a monstrosity in less skillful hands. As it is, the high sheer forward goes far toward balancing the deckhouse, an endeavor in which it is helped by the truncated after overhang and by the inverted dinghy on the forward deck. The result is a real deckhouse plus two other cabins, which few boats of this size and sailing ability can boast.

Cardhu's head is on the small side, though it is hard to see how it could have been enlarged without major changes elsewhere. The main cabin is cozier for the absence of pilot berths, which are not really needed because of the two deckhouse berths. The port berth extends into an alcove formed by two drawers on top and a locker inboard, a scheme that not only provides room for more goodies but also permits the bedding to be tucked out of sight in a moment. A modest galley is to port, and a chart table and an oilskin locker are to starboard. The reward for the somewhat skimpy cockpit, head, and galley is the deckhouse—a more than fair trade in northern climes but less of a bargain in warmer ones.

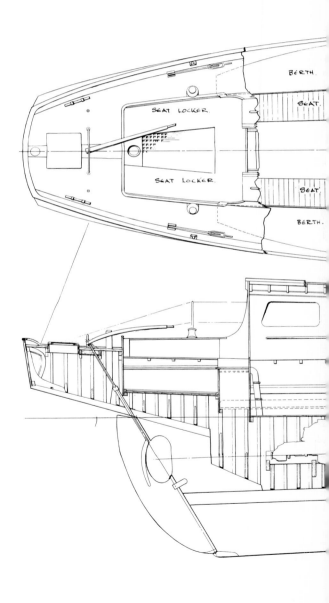

Cardhu's construction follows British tradition, with pitch-pine planking on laminated Canadian-rock-elm frames and steam-bent timbers. The center-line structure is oak, the deck and cabin house are teak, and the ballast keel is iron. The rig too owes more to the past than to the present, with spruce spars and galvanized plow-steel standing rigging, though sails and cordage are synthetics. The virtue of building a boat in so time-honored a manner is that a wider range of yards can do the job, which means a more reasonable cost. The penalty is more maintenance and a heavy displacement, but *Cardhu* has the sail to match her weight and so makes a fine cruiser.

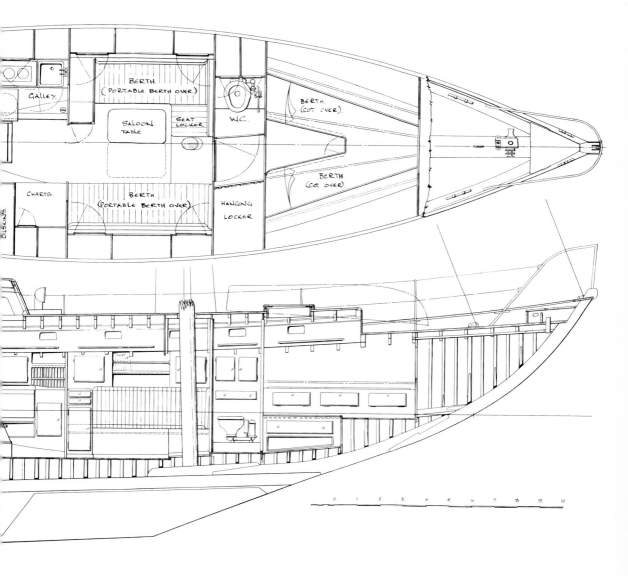

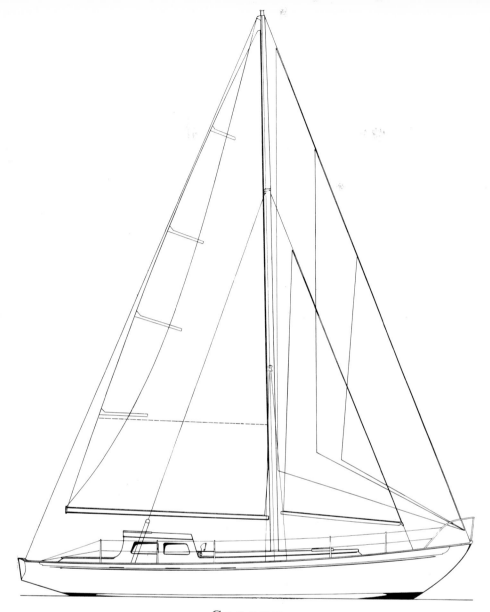

CARDHU

DESIGNER *Laurent Giles & Partners, Ltd., 4 Quay Hill, Lymington, England*

LOA   41 ft 4 in.

LWL   31 ft

BEAM   10 ft 9 in.

DRAFT   6 ft 3 in.

DISPLACEMENT   26,400 lb

SAIL AREA   848 ft²

ENGINE   Albin Mate D-411

FUEL   15 gal

WATER   92 gal

CONSTRUCTION   Pitch-pine planking on Canadian-rock-elm laminated frames, with centerline structure of oak; teak deck and deckworks; spruce spars

CARDHU *is a cruising cutter of heavy displacement designed by Laurent Giles. Her large dinghy fits neatly under the forestaysail boom.* (Beken)

CLIO

BRUNO VERONESE DESCRIBES HIMSELF AS AN amateur naval architect, but the yachts he has designed have been so distinguished in looks and ability that no lack of skill is implied in the adjective. He writes that "*Clio* was designed as a fast cruising yacht, with an easy motion at sea, and accommodation for four or five people, and may be considered a medium-displacement vessel. Her layout was planned in order to give the maximum comfort, accessibility and independence: there is also ample cockpit space. The companionway is amidships, starboard side, and leads to a sort of raised platform, where are the oilskin locker, chart-table, the door to the main cabin aft (where less motion is felt), to the toilet room, and access in the saloon forward. The toilet may be used for changing clothes, when swimming, the yacht being at anchor, having access to it without walking through the inside with dripping swimming trunks. There are plenty of lockers, wardrobes and drawers, where four people (including some ladies) may properly stow their belongings. In the forecastle (and thus out of sight) are the galley, icebox, anchor cable and sails stowage, besides a cot for a fifth occasional guest. This arrangement has been chosen as it keeps the inside of the yacht more tidy and especially less smelly, since it is well known that the draft inside a yacht is always from aft to forward.

"The yacht carries 0.6 tons of fresh water and has a range of 300 miles under power at economical speed (6 knots). A light 35 H.P. diesel Fiat engine is expected to give the yacht about 7 knots of cruising speed. It drives a two-blade feathering propeller, and is installed low down in the central section of the yacht, where it will help to increase stability, and is easily accessible removing the steps at both ends above. A special hatch shall be built in the roof of the deckhouse, of adequate size, to hoist the engine through whenever necessary.

"Construction is straightforward, with white oak stem and sternpost, iroko keel, yellow pine shelves and stringers, ash beams, glued mahogany hull, laminated locust frames and timbers, marine plywood bulkheads and coachroof tops, teak laid deck, cockpit, and superstructure, galvanized steel angle floors and knees, and spruce spars."

Though *Clio* is arranged with coastwise cruising in a warm climate in mind, little more than exchanging the locations of head and galley would be needed to fit her for more ambitious ventures. The after cabin is as useful on a long passage as it is in harbor, since the isolation and relative steadiness it provides help one to get rest under otherwise difficult conditions.

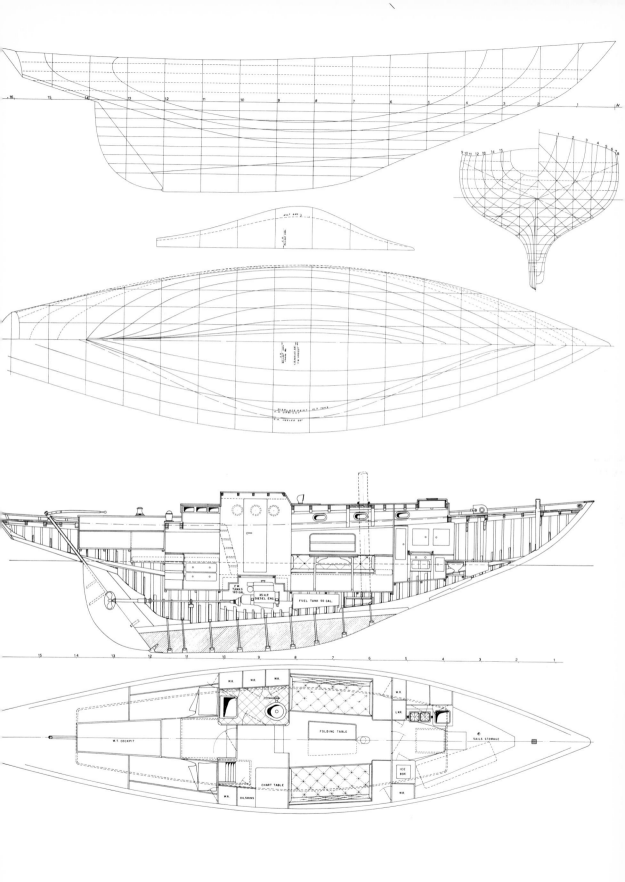

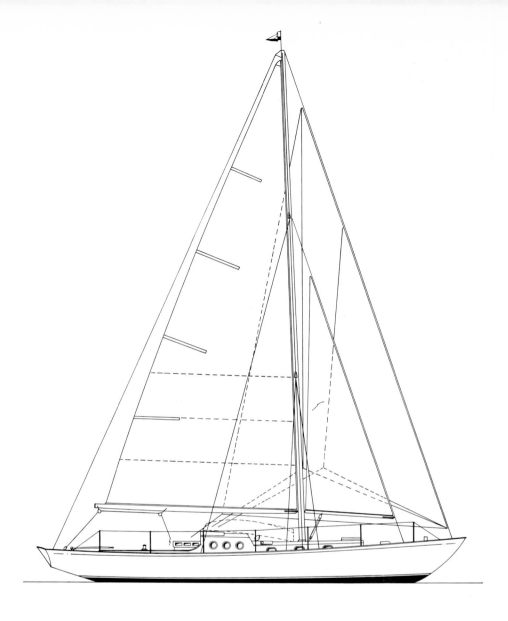

CLIO

DESIGNER *Bruno Veronese, Via Capo Santa Chiara, 25, Genoa, Italy*

LOA   43 ft

LWL   31 ft 6 in.

BEAM   11 ft

DRAFT   6 ft 6 in.

DISPLACEMENT   26,200 lb

BALLAST   10,400 lb of iron

SAIL AREA   900 ft²

ENGINE   Fiat diesel (35 hp)

FUEL   50 gal

WATER   120 gal

CONSTRUCTION   Mahogany planking on laminated-locust frames, with white-oak and iroko center-line structure; teak deck and deckworks; spruce spars

(TEXT CONTINUED FROM PAGE 94)

Another approach, which can be used with any kind of steel, is a special protective coating. Formerly, spraying with molten zinc was the preferred method, and it has the advantage of being effective against galvanic action as well as against rusting, but the coating must be both uniform and thick (a minimum figure I have seen quoted is 0.01 in.) to be of any real good, and it is hard to get paint to stick to zinc. Recently, synthetic resin coatings have been tried with generally good results, sometimes applied over a zinc coating—a combination that is perhaps the best, if most expensive, method of all. Steel hulls have been successfully coated both with epoxy compounds that were troweled on and with polyester resins containing chopped fiberglass that were sprayed on. One supposes that plenty of hand labor is required to smooth down the coatings, but all metal hulls require a certain amount of facing up with fillers to get an acceptable finish.

My own opinion is that it always pays to have the bilges of a steel hull sprayed with zinc, since it is hard to do much about a rusty bilge, but to have the rest simply sandblasted, primed, and painted according to the best modern practice is entirely acceptable if cost is a factor. Hugo van Kuyck's new *Askoy,* which he designed himself, was built in this manner, even to steel decks and cabin house, and it is a magnificent vessel in every respect. In general, then, rust is not inevitable with a steel hull, and it is possible to enjoy the very substantial benefits of this material without the penalty of poor appearance.

Electrolysis and galvanic action are not restricted in their effects to steel but can attack any submerged metal. In both processes, metal passes into solution owing to the flow of electric current between two immersed metallic objects (sea cocks, propellers, shafts, even fastenings) that are different in electrical potential. In electrolysis this difference in potential is imposed by an outside source—for instance, by grounding a piece of electrical apparatus to a particular underwater fitting—and can be avoided by using a two-wire ungrounded electrical system and, in the case of nonmetallic hulls, bonding all submerged fittings together with heavy copper conductors.

In galvanic action the difference in potential arises from the differing tendency of the various metals to lose electrons. When two dissimilar metals in electrical contact are placed in a liquid capable of conducting electricity, an electric current flows between them and ions of the more electropositive metal go into solution. The result is a self-contained battery that will continue to function until the corroded metal is completely eaten away. The following is a list of the metals common in boatbuilding, in increasing order of their electrochemical activity:

Mercury (found in some antifouling paints)
Monel
Passive stainless steel (rare)
Silicon bronze (Everdur is an example)
Copper (and copper antifouling paints)
Red brass
Aluminum bronze
Gunmetal
Yellow brass
Phosphor bronze
Manganese bronze

Lead
Active stainless steel (the most common)
Cast iron
Wrought iron
Mild steel
Aluminum
Cadmium
Zinc (and galvanized iron and steel)
Magnesium

For any pair of these metals immersed in seawater, the direction of current flow will be from the lower to the higher on the list; the lower one will corrode, the upper one will not. If a bronze propeller is installed on a shaft of ordinary steel, in short order the shaft will be eaten away, while the propeller will be untouched. However, if a zinc collar is fastened to the shaft, the current will flow from the zinc to both the steel shaft and the bronze propeller, and only the zinc will corrode. This is the principle underlying the use of sacrificial anodes of zinc or magnesium on boats with dissimilar metal appendages. An anode is simply a positive electrode, and in almost any marine galvanic situation, these metals have the more positive electrical potential. But even though such anodes can be valuable, it is still a good idea to keep any underwater metal parts close together in electrochemical activity unless they can be electrically insulated from one another. If a bronze fitting is necessary on an aluminum hull, for example, there should be plastic or rubber between them, since without electrical contact, no galvanic action can occur. Electrolysis and galvanic action are tiresome and potentially dangerous complications, but proper measures can be taken to keep them in check, and what is important is to see that no substitutions of the specified metals are made in the construction of a boat without the explicit approval of its designer.

Rather less of a menace but still sometimes annoying is the tendency of metal boats to develop condensation. If the interior has a wooden ceiling throughout, the problem is unlikely to be serious, but in any case it is easy enough when the boat is being built to have the inside of the hull smeared with a latex compound like those used to undercoat automobiles.

Aluminum is superior to steel on two counts: it is only about a third as heavy but more than half as strong for a given thickness, so rigidity as well as toughness can be provided in a light hull, and the alloys used in boatbuilding resist chemical

[OPPOSITE] *Designed by Arthur Robb for long passages at sea,* KOCHAB *has sailed perhaps 100,000 miles since her launching in 1956. Her dimensions are LOA 39 ft 4 in., LWL 29 ft, beam 10 ft 8 in., and draft 6 ft, and her sail area is about 750 ft². One of the owner's requirements was that the vessel be a handsome one, and certainly* KOCHAB's *looks match her ability.* (Beken)

corrosion (though not, of course, electrolysis and galvanic action). Taking everything into account except expense, aluminum is undoubtedly the best material of all for sailboat hulls because it provides the maximum in both security and performance. It is also undoubtedly the most costly. Aluminum is still too new as a boatbuilding material and presents too many specialized problems for there to be more than a handful of yards anywhere capable of turning out a good job. These yards seem to be uniformly expensive, and a moderate-size custom aluminum boat may well turn out to have a price tag double that of its wooden or steel sister—the former its equal in performance but not security, the latter its equal in security but not performance. I am not impressed with cheaper maintenance as an argument for aluminum, any more than I am with cheaper fuel costs as an argument for diesel engines; in each case there is undoubtedly some economy, but not nearly enough by itself to justify the vastly greater initial expense. How much hard cash the virtues of aluminum are worth is impossible to say, but each year a few people are willing to cough up what it takes and thus far have seemed pleased with their choice.

Boats of wood and metal require regular maintenance, and its expense in time and money is possibly the most variable factor of all in owning a boat. A man who does not mind working with sandpaper, paint, and varnish, who takes pains to use only the very best modern synthetic finishes, who can make minor repairs in wood and metal, who can tuck a splice and seize a slide, and who has the time to spare to make use of these talents may be able to reduce his yard bills to a modest minimum. This is not always possible, to be sure, and many people also prefer and find it more economical in the long run to do good work as doctors, lawyers, or Indian chiefs instead of indifferent work as amateur shipwrights. A typical boatyard in the New York City area charges an owner $6 to $7 per hour for labor, and the time some oaf spends in strolling from one end of the yard to the other in quest of an odd screw or a piece of sandpaper is not distinguished on the bill from the time a master joiner spends in fitting a graving piece that is invisible to the eye. The situation is less bleak elsewhere in the world, however, and even elsewhere in the United States.

If much work needs to be done and nearby yards are exorbitant, it may pay to take the boat to another area. But there I can say, from bitter experience, that one should first verify the competence of the distant yard in great detail, since one will not be there to keep track of the proceedings. I have left boats I have owned in Maine and Virginia without setting eyes on them from the time they were hauled until the time they were launched, and I could not have been happier with the results. But I have also left boats in two different Florida yards of the very highest repute, one of which turned out to be a wholly crooked operation (I was charged $157 for a teak block smaller than this book) and the other to be wholly incompetent (a catalog of their moronic doings is too long and too depressing to belong here, but I will mention that they clamped the intake hose of a bilge pump to the propeller shaft). Both of these yards are now building boats in addition to their other activities, no doubt to replace vessels they have ruined. The customary advice to find a good yard and stick with it is sound, and there *are* first-class yards here and there, but I can offer no help in how to find such a yard other than to suggest talking with people and seeing for oneself how the yard is run.

Because maintenance is such a pain in the neck, the freedom from deterioration of fiberglass is its biggest attraction. Fiberglass cannot rot or rust, needs no protection from the elements, is not attacked by worms, and is not subject to electrolytic or galvanic action. Given good design and workmanship, a fiberglass hull can be more than adequately strong, and the nature of its construction permits features that would be difficult or impossible in wood or metal. Most remarkable of all, many fiberglass boats are no more expensive than comparable ones built of other materials—a few are even cheaper—so they may be bargains in the long run.

For all its unquestionable advantages, fiberglass is still not the perfect hull material. In the first place, one must rely almost completely on the honesty and capability of the builders for a sound hull, since such shenanigans as leaving out a layer of fiberglass or substituting mat for the more expensive and stronger woven roving and such flaws as uneven distribution of the resin (or even voids) can be concealed beneath the shiny outside gel coat. It is much easier to survey wooden or metal hulls than fiberglass ones—although, of course, if it is sound to begin with, a fiberglass hull will stay that way indefinitely. Most builders of large fiberglass yachts today are responsible outfits, but if some sort of outside supervision is possible—for instance, by Lloyd's—it would seem worth the added cost in peace of mind alone.

Not everybody can enjoy the appearance and feel of fiberglass on deck and down below. For all its strength and inertness, I find fiberglass a cold, harsh material; and when the initial perfection of its surface becomes dull, blotchy, and disfigured by hairline cracks after a few years, it is not only we reactionaries who would rather have teak and mahogany to live with. Of course, the unpleasantness of fiberglass is no greater than that of steel or aluminum, but while no one would consider a yacht with metal inside as well as outside, many fiberglass boats make liberal use of this material in the accommodation. I owned a fiberglass sloop for two years, and the benefits of its sturdy hull were not enough to compensate for the sensation of being in a bathtub whenever I was aboard. The right way to do things is to have a fiberglass hull and perhaps a fiberglass deck, but to have the interior of wood and to use wood (preferably teak) for such items as cockpit coamings and seats. Then one has the best of both worlds, which is as it should be.

The major penalty that fiberglass construction exacts is the loss of freedom of choice. The cost of building a mold is such that it does not make economic sense unless a number of hulls are made from it, so one must take what is offered or leave it; there is no middle ground of custom construction. Hundreds of different fiberglass sailboats are on the market, to be sure, but very few of them are more than 40 ft in length, and of the ones that are, nearly all are identical in design concept (middle-distance racing), rig (masthead sloop or yawl), and accommodation (galley aft; four-berth main cabin, head, and double cabin forward). There are a few welcome exceptions, such as the 45-ft *Seafarer-45* designed by Sparkman & Stephens, the 49-ft *Glass Slipper* designed by E. G. van de Stadt, and the 52-ft sloop designed by William Tripp. Of course, some people will find conventional boats to their taste; but, generally speaking, it is necessary to go to custom construction in wood or metal to get one's heart's desire.

The problem of money is likely to be the deciding factor for many people in choosing the size yacht to have and the manner in which it is to be built and outfitted. It is not always easy to distinguish between good value and highway robbery at one extreme and between a genuine bargain and junk at the other. A well-designed and well-constructed new boat weighing between 15,000 and 45,000 lb and having minimum but adequate equipment would seem to me very reasonable at $1.50 per pound and expensive at $2.50 per pound—rather more than steak, but as in the case of steak, it may make more sense to pay a little more to a reliable supplier than risk poor quality from a cheap but untried source. The largest variation in construction costs is in wood and steel, since there are many builders all over the world experienced in using these materials. The basic cost, equipped, of a certain 40-footer might be as little as $25,000 in a good yard somewhere that happened to need the work or as much as $60,000 in another yard, no better than the first in quality of workmanship or materials but in an area with high labor rates and with no particular anxiety about getting the contract. Of course, one must figure in the cost of transport and duty if a boat is built abroad, and one should consider the value of having the builder nearby to make good any deficiencies that may turn up. Even so, there is no question that shopping around can make a big difference.

[VIII]

A Romantic Ketch for
the Home Builder:
PORPOISE

THE MODERN CRUISING SAILBOAT, WITH ITS clean lines and slick construction, is a marvelous thing, and who would want to turn back the clock to the days of clipper bows, carved trail boards, figureheads of naked ladies, steeved-up bowsprits complete with dolphin strikers and catheads, monkey rails with turned pillars, and dinghies on tail feathers? Surely only a madman would turn from the sensuous delights of fiberglass and aluminum back to wood, from a masthead sloop with a baby main to a double-headsail ketch, from a pointed keel 8 ft down to a long, straight keel 5 ft down, from lead ballast to (ye gods!) reinforced-concrete ballast? As it happens there are at least a few dozen madmen of this kind at large, for that is how many close relatives *Porpoise* has, and I have to confess that there are moments when

I wonder whether it is not the rest of us who are mad and they the only ones with clear minds. What, after all, does "efficiency" mean when applied to a yacht? Simply that it gives the greatest output of pleasure for the least input of money, effort, and discomfort, and by this criterion, *Porpoise* is surely more efficient than the latest ocean racer. *Porpoise* has the further advantage of being amenable to amateur construction; though it would not be a rapid job, since a professional builder would probably need about 4,500 man-hours and an amateur correspondingly longer. But whether they can have the ultimate joy of building *Porpoise* themselves or must hire alien hands to do so, there are people in this world for whom she is the only proper yacht, and I would find it hard to argue against their choice.

PORPOISE

Porpoise WAS DESIGNED BY THE TALENTED Seattle naval architect William Garden, whose versatility is such that another of his masterpieces, the 60-ft light-displacement sloop *Oceanus,* is about as different from *Porpoise* as

is possible. All that the two boats have in common is that each is an almost perfect vessel of its type. Here is how Garden describes *Porpoise*: "This 33-foot waterline ketch is a good compromise between pocketbook and optimum.

With a breadth of 13 feet, she has a length on deck of 42 feet 6 inches, and a moderate draft of 5 feet. This will increase by about 3 inches when loaded down in sea trim for a long voyage. The model is one we've found ideal for offshore voyaging, long on the keel to make her docile on the helm, clipper bow and a broad plank bowsprit to give the sail plan sufficient base and still balance, and a snug ketch rig which is ideally suited for chasing off before the wind under boisterous conditions. The tall mast well forward allows her to carry twin spinnakers, and with the four lower sails, several combinations can be carried; from the mizzen, main, and large genoa in light weather to the reefed main or trysail and staysail under adverse conditions. Trysail and mizzen are also duplicates to simplify the sail outfit.

"There is a tremendous amount of room on deck with her ample breadth of 13 feet and flush deck arrangement. From the fo'c'sle head, the deck sweeps aft to the transom without a break other than the small trunk and cockpit foot well. An Edson steerer is fitted aft and the cockpit extends forward to the trunk bulkhead with a raised threshold at the cabin access.

"The cabin plan is extremely flexible and allows four madeup berths, two amidships and two quarter berths aft. For most ocean passages, the forward cabin can be used for stowage and the crew can turn in amidship and aft where the motion is minimized. Another endearing feature will be found in the dinette area, directly opposite the galley, and a place where a meal can be served without disturbing crew members sleeping in the forward cabin. Quarter berths aft are well outboard port and starboard, and the engine box sides hinge away for complete access to the entire engine, making inspection or maintenance a relatively simple matter.

"The midship section is included to give an idea of her general proportions and form. She's built ruggedly but without excessive weight, frames being 1¾ by 2¼ inch bent oak on 12 inch center lines, and planking 1⅜ inch yellow cedar or mahogany, with a 1⅝ inch wale strake which fairs on into the clipper bow and is banded by double bronze half rounds.

"The Station 4 Section drawing shows the typical framing details through the dinette on the starboard side looking forward, the curved bulkhead being the separation between dinette and main saloon. The port section shows a typical mold with ribbands. Ballast can be reinforced concrete with scrap iron, cast iron or lead, depending on the pocketbook and whim of the builder. Several of this model are presently in the pre-construction or construction stage and the majority of them are fitting the reinforced concrete ballast keel.

"The plans are available with an overall deck length of 40 feet and with an outboard rudder as in the basic sketch, or with an overall deck length of 42 feet and 6 inches and an inboard rudder as shown in the detail drawing. Construction cost difference is negligible."

PORPOISE

DESIGNER *William Garden, 3040 West Commodore Way, Seattle, Washington*

LOA   40 ft (outboard rudder) or 42 ft 6 in. (inboard rudder)

LWL   33 ft

BEAM   13 ft

DRAFT   5 ft

BALLAST   7,500 lb of reinforced concrete

SAIL AREA   848 ft²

ENGINE   Mercedes-Benz OM636 (34 hp)

FUEL   70 gal

WATER   120 gal

CONSTRUCTION   Cedar or mahogany planking on oak frames; fiberglass-covered plywood deck; spruce spars

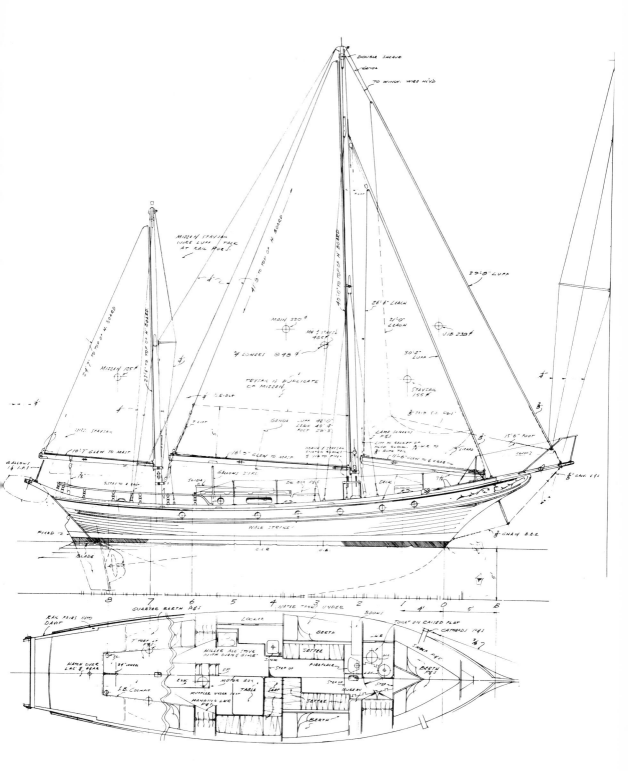

CHAPTER FOUR

The Rig

ASAILBOAT IS PROPELLED by the forces generated when moving air interacts with its sails. The amount of force produced depends upon a number of factors, some obvious (the sail area, for instance) and some subtle (the exact shape of each sail), and not all these factors can be adjusted to give the best possible performance without jeopardizing some other desirable attribute, such as stiffness or ease of handling. Unlike its hull, a yacht's sails require constant manipulation, but this is not necessarily a bad thing; indeed, much of the pleasure of sailing lies in the constant challenge to get the most out of the wind. How wonderful it is when everything is just right, all sails set perfectly and the yacht settled down to really moving along! How exquisite the anguish of knowing that something is just a trifle wrong, that maybe the difference of an inch in a sheet will make everything click—but which sheet? And trim an inch or slack an inch? Such are the delights of sailing.

In planning a yacht, the next step after deciding upon the size and shape of the hull is to choose the type of rig. Brigantines, schooners, gaff cutters with reefing bowsprits and housing topmasts—these are splendid to look at, particularly if their sails are red and they are silhouetted against a sunset, but they are also clumsy and inefficient unless much larger in size than the yachts being considered here. The real choice lies among the sloop, the cutter, the yawl, and the ketch, all with jib-headed (or "Bermudian") mainsails and mizzens. I would go even further and say that nothing but a masthead jibstay belongs on a cruiser, since by this simple expedient the nuisance of running backstays is eliminated. Actually, once the size of the hull is specified, the number of alternatives in rig is narrowed, since the size of the hull determines the sail area and since there is a limit to how large an individual sail can be before it becomes too much for a small crew. For this reason, it makes sense first to determine how much sail area cruising boats of different sizes need and only then go on to how this area should be arranged.

The primary factor in establishing the proper sail area is the wetted surface of the hull, since this is what determines the resistance of the hull at low speeds. A boat with enough sail to move well in light airs will surely have enough in stronger winds as well, while the converse is not necessarily true. Normally a sail area between two and two and a half times the wetted surface is chosen; the exact figure depends also on such other considerations as waterline length (relatively more sail for larger boats), type of hull (fat centerboarders need more sail than narrow keel-boats), and so on. A rough rule of thumb is that a boat whose displacement in pounds is D should have a sail area of at least $D^{\frac{2}{3}}$ in square feet, with the best amount, of course, depending upon the characteristics of the boat in question. For a 15,000-lb boat, this formula gives 610 ft²; for a 20,000-lb boat, it gives 740 ft²; and for a 25,000-lb boat, it gives 850 ft², to cite a few examples. This is a very crude way to arrive at a minimum-sail-area figure, but I find it convenient (like the equally approximate formula for displacement as a function of waterline length in a previous chapter) as a handy means of comparing designs with one another without going through the labor of calculating their wetted surfaces.

I believe that the majority of auxiliary sailboats today carry rigs that are too small for both performance and convenience. No cruiser should need either half a gale or oversize genoas and spinnakers in order to really go, yet that is precisely the case with most of the boats designed and built in recent years. Except possibly in the neighborhood of Patagonia, most weather contains a good percentage of light winds, and one of the keener joys of sailing is to ghost along with only zephyrs about. Here the culprit is unquestionably the fact that in computing a yacht's racing rating, the basic area of its sails is heavily taxed. To quote from Illingworth: "If one carries an oversize sail area, for the size of the boat, the rating rises out of proportion to the advantage which it confers as regards speed." Accordingly the serious racing boat is obligated to carry the very minimum of sail and to rely upon exploiting it to the utmost, which means a large crew and constant attention if the boat is to move well. On the other hand, the pure cruiser can carry any amount of sail appropriate to its needs so arranged as to be easy to cope with, which means as much or more speed with a small crew as well as less effort for them. It is a misconception that the proper cruiser should be underrigged; on the contrary, it should have plenty of sail and should be able to sail circles around any racing boat with a crew of the same strength.

There are other reasons behind the shrunken rigs of most ocean racers that compound the effect of the high tax on sail area. Let us suppose for the sake of argument that the rating rules *are* fair in that they assess sail area in terms of actual effect on speed (which they do not). Boat A has more sail than the otherwise identical boat B and carries a higher rating, but, by hypothesis, it will move sufficiently faster in light to moderate airs to match boat B on corrected time. In moderate to strong winds, however, boat A has to shorten down, while boat B does not, both travel at the same speed, and boat B is way ahead on corrected time. So boat B has the same chance of racing success in light going as boat A, even though slower through the water, and a far better chance in heavy going; boat B is the one that will end the season with the most silverware.

Yet another consideration is the manner in which rating formulas compute sail area. The weight in the formula given to headsails turns out to be so small rela-

[OPPOSITE] *Scores of 40-ft stock Concordia yawls like* SKYE *have provided their owners with first-class cruising at a reasonable price.* (Rosenfeld)

tive to their actual propulsive efficiency that a small main is an advantage in racing. Thus mainsails on racing boats often terminate well below the masthead, and they would be smaller still if the various rules did not expressly prohibit more than a certain maximum distance between the mainsail head and the top of the jibstay. All well and good, except that it is often easier to set, trim, lower, and stow a mainsail than an overlarge genoa or spinnaker. The rating formulas also favor small mains by taxing the part of a headsail that is aft of the mast only lightly. This is reasonable, since the overlapping part is less efficient than the rest, and there is, all else equal, something to be said for a snug rig. The CCA and RORC rules start to count the extra areas of overlapping jibs only when they are about half again longer at the foot than the base of the foretriangle, and the penalty is a light one until the overlap is about 180 percent of the foretriangle base. It is clearly beneficial to a racing boat to use monstrous headsails in light to moderate winds despite the difficulty in handling them and the need to change them with each change in wind speed or direction.

Quite apart from racing considerations, a small rig for cruisers is often advocated on the grounds that too much sail means a tender boat. I am not impressed with this train of thought, because a slight increase in beam does wonders for initial stability without adding more than a trifle to wetted surface, and a skilled hand can draw quite a bit of beam in a set of lines without affecting speed or windward ability adversely. One wants speed and ease of handling in a cruising boat, pleasure for the few instead of work for the many, and it is a big help to have ample sail.

It must seem paradoxical to claim that a sizable rig is less trouble than a modest one, yet my experience shows this to be true. The point is that with area to spare, one can arrange matters in a seamanlike manner—a well-divided rig, headsails with only moderate overlaps—without worrying about perfect efficiency in terms of CCA or RORC rating.

Because the simplest and most efficient rig of all is the masthead sloop, it is the only one that makes sense for vessels less than, say, 36 ft long overall, which need all the help they can get. The biggest jib is still not beyond the ability of one man, aided by intelligent gear, to set, sheet, and hand by himself, and roller reefing can be reasonably satisfactory in a small boat. It is hard to see what advantages the tiny yawl or ketch has that offset its reduced performance and greater expense. The mizzenmast, its standing and running rigging, the sail itself, and a mizzen staysail all add up to a sum better employed in getting a bigger boat in the first place; it is astonishing how much difference in comfort and speed even the smallest enlargement of a minimum boat makes. And comfort and speed are more important to seaworthiness than a handy post to lean against.

In a medium-sized boat the virtues of the cutter and yawl become significant. Two huge sails can be a problem at times, so breaking up a large sail area into smaller parcels is sensible provided that the proportions are correct and an allowance is made for the loss in efficiency. Just where the dividing line comes depends upon the boat. After crossing the Atlantic in a gaff ketch in 1920, Uffa Fox concluded that "one man could reef or stow a 500 square foot mainsail in all weathers, but not a larger sail," while Eric Hiscock puts the upper limit at 400 ft². I feel the criterion that one man be able to secure the mainsail is a sound one for a cruising boat of any size, but it seems to me that there is a lot of difference between the

(TEXT CONTINUED ON PAGE 131)

[I X]

Three Ketches:

RIWARU, MELUSINE II, &
LADY HELENE

WHEN THE SAIL AREA OF A PROJECTED cruising boat approaches 1,000 ft², the ketch rig changes in status from merely a possible alternative to an active candidate. A modern yacht large enough to warrant this much sail is also large enough to have it split up thoroughly without injury to performance, something that was impossible in the days of small overhangs and low, inefficient sail plans. The three ketches described here all have sail areas in the neighborhood of 1,000 ft² and are about the same in size, but there they part company: in *Riwaru,* the emphasis is on a wide cruising range; in *Melusine II,* speed under sail is stressed; while in *Lady Helene,* ability under

power and comfort in port are major considerations. All three have been successful in their separate ways, and it seems unlikely that their owners would be especially happy to trade with any of the others. Instead of three solutions to the same problem, these ketches represent solutions to very different problems, and it is worth noting the various features in each design which are necessary to its ambitions yet which are incompatible with the ambitions of the others. All this emphasizes the basic point that there is no "perfect" yacht of any size or type but instead an infinity of proper ones to match against one's needs and dreams.

RIWARU

A LAURENT GILES DESIGN, *Riwaru* IS PROportioned and laid out for what might be termed "serious cruising"—long periods of independence from the shore, whether along the coast or at sea. The ample beam and heavy displacement mean that *Riwaru* should sail on her bottom despite the moderate draft of less than 6 ft, with an easy motion in a seaway.

Two items on the sail plan will bring an appreciative nod from experienced cruising men— the upright dinghy and the boomed forestaysail with its row of reef points. As in other cruising boats from the Giles board, *Riwaru* has enough sail area to push her along, and it is so disposed as to make for easy handling.

Riwaru's accommodation is similar to that of

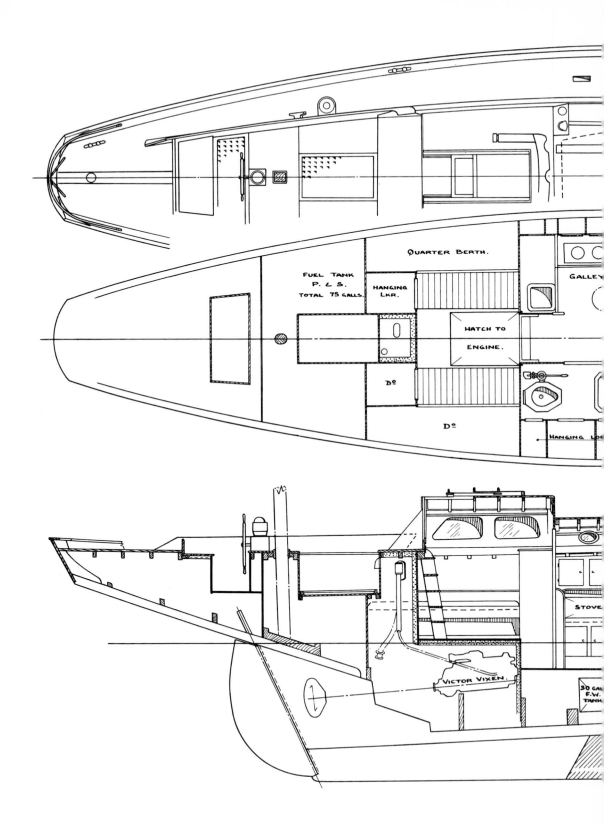

QUARTER BERTH.

FUEL TANK
P. & S.
TOTAL 75 GALLS.

HANGING
LKR.

GALLEY

HATCH TO

ENGINE.

Dᵒ

Dᵒ

HANGING LO

STOVE

VICTOR VIXEN.

30 GAL
F.W.
TANK

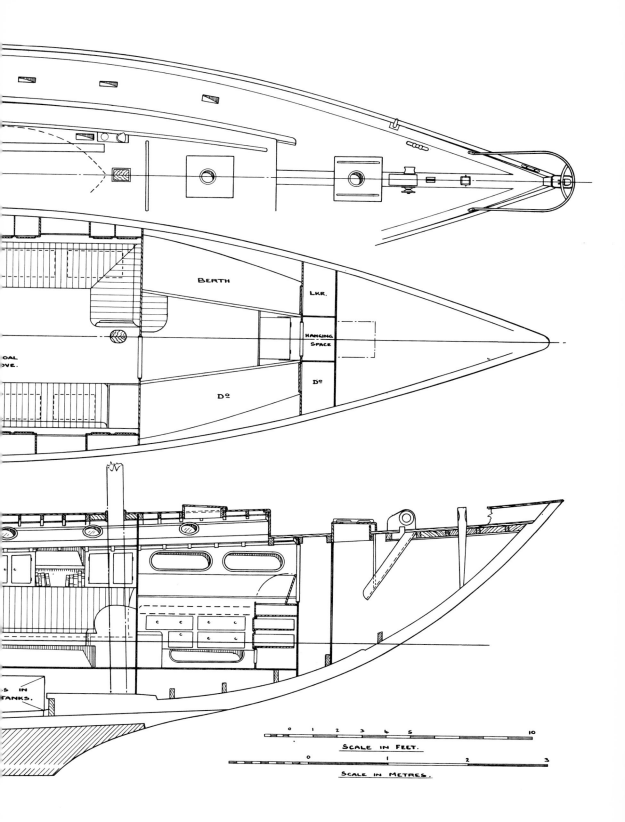

BERTH

LKR.

HANGING
SPACE

COAL
OVE.

Dᵒ

Dᵒ

S IN
TANKS.

SCALE IN FEET.

SCALE IN METRES.

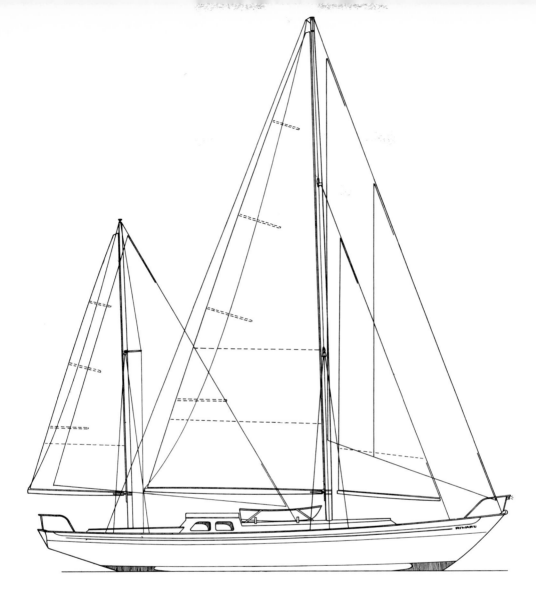

the smaller *Cardhu,* but the additional space means that what was a tight fit in *Cardhu* is now agreeably roomy. The forward cabin is sufficiently far aft to have headroom throughout, adequate stowage (ten drawers plus several lockers), a separate seat, and enough floor area for two people to turn around in. The forepeak itself is separated from the accommodation by a solid bulkhead, which makes the forward cabin a dead end rather than a passageway.

Access to the forepeak is through a hatch on deck, and no doubt steps are fitted on the bulkhead to permit easy entry and exit. The main cabin has an L-shaped settee to port and a transom to starboard with lockers and bookshelves above them instead of pilot berths. A Pansy heating stove will take any chill from the air, though it is unable to cope with really cold weather, and its location adjacent to the head is a happy thought. The deckhouse has

RIWARU, designed by Laurent Giles, is a cruising ketch of character and ability. (Beken)

two quarter berths with seats inboard, a good arrangement, and a hinged chart table could be worked in here, though one is not shown. The hanging lockers aft are exceptionally well located for oilskins and seaboots, since they are handy to the companionway, and the heat from the muffler will dry them out whenever the engine is run. The divided cockpit is not ideal, but this is not the best of all possible worlds, and the cross deck does help with the mizzenmast, the steering gear, and the compass. To console the helmsman for not being able to reach the jib-sheet winches, he is given a real seat with a backrest.

The tankage of 187 gal of water and 94 gal of diesel fuel is exceptional in an auxiliary of this size and further testifies to her seriousness of purpose. Built of teak on oak, *Riwaru* is a solid ship that should give many decades of notable service.

RIWARU

DESIGNER *Laurent Giles & Partners, Ltd., 4 Quay Hill, Lymington, England*

LOA 48 ft 9 in.
LWL 33 ft 6 in.
BEAM 11 ft 4 in.
DRAFT 5 ft 10 in.
DISPLACEMENT 34,000 lb
SAIL AREA 1,076 ft²

ENGINE Coventry Victor Vixen diesel
FUEL 94 gal
WATER 187 gal
CONSTRUCTION Teak planking on oak frames and center-line structure; teak deck and deckworks; spruce spars

MELUSINE II

ALMOST THE SAME IN WATERLINE and over-all lengths and with the same sail area in relation to displacement as *Riwaru, Melusine II,* by Illingworth & Primrose, nevertheless represents an entirely different conception of a cruising ketch. While *Riwaru* has a heavy displacement for her length, good beam, shoal draft, and a high freeboard, *Melusine II* is a light boat, narrow and deep, with a low profile. Where *Riwaru* has a boomed and reefable forestaysail, *Melusine II* has a choice of no less than three forestaysails, all loose-footed and two of them overlapping the mast. *Riwaru*'s deckhouse is a pleasant place to sit in port and under way; *Melusine*'s deckhouse is strictly for the cook and navigator, who can chock themselves in place neatly against the engine box in a seaway.

Riwaru carries plenty of fuel, and her propeller is well immersed for efficiency; *Melusine* has a smaller fuel tankage, and while her propeller just below the surface means little drag under sail, it also means that much of the engine power output is wasted. Clearly *Melusine II* does not conform to the conventional idea of a cruising yacht, but just as clearly all the departures from custom have specific purposes. By being light for her size, *Melusine II* is correspondingly cheap for her size without compromising quality. Light-displacement boats are sensitive to too much beam, so *Melusine II* is narrow, and her ballast must be slung lower to achieve the required stiffness. Since speed under sail is the goal, overlapping headsails and a poor location for the propeller are accepted as ap-

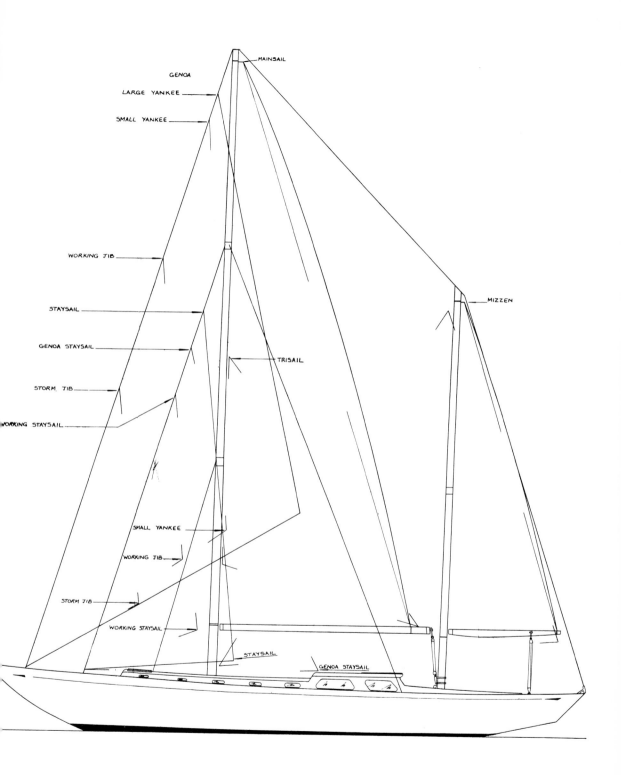

GENOA

MAINSAIL

LARGE YANKEE

SMALL YANKEE

WORKING JIB

STAYSAIL

GENOA STAYSAIL

STORM JIB

WORKING STAYSAIL

TRISAIL

MIZZEN

SMALL YANKEE

WORKING JIB

STORM JIB

WORKING STAYSAIL

STAYSAIL

GENOA STAYSAIL

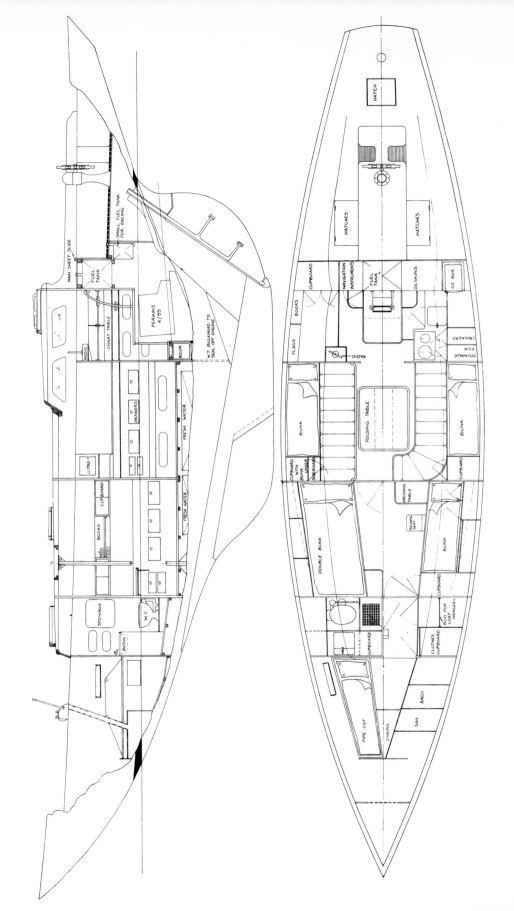

M E L U S I N E   I I

DESIGNER *Illingworth & Primrose, 36 North Street, Emsworth, England*

LOA 49 ft	DISPLACEMENT 27,800 lb
LWL 33 ft	SAIL AREA 910 ft²
BEAM 10 ft 9 in.	ENGINE Perkins 4-107 diesel (47 hp)
DRAFT 7 ft	

propriate means toward achieving it. There is as much to be said in favor of *Melusine II* as in favor of *Riwaru,* and which makes the better cruiser depends entirely upon who is doing the cruising.

Captain Illingworth has reported on the proof of this particular pudding: "The 33′ waterline design *Melusine II* has been a very great success. She has cruised everywhere in Europe from the Baltic to the Greek islands. I can say from personal experience that she is one of the most sea kindly boats I have ever sailed in and at the same time is extremely rapid. The ketch rig enables her to give a really excellent performance without the mainsail which is a convenience in heavy weather. Also in light weather when a good mizzen staysail is added in place of the mainsail a large awning can be spread over the centre of the yacht."

The rig is an interesting one. There is no independent main backstay, but instead a triatic stay running to the mizzen masthead from which the mizzen backstay goes to the stern. Because the mainsail has the high aspect ratio of 3:1, a conventional backstay would have added a much greater compressive load to the mast for the same support to the jibstay. Having less compression to stand up to, the mast can have a smaller section; but with the forestay so high up, there is the problem of keeping the lower part of such a mast straight—hence the inner forestay in place of a pair of forward lower shrouds. With a stouter mast and a slightly broader and less lofty sail plan, the masts could be stayed independently with a light triatic for help but not for exclusive support, the inner forestay given an honorable burial at sea beyond the continental shelf, and the running backstays brought forward to permit short tacking without continually having to set up and release them. Undoubtedly a skinny mast is lighter in weight and interferes less with the flow of air to the main, and square foot for square foot, the sail plan shown is probably the most effective in a ketch rig, but a modest compromise here would seem possible without violating the spirit in which the design was conceived and executed.

The owner's stateroom in *Melusine II* is forward of the main cabin and has a double berth plus a single one, a dressing table with seat, and adequate stowage space. However, the price of having this stateroom in a comfortable and roomy part of the ship is that it thereby constitutes the passageway to the forward cabin and to the only head—a considerable price. The forward cabin has a pipe berth to starboard and sail bins to port, and there are two pilot berths in the main cabin in addition to the settees. As already noted, the galley and chart table are fine at sea, but in harbor few cooks will be happy with so little space.

LADY HELENE

THE THIRD OF THIS TRIO OF KETCHES also has a distinctive personality. *Lady Helene* is called a "full-powered auxiliary" by Philip Ross of her designers, John G. Alden & Co., Inc., who describes her as combining "the virtues of a fast and able sailing yacht with the plush accommodations and comfort only found in power yachts. Because many busy men who enjoy the pleasures of sailing have limited time to use their boats and because many a cruise has been plagued by head winds and flat calms, the full-powered auxiliary has a large engine installed, capable of moving the vessel at a cruising speed of from 8 to 9 knots. With this speed and power, a short cruise can include a broad itinerary without the concern of getting back on time if unfavorable weather develops and permits maximum time for sailing. The basic difference between the full-powered auxiliary and the motor sailer is that the former is basically a sail boat with good sailing capabilities fitted with a large engine, whereas the latter is primarily a power boat with some sailing capabilities.

"The dominant theme of the *Lady Helene* is the 'sailing deck house' with the open compartment concept carried through to the galley and lower cabins. Those who want to be out in the sea air and weather can remain in the cockpit, whereas those who want protection, but still enjoy the sea view, can lounge in the deck house. To make the *Lady Helene* exceptionally livable, a place for everything was worked out. Eighteen drawers, three large clothing lockers and ten miscellaneous lockers were worked into the various compartments. Liberal sleeping accommodations for six are available in three separate areas.

"The galley boasts a full-sized, four-burner, stainless steel gas stove with oven and broiler, electric refrigeration, and hot and cold pressure water. For breakfast and snack time, a double folding table hinges down from the bulkhead. This table is opposite the galley and adds to the counter space when the cook is preparing meals.

"The deck house lounge is a versatile area with many uses. A convertible divan and two upholstered swivel chairs set the theme for the lounge and the addition of an interesting table with adjustable legs shifts the use to dining. When the table is stored under the divan and the divan is opened sideways, the lounge is converted to a sleeping area. In order to seat a large gathering of people and have the feeling of being together, each area opens into the other to form one continuous flow of seating and space. Because the elements and the sea remain the same to all vessels, all furniture is bolted down. The deck house might not appeal to everyone, but for those who enjoy the openness and the pleasure of watching the views both standing and sitting, a very careful balance of dimensions was worked out between the top and bottom of the windows, the elevation of the chairs and the eye level of tall and short people, both standing and sitting."

Quite apart from her accommodation, *Lady Helene* is worthy of study. She has a broad beam and high topsides, but is saved from dumpiness by the sweep of her forward overhang and the very careful treatment of the deckhouse. The dinghy on stern davits is hardly a seagoing proposition, but there is plenty of room for it on the flush deck when the boat is offshore, while the davits are convenient indeed for coastwise cruising. Advantage is taken of the large deckhouse and clear deck by the installation of an inside steering position, and the deckhouse windows have electric wipers to keep them clear of rain and spray. With radar, loran, automatic pilot, depth-sounder, radiotelephone, and electric refrigeration, *Lady Helene* is very

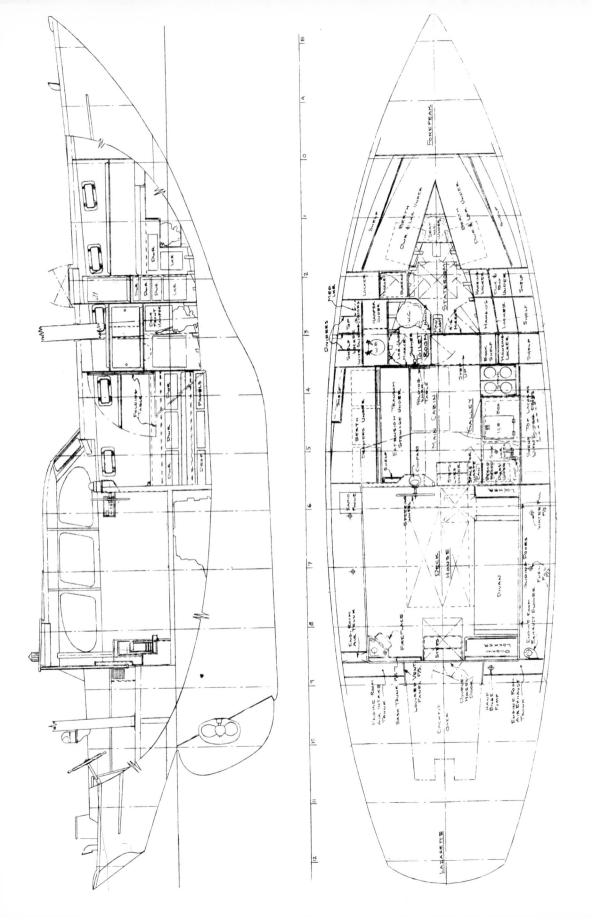

LADY HELENE *is an Alden ketch that combines ability at sea with comfort in port to an unusual degree. Seldom does a sailboat only a little more than 47 ft long overall have a flush deck with headroom underneath, a luxurious deckhouse with an inside steering station (and visibility from it), and a radar installation.* (Fortier)

well equipped for a sailboat less than 32 ft long on the waterline, and one can only hope that nothing goes wrong with her electrical system. A somewhat smaller version of *Lady Helene*, the 44-ft LOA *Countess*, is available in fiberglass.

Lady Helene is as convincing an exponent of a certain style of cruising as *Riwaru* and *Melusine II* are of other styles, and all three vessels show that given enough boat to work with and a reasonable set of requirements, a capable and sympathetic designer can turn out a handsome cruiser.

L A D Y   H E L E N E

DESIGNER   *John G. Alden & Co., Inc., 131 State Street, Boston, Massachusetts*

LOA   47 ft 4 in.

LWL   31 ft 8 in.

BEAM   12 ft 1 in.

DRAFT   5 ft 4 in.

DISPLACEMENT   28,000 lb

BALLAST   9,000 lb of lead

SAIL AREA   942 ft²

ENGINE   Barr-Ford FDY 330 (96 hp)

FUEL   90 gal

WATER   150

CONSTRUCTION   Philippine-mahogany-over-cedar double planking on oak frames, with oak center-line structure; teak-over-plywood deck and Honduras-mahogany deckworks; spruce spars

(TEXT CONTINUED FROM PAGE 116)

handling of a main of a given area on a narrow sloop and on a beamy ketch, to give two extremes. I myself find it only a trifle harder to cope with the 660-ft^2 main in my present ketch than it was to cope with the 260-ft^2 main in a sloop I formerly owned, and the 235-ft^2 mizzen of the ketch is a joke to stow compared with the sloop's main. Of course, I have taken pains to make the large main tractable, with soft rather than hard Dacron cloth, a reel halyard winch, a light downhaul secured between the headboard and a slide 20 ft below it, and so on; but these measures only emphasize that no arbitrary area limit can be set. Still, there *is* such a thing as too large a main for comfort in a shorthanded cruising boat, and it is somewhere between 350 and 650 ft^2. In the case of a sloop, the lower figure is probably about right, though it might be raised by 50 to 75 ft^2 in the case of an especially stiff vessel.

A cutter is basically a sloop with two headsails instead of one. Thus the total sail area is broken up into three pieces instead of two, with more area in the fore-triangle than in the mainsail. Generally a jib topsail with a high clew is set on a stay that goes to the masthead, and a low-cut forestaysail is set on a forestay parallel to the jibstay and some distance aft of it. With three sheets to play with, it is easy to balance a cutter on any point of sailing. In a properly designed cutter, the main has about the same area as the single-reefed main of a comparable sloop. The first step in reducing sail in a cutter is usually simply to hand the forestaysail, which seldom affects the balance of the boat and, since the forestaysail is well inboard, is no great chore. In a sloop, one must either reef the main or change jibs. In serious weather, it is often possible to proceed under forestaysail alone, while to achieve the same degree of sail reduction while retaining balance in a sloop requires both changing to a storm jib and either tucking a deep reef in the main or replacing it with a trysail —which means substantially more work, and work that must be done under un-congenial circumstances.

Despite its valuable qualities, the cutter rig has been more or less neglected in recent years. There are two chief reasons for this neglect. First, modern materials and equipment no longer make it mandatory to break up a masthead foretriangle; stronger hulls, spars, and rigging permit a single headsail and backstay to carry the full load without the mast breaking, and more powerful winches enable ordinary human beings to sheet a masthead genoa. Second, as has been said, much of the area of a genoa is "free," so most rigs are drawn in the expectation that genoas with substantial overlaps will be used until the wind really whistles.

It would seem, then, that the cutter is simply an anachronism, as doomed as the dodo to extinction. This is not far from true in the United States, where the typical beaminess of the hulls makes genoas very efficient, and would no doubt be true abroad except that European boats tend to be narrower and so are less able to exploit genoas. (A genoa needs a wide deck aft to be sheeted properly.) Further, the RORC method of measuring sail area favors a cutter with both overlapping forestaysail and overlapping jib topsail. In any case, the cutter can be a welcome rig for the cruising sailor who couldn't care less about The Rule. A proper cruising cutter has a larger foretriangle than a comparable racing masthead sloop, so that with forestaysail and jib topsail its sail area is the same as that of the sloop with its biggest genoa. Thus in light airs the cutter sets as much sail but in smaller units, which are less trouble to handle—indeed, if the forestaysail is on a boom and therefore self-tending when coming about, very much less trouble to handle. In moderate airs, when all hands on the sloop are messing about on the foredeck to change down to a smaller genoa, the cutter's crew merely has another beer, since its smaller sails are not so sensitive to wind strength. If the wind does pipe up a bit, one man in the cutter hands its forestaysail in no time flat, while the lads on the sloop are again taking off one genoa and setting a still smaller one, perhaps getting their pants wet in the process. And so it goes, with both boats sailing together at the same speed all the time but the cutter's crew having much less work to do. (Actually, since the sloop is bareheaded whenever the jib is being changed, the cutter is probably ahead of it.) In racing, of course, the higher-rated sail area of the cutter means that it must give time to the sloop, so it will always lose on corrected time; but for cruising, the cutter has the edge, one might say.

It is not a bad idea to fit the forestay of a cutter with a quick-release lever fitting, somewhat like a backstay lever, to permit the forestay to be freed readily. When there are only cat's-paws about, a light overlapping genoa can be set to good effect, and a removable forestay can be secured amidships to permit tacking or jibing such a drifter; or if the mast needs the additional support, the stay can be freed momentarily and then set up afterward. To windward or reaching in a breeze of Force 3 or thereabouts, though, it should be possible to shift to a double-head rig without losing drive.

The various arguments for the cutter lose much of their point in small yachts, where even the largest genoa is still a one-man job. At an over-all length of 36 ft or so, however, a masthead sloop is getting to be a big package to handle, and a cutter is worth looking into. A yawl, too, is worth looking into in such a case; and since in a yawl, part of the sail area is shifted to the mizzen and it also remains controllable under jib and mizzen alone, one need not contemplate a double-head rig in a yawl until it reaches a length of 40 to 50 ft overall.

Of all of the modern rigs, the yawl is the most peculiar-looking to the land-lubber. Why that cute little sail at the back end? To which many a sailor will reply, "The £%§&φ rule!" Actually, while it is true that much of the popularity of yawls can be traced to their kind treatment by rating formulas (kinder in the past than in the present, however), they do offer certain advantages. After all, mizzen-masts are nice to lean against and also provide a perch from which to fly a private signal. Further, the mizzen is often helpful as a balancing sail, and a mizzen staysail provides a painless way to augment sail when off the wind. Most significant of the yawl's virtues, to my mind, is that it is possible to reduce sail area quickly without losing maneuverability by just dropping the main. It may be a sudden squall coming up or a desire to sail slowly in unfamiliar waters, but there are times when one wants to take it easy without having to go to the trouble of reefing or changing sails, and at such times a yawl wins out over most sloops and cutters. I say "most" because there are some boats that can be taken on any point of sailing under headsails or mainsails alone with no difficulty, and I would certainly prefer a single-masted vessel with such good balance to an ill-mannered two-master.

But things are seldom wholly black and white, and for shorthanded cruising in a medium-sized boat—say, 36 to 50 ft overall—the yawl rig has much to offer. Below 36 ft overall, the mizzen on a yawl is usually too tiny to compensate for the windage of its spars and rigging, and the mizzen staysail that can be set is hardly larger than a handkerchief. Between 36 and 40 ft overall, it all depends on the boat and the tastes of its crew; some of the popularity of small yawls is surely due to racing and not cruising considerations. From 45 ft up, the ketch becomes a competitor, and whether a yawl with a biggish mizzen or a ketch with a smallish mizzen is better depends on the boat and to some extent is a matter of splitting hairs. Past 50 ft overall, though, it is a rare yawl that can be readily handled by a man and his wife alone.

In a sizable cruising boat, the ketch rig is hard to beat. It is very easy to handle, both because none of the sails is unduly large and because sail can be reduced in successive stages without reefing. The spars are moderate in length, and with the help of a triatic stay from the mainmast to the mizzen and a standing backstay from the mizzen to a boomkin, they can be superbly stayed. The center of effort is lower than in other rigs of the same total area, which contributes to stiffness and thus provides more latitude in deciding when to shorten sail. Off the wind, a huge mizzen staysail can be set to give a substantial boost at the expense of very little effort; and in strong winds in a seaway, the combination of jib and mizzen staysail with main and mizzen stowed frees one from worry about accidental jibes, dipping booms, chafe, and so on. All in all, the ketch rig is flexible and splendidly seaworthy.

The only thing wrong with the ketch rig is that it is relatively inefficient to windward and running free. On the wind, the main interferes with the mizzen, though full and by, the mizzen does help. Downwind, the mizzen interferes with the flow of air to main, and, in addition, the shorter mainmast means a smaller main and spinnaker. A bleak picture, it would seem; but on a reach and in heavy weather, the ketch rig redeems itself. Reaching with spinnaker or a big jib, mainsail, mizzen staysail, and mizzen all up and pulling, one has a great deal of power to drive the ship without any of the elements that provide this power being unduly large or hard to control. When it blows up to the point where other rigs must have their headsails changed or their mainsails reefed, the ketch need only drop an appropriate sail, a fairly easy job in any case but made easier here by the small size of each of the sails relative to the size of ship. On the one hand, then, the ketch does not sparkle to windward or on a run in light and moderate airs; on the other, it is fine when reaching and altogether splendid when the wind blows up.

Very well, one might say, the obvious cure for what ails the ketch is to increase the size of the rig so that it is large enough to cope with light weather on and off the wind, an increase that will not prejudice its handiness since sail can be so readily shortened. In practice, the only two ways to effect such an enlargement of sail area are to spread the rig out further with a bowsprit forward and a lot of overhang of the mizzen boom aft or else to go to a lighter displacement than normal. Neither alternative is wholly desirable in a cruising boat; an all-inboard rig is safer and more convenient, while moderate displacement means greater all-round comfort.

Because of the above considerations, the ketch rig is seldom used in vessels small enough to be no great burden to a modest crew when rigged as cutters or yawls. The dividing line is a mainsail area in the neighborhood of 500 to 550 ft². If one wants a larger yacht yet does not feel happy about coping with monstrous expanses of Dacron and nylon, the best answer is a ketch. After all, the lack of efficiency to windward and downwind is only a relative one: a big ketch will still go faster than a smaller yawl whose main is the same size. And modest displacement in a big ketch need mean little sacrifice of looks or sea-kindliness as compared

with what is lost in a small light-displacement boat. In a ketch between 50 and 60 ft overall, I believe one can come quite close to having one's cake and eating it too: a fast boat that provides indecent comfort at sea and in port, yet a rig that is docile at all times.

If I seem unduly bullish on ketches, it is because I am trying to compensate for the bad name their indifferent racing performance has given them, a bad name that should properly be given instead to the measurement rules by which they are rated. A large ketch is a far superior cruising boat than a large sloop, yet the ketch cannot compete on equal terms with the sloop in today's ocean racing. The result is that there are not many ketches around, except for ketch-rigged motor sailers, which is rather a pity.

My own knowledge of ketches has come from sailing my 58-ft ketch, *Minots Light,* more than twenty thousand miles in the past five years. In that period we reefed the main exactly once (except for practice drills), and even that time it was more in a spirit of adventure than of necessity. All my offshore sailing in *Minots Light* has been with total crews of three to five adults, of whom one or two were women, except for an Atlantic crossing when we were five men and two women. Even the latter passage could have been made quite well with a smaller complement aboard. My wife and I and our three children live aboard while cruising for four or five months each year, often with several guests, without claustrophobia, yet two people on deck can do everything that needs doing except play spinnaker. In 1962 my wife and I saw the *America*'s Cup races off Newport and took inordinate pleasure in watching eleven husky characters getting a workout on each boat, both of which have comparable displacements and sail areas to *Minots Light,* which the two of us had sailed there by ourselves. Of course, seventeen winches, braided sheets, a boomed forestaysail, light downhauls on the upper luff of each sail, and other laborsaving devices do their part, but that is what they were invented for, and not to exploit them seems foolish.

A number of subsidiary questions arise in connection with the design of a rig. One is the matter of a bowsprit, which provides a way to extend the base of the foretriangle without elongating the hull. In the old days, when boats were heavy, rigs were low and inefficient, and the plumb stem was regarded as the apex of seaworthiness, bowsprits were almost invariably found on sailing vessels of all kinds. Today boats are light, rigs are tall and efficient, and the value of an adequate bow overhang is generally appreciated, with the result that bowsprits rarely are necessary. Perhaps the only legitimate excuse for designing a modern boat with a sprit is in the case of a ketch that has no other way to secure the sail area it requires. Sometimes a boat turns out to be underrigged or to have excessive weather helm, in which case a sprit can be added afterward as a remedy; I once owned a cutter with a bowsprit that had begun life as a sloop without one, and the improvement

[OPPOSITE] *The aluminum ketch* SYRA *was designed and built by Robert Derecktor. Her quadrilateral mainsail has a half-wishbone aloft (it is to windward in the photograph but its shadow is visible) which sheets to the mizzenmast as well as a conventional boom at the foot. A mainsail of this kind permits a substantial sail area to be set, but it is not the simplest rig to cope with. The deck layout is also unconventional: note the twin companionways on either side of the mizzenmast, the oversize steering wheel, and the dinghy stowage on the boomkin. (Rosenfeld)*

in its performance was marked. However, a really badly balanced boat can seldom be helped by a rig change—the fault is with the hull, and only altering the hull can improve matters.

Two reasons occasionally cited for having a bowsprit are that it makes anchor handling easier and that in some instances it lowers the rating a trifle over what it would be if the bow were drawn out by the same amount. The latter is of no interest here, and I think the former is an exaggeration. It *is* nice to be able to cat an anchor alongside a bowsprit, but Danforths and CQR's of the right size are light enough in nearly any yacht to be gotten on deck and secured by one man.

To be sure, modern bowsprits pose few of the terrors of their ancestors. Today they consist of frameworks of steel tubing with grating platforms and pulpits, so that they are reasonably safe to work on if perhaps not too convenient. Because of this, it is not necessary either to risk one's life on a slippery, narrow stick to change jibs or else to have a jibstay that can be brought inboard for this purpose, which means that it cannot ever be set up really tight. Still, bowsprits are excrescences, and one is better off without them if they can be avoided.

A boomkin is in a category quite different from that of its cousin at the other end of the boat. In many ketches and in some yawls, a short boomkin makes it possible to have a permanent mizzen backstay, an improvement over running backstays with little drift when a mizzen staysail is set. In conjunction with a light triatic stay to the main masthead, a permanent mizzen backstay stiffens the whole rig; the triatic and its fittings should be designed to fail in the event either mast breaks, so that only one will be lost. In a yawl with stout aluminum spars, the need for a fixed mizzen backstay is not great; but in a ketch with wooden spars, it is often desirable. The mizzen staysail of a ketch may be comparable in area to the mainsail, and it can produce a mighty pull at times.

Another question to be decided at the start is what kind of reefing arrangement to have. I suspect that much of the current trend toward roller reefing is the result of collective brainwashing and is not based on actual experience. For every argument in favor of roller reefing, there is an argument against it; and the more one has been at sea with both reefing systems, the less dogmatic one becomes. This ambiguity is less pronounced when a particular boat is considered, because it may have certain characteristics that point directly one way or the other, but it seems hardly warranted to be wholly for or against roller reefing in general.

The overriding virtue of roller reefing is that with it one man can amble forward, casually slack the main halyard, and effortlessly turn a crank that rolls the main around the boom until its area has been reduced by the amount required. At least, that is the theory. I have had two boats fitted with roller reefing, and in neither was the process of rolling in a reef so simple and painless if a properly setting sail was to result. Still, there is no question that rolling in a reef is substantially easier than tying one in and that with a correctly shaped boom (including a cutaway portion near the gooseneck to take the luff rope) a perfectly acceptable single reef can be taken quickly with minimum effort. By the time 30 to 40 percent of the sail has been rolled up, though, it is less likely to look good, and windward ability under shortened sail is not something that should be compromised. A worthwhile precaution is to have a row of eyelets placed where a normal double reef would be, and one can then roll the sail down far enough to make running a lacing through the eyelets and hardening it down a feasible job shorthanded. The eyelets are worth having in any event in case the reefing gear should suffer a temporary embarrassment, which has been known to happen.

There is no point in contrasting a good roller-reefing installation with a poor conventional one, as is often done, since the former is no more inevitable than the latter. Given a stout gallows for the boom, sheaves on the boom at the positions of the cringles in the leech, and a winch to do the pulling down, tying in a reef while the sail is still up is a practical proposition even for a small crew. A light line permanently rove through each cringle permits passing a heavier reefing pennant through when needed without either having to climb up on the boom or having to suffer the windage and possible chafe of the latter at other times. A gallows is actually not mandatory, since the boom can be held fairly firmly by the combined action of topping lift, mainsheet, and a vang led to the lee rail, but it does make the job safer and less of a struggle. Still, no matter how good the mechanical arrangement is, tying in a reef by hand with the sail up is more work for more people than rolling in the same reef, though not necessarily very much more of either.

What, then, are the advantages of conventional reefing that may be enough to offset its inconvenience? First of all, it provides for a well-setting sail at all times. Second, when the sail is down, it is harder to roll in a reef than it is to tie one in. No more crew are needed to tie in a reef on a furled sail than the number needed to get it down, while rolling in a good reef under similar circumstances when the wind is blowing is quite a trick. The ability to reef the main before setting out from port is at times worth having, and a boat with a divided rig can usually afford (except when racing) to hand the main in order to reef it and will still be able to remain on or near the desired course. A vang can be rigged anywhere on a conventional boom at any time, which seems to me especially advantageous under gale conditions. The topping lift can be led to a tackle on a track on the side of the boom, making adjustment possible without the complication of a block aloft and the windage of another wire down the mast—although there are some who prefer the latter scheme. It is possible to have one or two winches at the forward end of a fixed boom for trimming a jib or spinnaker whose sheet is led to the end of the boom; adjusting the mainsheet or mizzen sheet then automatically adjusts the other sail as well, a not inconsiderable bonus. Also, with roller reefing, the mainsheet must lead directly from the boom end. Usually this means that the sheet must be trimmed from the after end of the cockpit, so that if there is a tiller the helmsman cannot reach the sheet, and if there is a wheel there may not be room for anybody else to do so. With a fixed boom, the mainsheet can be led to a reinforced pedestal just in front of the wheel or forward to the cabin house or almost anywhere else that makes sense. Distributing the points of attachment of the mainsheet also reduces the tendency of the boom to bend and so permits a lighter boom.

Balancing the merits and demerits of each scheme as applied to cruising boats, it all boils down to the question of how often it will be necessary to reef and how urgently this will have to be accomplished. In a fairly large, stiff boat with a divided rig whose main contains less than perhaps 45 percent of the total sail area, I doubt that roller reefing is worth the sacrifice of a fixed boom. On the other hand, most cruising sloops are the better for roller reefing, since rolling up some of the main, however sloppy the result, is quicker and easier than shifting jibs and less apt to set one excessively off course in the process. In a cutter or yawl of moderate size, I think roller reefing is more likely to be worthwhile than not, but no general rule is possible. A ketch of any size should be happier with conventional reefing.

Like roller reefing, roller furling for jibs has its enthusiastic advocates and equally enthusiastic detractors. This old dodge involves a jib set flying with a swivel at its head and a reel at its foot. The reel is wound with light wire, so that hauling in the wire rotates the jib luff and thereby rolls the jib up on itself. Instead of lugging a jib up forward, hanking it on, attaching its sheets and halyard, and then sweating it up, all one need do with a furled jib is release the furling line and pull on the sheet to unroll it. Instead of going forward to fight the jib to the deck, unhank it, and bag and stow it, the procedure is merely to tug the furling line while seated in the cockpit. Nobody ever need set foot on the foredeck, and even the largest jib can be rolled up in a squall. With a double-head rig, part of a large roller-furling jib topsail or genoa can be rolled up to make coming about easier; sometimes, if the jib is correctly cut, it can be set only partially unrolled instead of changing to a smaller sail. A marvelous picture, so alluring that one wonders why every boat is not equipped with a roller-furling jib.

In real life, roller furling is not all that wonderful, though it does have a certain range of usefulness. Different people have different objections, but I do not feel that those based on doubts as to the reliability of the furling apparatus are too well founded. The Merriman swivel-and-drum gear that I have used is quite sturdy and robust, and I know a man who sailed from Los Angeles westward across the Pacific and Indian Oceans to Malta with a roller jib and had no trouble with it at all. The objection that really counts is the difficulty of getting a straight luff on a sail set flying. A jib with a sagging luff is no good at all to windward, and if one tries to point high with it, the results are lots of leeway and low forward speed, a discouraging combination. This is less of a problem in a sail of moderate size in a small boat, where a reasonable mechanical advantage will get the halyard up tight enough. In *Nipinke,* my little cutter, a roller-furling jib topsail was fairly satisfactory on the wind, and inefficiency was tolerable in exchange for never having to go out on the bowsprit. However, a similar sail on *Minots Light* was a failure despite a luff wire identical with the head stay and a heavy two-part wire halyard leading to a geared winch; even when the backstay turnbuckles were used for the final hardening of the halyard, the jib luff curved well out to leeward when on the wind. Further, the sail, though not large for the boat, was still a big fellow, and rolling it up was a time- and effort-consuming process, more of a chore than handing an ordinary jib of that size usually is. But my chief complaint is poor performance to windward.

On the balance, then, I cannot recommend roller jibs for serious windward work in moderate to large vessels, certainly not for genoas in boats more than 40 to 45 ft in over-all length. In a boat smaller than this or in a somewhat larger ketch, a roller jib might turn out to be satisfactory if plenty of mechanical advantage is provided to get the halyard taut. In particular, roller furling can be a help in a double-head rig, where it is difficult to get the jib past the forestay when coming about. Where roller furling is most useful, in my opinion, is in a motor sailer, where the engine normally does the work going to windward anyway. Once the wind is a few points free, a roller jib is just as good as any other and is easier to cope with, especially if the boat has a bowsprit, as do most motor sailers with pretensions to sailing ability.

Another ambiguous item is a jib boom or forestaysail boom. As usual, on the one hand, it offers convenience; on the other, loss of efficiency. The main convenience comes from the fact that a boomed sail is self-tending when coming about, so that all one need do is turn the wheel and over she goes. Subsidiary advantages include a built-in tackle that makes it less work to trim the sheet and the simplicity of setting or handling the sail, the more so if a removable topping lift is fitted (the spinnaker-pole lift is fine for this purpose). The loss of efficiency is real, but if the boat has an ample rig it is certainly tolerable. In an underrigged vessel that cannot get out of its own way in a gale without an overlapping genoa, of course, a boomed jib is impossible, which is a further argument for an adequate sail plan.

A scheme alleged to increase the efficiency of a boomed jib is to have the boom pivot a short distance aft of the stay, so that slacking the sheet automatically provides more draft to the sail and trimming the sheet flattens the sail. The ordinary procedure is to lace the jib to a boom whose forward end is secured to the stay. I have sailed with both kinds of boomed jibs, and my impression is that the best results to windward come from a jib laced to a thin boom that bends in just the right way, while on a reach the independent boom is superior. The trouble with the latter to windward is that the draft tends to come in the middle of the sail instead of near the luff. Nevertheless, I prefer the independent boom because it is secured only to the clew of the sail and therefore the latter can be detached for use in the normal way in a moment. Releasing another pin at the pivot and unscrewing the shackle on the traveler frees the boom entirely for stowage in chocks along the rail. If one feels lazy, the boom is there; while if one feels ambitious, it can be removed with no trouble.

With double headsails in a cruising yacht, a boomed forestaysail means only one pair of sheets to worry about when tacking instead of two. So while it is pretty much a matter of taste whether to fit a jibboom when there is only a single headsail, the pros outweigh the cons in the case of the forestaysail boom when there are two headsails.

It is sometimes thought that since much ocean cruising is done in the trade winds, it is only sensible to have a rig designed chiefly for downwind sailing in a yacht meant for long-distance cruising. But experience shows that it is wise not to go overboard in the sacrifice of all-round ability, as Eric Hiscock has emphasized: "So much has been written about the delights of this kind of sailing, when, it is said, the twins are set and the vessel left to run unattended on her way while the crew bask in the sunshine and grow fatter day by day, that those who have not sailed in them may imagine the trade wind areas to be permanently blessed with moderate winds blowing always from astern, smooth seas and continuous sunshine. Unfortunately this is not true. More often than not the wind is too far out on the quarter or the beam to allow the self-steering rig to work; in 400 days of ocean sailing I find that *Wanderer*'s twins were used during only thirty-eight days." A point to be kept in mind even when fitting gear for a pair of running sails, then, is that shifting back and forth to fore-and-aft sails should not be too much of a project.

[X]

A Cutter and Two Sloops:
THUNDERHEAD, DISCOVERY,
& K-50

THERE WILL ALWAYS BE SAILORS FOR WHOM the simplicity and efficiency of the masthead sloop (or cutter) make it the only rig to have. But lovers of the single stick may still differ widely in their other tastes, and the three yachts shown here, though similar in sail plan and hull dimensions, are decidedly different in flesh and spirit. Their respective designers, Philip Rhodes, William Garden, and Paul Kettenburg, are from widely separated parts of the United States, and it is not too hard to guess who has his home in New York, who in San Diego, and who in Seattle on the basis of their creations—or, for that matter, to guess which boat would be ideal for a weekend spin to Catalina, for a cruise Down East to Maine, and for a passage through the inside route to Alaska.

THUNDERHEAD

IT HAS BEEN MY PRIVILEGE TO SEE *Thunderhead* in her home grounds of Long Island Sound any number of times, and she has never failed to stand out from other boats nearby. A clipper-bowed cutter under way makes a brave sight, and I have no doubt that much of *Thunderhead*'s racing success is due to accidental jibes by competing boats whose helmsmen could not take their eyes off her. It is interesting that *Thunderhead*'s good looks are only hinted at in her plans. I for one would never have thought from her profile drawing that she would turn out to be so handsome in three dimensions, which goes to show how essential it is that a yacht designer be an artist as well as an engineer.

Thunderhead was meant for racing as well as cruising, but racing considerations do not seem to have dominated over common sense except in the choice of a gasoline engine. *Thunderhead*'s bronze centerboard means that her hull draft is only 5 ft 6 in., a modest figure for so able and substantial a vessel; a virtual sister ship has been built on the West Coast with a normal keel that draws 7 ft 6 in.

Mr. Rhodes has provided the following comments on *Thunderhead*: "The helmsman sits slightly above deck level abaft a pedestal wheel and binnacle. All winches are forward of him, but the runner levers are aft where he can handle them. The cockpit sole is lowered for-

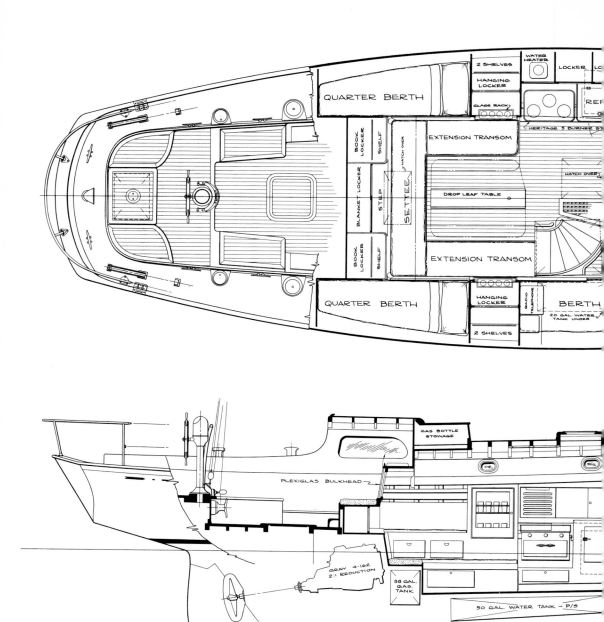

QUARTER BERTH

2 SHELVES

HANGING
LOCKER

WATER
HEATER

LOCKER LO

GLASS RACK)

REF

HERITAGE 5 BURNER S

BOOK
LOCKER

BLANKET LOCKER

SHELF

STEP

SETTEE

HATCH OVER

EXTENSION TRANSOM

DROP LEAF TABLE

HATCH OVER

BOOK
LOCKER

SHELF

EXTENSION TRANSOM

QUARTER BERTH

HANGING
LOCKER

RADIO
TELEPHONE

BERTH

20 GAL WATER
TANK UNDER

2 SHELVES

GAS BOTTLE
STOWAGE

PLEXIGLAS BULKHEAD

GRAY 4-162
2:1 REDUCTION

38 GAL.
GAS.
TANK

50 GAL WATER TANK - P/S

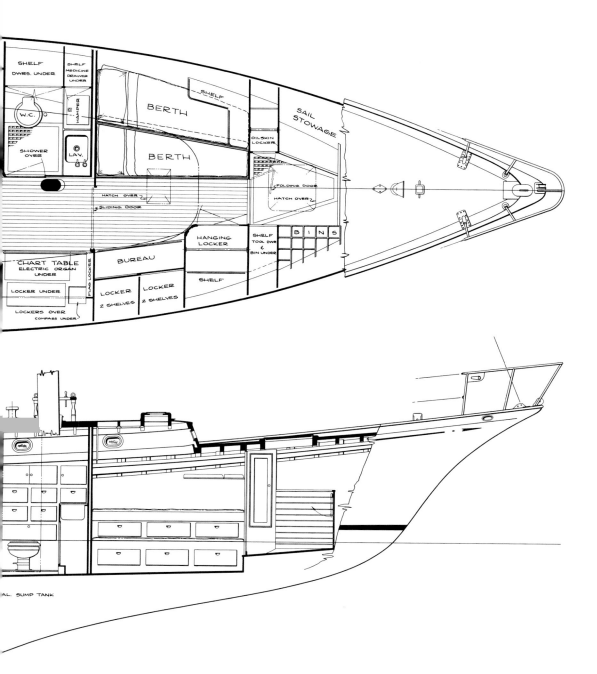

SHELF
DWRS. UNDER

SHELF
MEDICINE
DRAWER
UNDER

W.C.

HAMPER

BERTH

SHELF

SAIL
STOWAGE

SHOWER
OVER

LAV.

BERTH

OILSKIN
LOCKER

HATCH OVER?

SLIDING DOOR

FOLDING DOOR

HATCH OVER?

CHART TABLE
ELECTRIC ORGAN
UNDER

BUREAU

HANGING
LOCKER

SHELF
TOOL DWR
&
BIN UNDER

B I N S

LOCKER UNDER

FLAG LOCKER

LOCKER
2 SHELVES

LOCKER
2 SHELVES

SHELF

LOCKERS OVER
COMPASS UNDER

AL. SUMP TANK

ward of the binnacle so that the coaming and sheet winches are waist high to the crew and, therefore, much easier to use. At the forward end of the cockpit is a shelter with transverse seat. The instruments are located in the protection of the shelter, which also has a chart board that hinges down from the shelter roof, always immediately available for reference. There is a cast bronze framed hatch in the cockpit sole for access to the motor. Under the shelter, a hatch is provided so that one can enter the main cabin. The main companionway access is from the starboard side deck, the hatch slide being on the trunk top.

"An unusual feature is that the bulkhead at the after end of the trunk, which separates the main cabin from the cockpit, is made of Plexiglas. This lets in a lot of light and permits those below to see what is taking place in the cockpit. With the shelter hatch open those below, especially the navigator, can converse freely with those in the cockpit and always see the other party. The shelter is a real blessing for the crew in bad weather and the protected hatch is very useful for passing up food, drink, cigarettes, etc.

"There is a big U-shaped seat, or triclinium, surrounding the mess table aft which is supported by the bronze centerboard trunk. This is flanked by out-of-the-way quarter berths and some large lockers. The seats are extension transoms so that four persons can sleep aft. At the aft end of the transoms are small but adequate doors for access to the motor, batteries, and so on.

"The companionway ladder is really a beautiful circular stairway, turning 90°, with an attractive chrome balustrade. Outboard is a well-concealed berth for the navigator. Opposite, on the port side, is the galley. Here we have a stainless steel Heritage five-burner gas stove, an electric refrigerator with freezer compartment, gas hot water heater, stainless steel dresser top and sink, and racks for dishes and lockers for pots and pans.

"Forward of the galley is a generous toilet

The cutter THUNDERHEAD *is one of Philip Rhodes's happiest creations. The forward end of the cockpit is well protected by the fixed shelter.* (Rosenfeld)

room, which has a shower, linen lockers, a clothes hamper and a large number of drawers. The shower and wash basin are supplied with hot and cold running water and the shower drains through a teak grating to a sump tank equipped with an electric pump.

"Opposite the toilet are the chart table and flag locker. Proper stowage is provided for all navigational equipment. Here again is another novelty: the chart table top hinges up, exposing a small electric organ! The wide open treatment of this combination dining saloon, main cabin, galley, and chart room creates an unbelievable sense of spaciousness. With the plexiglas bulkhead at the after end of the cabin, the vista is startling. The entire interior is of Farican mahogany, rubbed to a satin finish. The sole is teak splined with holly.

"Forward, separated by a transverse bulkhead, is the owner's cabin. There are two berths to port and on the starboard side there are wardrobes and a handsome dressing table with hinged stool. Forward is a large forepeak with bins for sails and gear all very carefully arranged. Above is a flush cast bronze framed hatch.

"The quarters below decks are well-lighted with ports and skylights and especial care has been given to adequate ventilation with numerous cowls on baffle boxes. The forward end of the trunk cabin is circular, which adds to the free and clear deck space. The side decks are wider than usual and the forward deck is uncluttered to make for easier sail handling. The deck is laid in narrow strakes of Port Orford cedar and payed with 3-M compound. Deck joinerwork and rail caps are of Honduras mahogany."

THUNDERHEAD

DESIGNER   *Philip L. Rhodes, 369 Lexington Avenue, New York City*

LOA   48 ft 9 in.

LWL   37 ft

BEAM   13 ft

DRAFT   5 ft 6 in. centerboard up, 9 ft 11 in. centerboard down

SAIL AREA   964 ft²

ENGINE   Graymarine 4-162 (63 hp)

FUEL   38 gal

WATER   120 gal

CONSTRUCTION   Double planking of African mahogany on laminated-oak frames and teak keel; bronze-weldment floors, mast step, centerboard trunk, and web frames at the mast; standing rigging of stainless-steel wire rope with swaged terminals; running rigging of stainless-steel and Dacron rope, hollow-spruce spars

DISCOVERY

WILLIAM GARDEN HAS BEEN RESPONSIBLE FOR many original ideas in the design of cruising yachts, and almost every set of plans he turns out shows the influence of a restless imagination—an imagination, I should add, that is controlled and directed by his feeling for the sea, so that Garden boats always seem to fit into the tradition of the Grand Banks fishing schooner and the opium clipper, however equipped they may be with innovations of all kinds. *Discovery* is no exception, and she remains a ship rather than a toy despite her clean rig, large deckhouse windows, after cabin, and davit-launched dinghy on the counter. Afloat, *Discovery* shows herself worthy of being the namesake of Cook's flagship, and it is hard to imagine her staying in her Puget Sound home for very long.

Mr. Garden has commented that *Discovery* turned out to be "a wonderful boat under sail—

fast and comfortable. She has 400 gallons of diesel oil under the saloon sole, giving her an excellent cruising radius under power. A close sister ship ran under power from Seattle to San Francisco last summer on just half her fuel. This means a range of about 1600 miles at 7 knots, or about 7½ knots in smooth water. The hull form incorporates a broad shallow keel measuring about 24 inches across the garboard. The accommodation plan is shown quite clearly on the drawing. For extended cruising, however, such as a world voyage, I think a single cabin arrangement would be much better; perhaps with quarter berths port and starboard of the engine area where a couple of members of the crew could sleep in the point of least motion. While the double cabin arrangement does give wonderful privacy on short cruises for two couples, it has the disadvantages of being hard to heat and difficult of access under severe conditions."

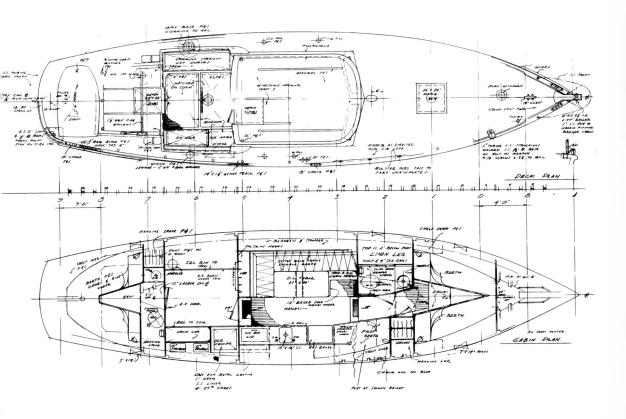

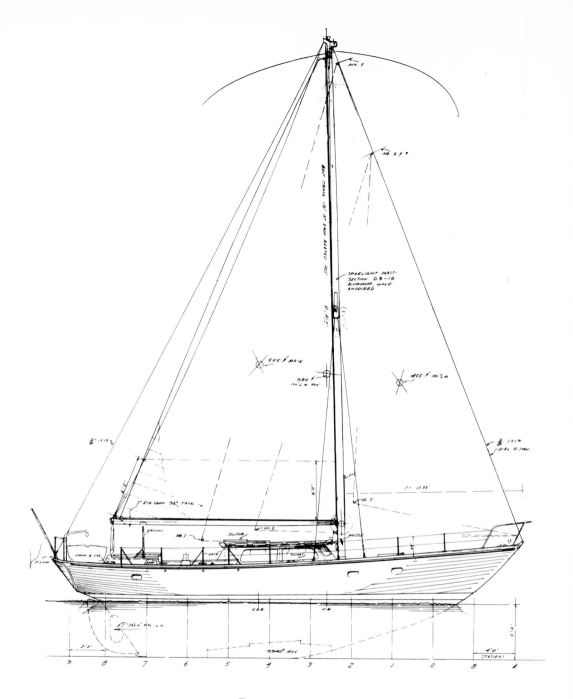

DISCOVERY

DESIGNER *William Garden, 3040 West Commodore Way, Seattle, Washington*

LOA 46 ft

LWL 34 ft 9 in.

BEAM 11 ft 6 in.

DRAFT 5 ft 6 in.

BALLAST 9,000 lb of iron

SAIL AREA 960 ft²

ENGINE Diesel

FUEL 400 gal

WATER 200 gal

K-50

HER DESIGNER CLAIMS FOR *K-50* that she combines "motor sailer accommodations with the speed of a racing boat," which is undoubtedly true even though not as much of a compliment as it seems, since most racing boats are more notable for low ratings than for high speeds. But blurbs are meant to impress the landlubber, and the sailor needs no coaching to draw his own conclusions from the plans. The hull has sweet lines and the sail area is ample, so *K-50* should move well under sail, and the elongated deckhouse does indeed make possible a roomy interior. In fact, by taking the deckhouse seriously, the designer has been able to do more than just provide ten picture windows to be shuttered on a rough passage. The engine can be placed low and amidships, together with tanks for 200 gal each of fuel and water, and there is considerable stowage space under the

galley sole as well. Raising the main-cabin sole above the waterline means that it is unusually wide, and the galley benefits from the added space as well. The deckhouse top and sides extend aft to protect the forward part of the cockpit, a very fine feature. Unfortunately the deckhouse is too long for a dinghy to fit between it and the mast, and when one is carried it cannot help looking like an afterthought, thereby spoiling the otherwise clean lines of the hull and deck.

The accommodation is an interesting one, with six of its nine berths in the form of three doubles, and if the chart table is in place over the quarter berth, there is not a single proper seagoing berth. Since the *K-50* is a popular class —nineteen of them have been built in a relatively short time—one can only surmise the normal manner of sailing in southern Cali-

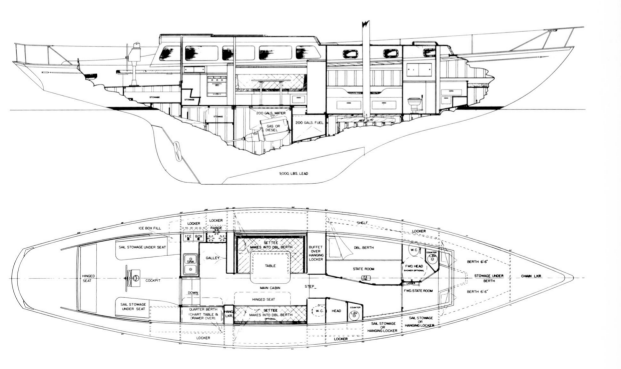

fornia. But however out of place a *K-50* might be in Pentland Firth or the Strait of Magellan, there are many regions where it is exactly suited to the prevailing conditions, and unkind remarks about this really quite clever design could come only from envy of those able to enjoy such conditions.

K - 5 0

DESIGNER   *Paul A. Kettenburg, 2810 Carleton Street, San Diego, California*

LOA   50 ft 9 in.

LWL   34 ft 6 in.

BEAM   13 ft

DRAFT   6 ft 10 in.

DISPLACEMENT   29,000 lb

BALLAST   9,000 lb of lead

SAIL AREA   987 ft²

ENGINE   Chrysler M225 or General Motors 3-53 diesel

FUEL   200 gal

WATER   200 gal

CONSTRUCTION   Philippine-mahogany planking on white-oak frames, with Douglas-fir and apitong center-line structure; fiberglass-covered plywood deck and Honduras-mahogany deckworks; spruce spars

The Kettenburg K-50 is a masthead sloop popular on the U.S. West Coast. (Merrick)

CHAPTER FIVE

Spars, Rigging, and Sails

W HEN THE TYPE of rig and its proportions have been chosen, the problem changes from What? to How? The introduction of aluminum spars, stainless-steel standing rigging with swaged fittings, and sails and running rigging of synthetic fibers has been a blessing to all sailors, for these materials are superior in efficiency, reliability, ease of handling, and longevity to what they replace. Until recently, the hull of a sailboat was sturdier than its rig; but now, if anything, the reverse is true and hulls have had to be made stronger than ever, which means, since wind and sea have not changed, that margins of safety are greater all around. Mistakes in judgment no longer need result in blown-out sails or a mast collapse. Of course, the intrinsic superiority of the new materials does not mean that careless design or sloppy workmanship can be tolerated, and attention must be paid to such new problems as insulating bronze winches and fittings from aluminum spars; but on the whole there is less likelihood of built-in-flaws, and the risk of hidden deterioration is now a minor one.

For all the advantages of aluminum, it is not necessarily worthwhile to replace an existing wooden mast in a cruising boat if it is still adequate. The benefits of aluminum are simply not great enough in most cases to justify throwing away a good mast with many years of life left in it. However, I personally would not even consider wood when a new mast is involved. A new aluminum mast is somewhat more expensive than a new wooden one, but in the long run the freedom from deterioration and maintenance of the former goes far toward evening the score. Even if this were not so, an aluminum mast would still pay its way, since it is both lighter in weight and smaller in cross section than a wooden one. Weight aloft reduces stability to a marked extent owing to the long lever arm, and a thick mast interferes excessively with airflow to the mainsail and so reduces its propulsive efficiency. Most of the drive of a mainsail before it is stalled—that is, to windward and on a reach—is developed near the luff, and the less turbulence in the airstream due to the mast, the better.

While granting all this, some people still prefer wood on the not indefensible grounds that varnished spruce is more pleasing to the eye than bare aluminum. In the case of an all-fiberglass boat, with a fiberglass deck and cabin house as well as

Wet and cold and the prospect of worse to come: the test of a good cruiser is not only whether she can take such conditions without difficulty, but also whether within her can be found warm, dry comfort afterward. (Beken)

hull, I must say that I think bare aluminum adds to rather than detracts from the picture, which is one of uncompromising modernity and ruthless efficiency, a kind of nautical exemplar of the principle that the end justifies the means—the end here being toughness and freedom from maintenance, the means being the use of materials that have an aura of coldness at best and plain ugliness at worst. But so far as I know, there is no legislation that prohibits the anodizing or painting of aluminum spars, and sailors who dislike the unadorned facts of contemporary technology are free to do either. *Simba,* Ralph Greenlee's beautiful yawl, has a hull of varnished mahogany and aluminum masts painted white, and I cannot believe that it would look any better with spruce masts instead. However, sometimes bare aluminum is best even in a conventional vessel. When Hans Van Nes replaced the aged wooden masts of the schooner *Chauve Souris,* the slender, silvery new aluminum ones went very well with the brilliant blue of the hull and gave the boat an air of elegance that had been absent before. Aluminum spars anodized to a gold color are common in England and look very well indeed.

Because excess weight aloft and a large mast cross section are both bad, one might think that the thing to do is to have a narrow mast stiffened with several sets of shrouds and spreaders. However, spreaders and shrouds are hardly buoyant and offer considerable wind resistance as well, so the choice between a sturdy mast with a minimum of rigging and a thin one with more rigging is not always easy to make. Beam enters here also, since a wide base for the shrouds permits a large enough angle between the upper shrouds and the mast for adequate support even with a single pair of spreaders, while a narrow base means that two pairs of spreaders are needed. Even in a fat boat, multiple spreaders are sometimes used, enabling the spreaders to be shorter and thereby making it possible to trim overlapping headsails properly. In America, the decision most often goes to one set of spreaders in the case of aluminum masts; in Europe, to two sets of spreaders. To reduce the number of things that can go wrong, I feel that it is preferable to use a single-spreader rig whenever it makes sense structurally—say, up to 60 ft above deck in the case of an aluminum mast. I feel safer with a small number of large fittings than with a large number of small fittings, since *any* fitting that lets go in the rigging can have catastrophic results.

Standing rigging these days is almost always 1×19 stainless-steel wire with swaged fittings, a neat, strong combination that has given excellent results. In swaging, the end of the wire is inserted into a socket in the shank of an appropriate stainless-steel terminal, which is then squeezed under high pressure until the

The little ketch MARCO POLO *has made many long voyages with small crews, including a circumnavigation of the world and a largely single-handed passage from New Zealand to Denmark, and those who have sailed aboard her recall the experience with fondness. However, much of her comfort at sea, as with other boats of this type, derives from her slowness, which denies her crews the deep pleasure to be found in speed under sail. A more modern boat with overhangs, finer lines, less wetted surface, and a more efficient rig will be faster, abler, and easier to handle than* MARCO POLO *while being no harder on the crew if not pressed too hard.*

shank actually flows around the wire. In time—perhaps in ten or fifteen years—the terminal may begin to develop tiny cracks, which may grow and eventually lead to failure. One theory has it that the cracks are due to corrosion, so that keeping the socket opening sealed with Rustoleum or grease will prolong the life of the fitting. In any case, there is no question that the stainless-steel wire–swaged-fitting combination is strong, stretches little under load, and is unlikely to let go without giving warning signs which regular inspection can reveal before it is too late. Other methods in use involve a fitting clamped onto the splayed end of the wire or secured there with the help of solder poured in to prevent the wire end from pulling out, but their chief virtue seems to be that no special tools are needed. I still think swaging does the neatest and most foolproof job, though the other techniques may well be as strong and are somewhat cheaper.

If running backstays are to be fitted in a cruising boat, much of the hazard and nuisance that often accompany them can be avoided by three measures. First, the mast should be so designed that the sole function of the runners is to keep the forestay taut when going to windward in moderate or strong breezes; in light airs and downwind, no runner should be needed, and at no time should the safety of the mast depend upon them. To permit the runners to play secondary rather than primary roles, a standing backstay and a pair of jumper stays (their struts braced together for added security and to prevent fouling) are usually adequate. With an aluminum mast, the jumpers may not even be needed. Second, the "drift" of the runners—that is, their distance aft of the mast—should be small enough to make it unnecessary to slack the lee runner when coming about. A runner drift about equal to the distance between the forestay foot and the mast is preferable from a structural point of view, but if reducing the drift by the few feet that may be required turns out to make any real difference, it is more sensible to beef up the runners than to have to work them constantly when short-tacking. The third measure is to have the runners lead to levers rather than to winches. True, one cannot "play the mast" with a lever, but who wants to? A backstay lever is fast, safe, and simplicity itself to operate, three attributes not shared by a backstay winch, and I would fit levers no matter how rarely the runners are needed; the stronger the wind, the more likely it is that they will be required, but these are the same circumstances under which foul-ups are apt to occur unless all gear is as straightforward as possible.

Rigging hardware—turnbuckles, toggles, shackles, tangs, pins—varies widely in design and construction, and since hardware failures are far more common than failures of the wire itself, the prudent sailor pays close attention to his fittings. A fitting that lets go may mean the loss of a mast, hardly an attractive prospect, yet inadequate or faulty fittings are on the market and, one must conclude, are bought and installed. I myself have had a backstay turnbuckle part during a Gulf Stream squall, naturally at 0300, and though the mast held, I do not look back at the event with relish. As I screwed together a series of shackles to replace the turnbuckle, I resolved to have nothing but the very best hardware in the future as well as to carry spares for everything. But as I soon found out, the best is often outrageously expensive: to replace all my forged-bronze turnbuckles with stainless ones machined from bar stock would have cost more than $600, for example. And there are certain applications for which no adequate fittings exist, though most of them are in the realm of running rather than standing rigging.

I find it curious that, according to my observations, most American yachts are fitted with bronze turnbuckles, most British yachts with galvanized-steel ones, and most Scandinavian yachts with stainless-steel ones. It seems unlikely that sailing conditions vary so widely among these countries that the different materials all represent the optimum choices, and one must conclude that habit and prejudice are to some degree involved. An objective comparison is therefore interesting. A typical size for a turnbuckle on a cruising boat of intermediate size is $\frac{1}{2}$ in., which normally is used with $\frac{1}{4}$-in. 1×19 stainless-steel wire. The approximate tensile strength of a $\frac{1}{2}$-in. stainless-steel turnbuckle is quoted by a reputable manufacturer as 14,200 lb, and its price in the United States is about $25. Comparable figures for a $\frac{1}{2}$-in. forged-bronze turnbuckle (cast bronze is apt to have voids and so is out of the running) are 10,500 lb and $11, and for a $\frac{1}{2}$-in. galvanized forged-steel turnbuckle they are 7,500 lb and $4. Since the breaking strength of $\frac{1}{4}$-in. wire is quoted as 8,200 lb, there is obviously a large margin of safety with the stainless-steel turnbuckle, a smaller but still substantial one with the bronze turnbuckle, while the galvanized-steel turnbuckle is not up to the job, and a larger, heavier, and more inconvenient (though still cheap) size is required. The stainless-steel turnbuckle is so strong, in fact, that one might even consider one size smaller, $\frac{7}{16}$ in., whose approximate strength is 11,500 lb and which saves $\frac{1}{4}$ lb in weight and $5 in cost.

It is hard to escape the conclusion that bronze offers the best combination of strength, freedom from deterioration, and expense. In all fairness, it must be said that stainless-steel fittings are cheaper in Scandinavia than elsewhere, while bronze is regarded with suspicion, so they are just as reasonable a choice there as bronze is in America. In Great Britain, on the other hand, appearance is seldom a consideration where yachts are concerned, so the disproportionate size and liability to corrosion of galvanized steel are accepted in exchange for low cost.

There is more to the matter than tensile strength. It is pointless for any link in a particular chain to be stronger than the others if all are subjected to the same load, but the different links between mast tang and chain plate actually experience stresses of a different kind and therefore may well need to have different characteristics. The source of the problem is that the lee rigging is slack and flexes, while the headstay—and the forestay if a sail is set on it—takes on a definite sag to leeward. Unless the fittings at the ends of the wire are able to align themselves with the wire at all times, the resulting unfair strains on them will lead in time to fatigue failure. The customary remedy is to install toggles between each turnbuckle and its chain plate; and in the case of the headstay, which is further abused when reaching under spinnaker with the pole against it, to install an additional toggle at the masthead. However, when a stay is really taut, the friction between pins and toggle may not actually permit full alignment, and some bending strain on the turnbuckle will be present. A stout turnbuckle in excess of nominal requirements is therefore likely to last longer than one that is just adequate but no more. Even so, bronze is an acceptable choice as a material for rigging hardware; but if money were no consideration, I would certainly have stainless steel.

Another problem is faulty hardware. I know a man who went out for a sail in a brand-new sloop and, when he went on the wind for the first time, the shroud toggles fractured and the mast went over the side. The manufacturer, shown the remains of his product, cheerfully replaced the toggles. The only way to be 100 percent sure is to X-ray all fittings, but one can get pretty close to that by installing only forged or extruded fittings or fittings machined from bar stock. Another point worth keeping in mind is that shackles have in general proved unreliable in standing rigging and do not belong there; if flexibility or a change in pin axis is required, a toggle should be employed.

An unsung part of the rigging is the topping lift. In some flat-out racers, topping lifts are considered expendable, being replaced in port with a halyard and at sea by prayer. In small boats this is perhaps all right, but in larger ones topping lifts can come in very handy. This is not a sailing treatise, but I bring up the matter of the topping lift because there is a tendency these days to regard its actually trifling windage as unacceptable and to leave it out in consequence. A sturdy topping lift means that one can dispense with a boom crutch, allowing the weight of the boom and furled sail to rest on the lift with a line off to the rail to hold the boom steady in collaboration with the mainsheet. If there is a permanent gallows for the boom, the lift is used to raise the boom prior to making sail and to hold the boom while the sail is dropped. If the halyard parts or its reel winch slips—infrequent but not unknown events—the lift will keep the boom from crashing down, perhaps on the helmsman's head if the vessel is on the wind at the time. And, not least, a proper topping lift that runs from the boom end through a masthead block and down the side of the mast (or out to the rail) provides an alternative means of going aloft. This is especially vital in a nonmasthead rig, where failure of the main halyard or its jamming aloft otherwise leaves only the flag halyard to ascend with. Even if one is bashing along under full sail, such a topping lift permits somebody to go aloft in safety. A length of strong shock cord leading down from the running part of the lift 10 ft or so above deck keeps the lift under control.

Synthetic fabrics have replaced cotton for sailcloth because of their superiority on every important count: the synthetics are stronger, have an indefinite life, are not attacked by mildew if stowed while wet, and have a smoother surface that enhances their effectiveness to windward. The elasticity of nylon particularly suits it for spinnakers, mizzen staysails, and spinnaker staysails; while for jibs, mains, and mizzens, Dacron (or Terylene in England) is excellent. The weight of cloth to be used in the various sails is usually specified by the designer, but often the sailmaker will have somewhat different ideas as to what is most suitable. It is quite essential to have exactly the right weight in the case of the mainsail and, if they exist, the mizzen and boomed forestaysail as well. These are the sails that must function under the widest range of conditions, and they cannot do so properly if they are too light or too heavy. Sol Lamport, who is one of the chief American suppliers of sailcloth, has a simple formula to arrive at the weight of Dacron fabric to be used for working sails: one-tenth of the sum of the over-all length of the boat and the length of the mainsail luff. This formula yields ounces per yard for the standard American width of 28½ in.; while approximate, it is still handy as a general guide. The mizzen in the case of a yawl or ketch should be a few ounces lighter than the main, but the working forestaysail in a boat with a double-head rig should be of about the same weight as the main, since it will be expected to function in strong winds.

Given any ambiguity in choice of mainsail material, I myself would always choose the lighter alternative for a cruising boat of any size. Sooner or later every sail must come down, and the less of a battle that is involved, the better. Further, the lighter sail will be better in light airs, which lessens somewhat one's dependence on fancy lingerie. No question of strength is involved here, since much lighter fabrics

(TEXT CONTINUED ON PAGE 170)

[X I]

Two Unusual Cruising Ketches:

BLUEBIRD OF THORNE &

GOUDEN DRAAK

THESE TWO MOST INTERESTING VESSELS have more in common than their ketch rigs, for both were designed for fast, comfortable cruising by extremely experienced owners who knew what they wanted. Both have had thousands of miles of blue water under them in the short time since their building, and their fortunate owners have had the pleasure of enjoying the success of their unconventional ideas.

What is fascinating is to see how unlike each other the boats are despite quite similar design objectives, with differences that arise from the different personalities and prejudices (or, perhaps better, lack of prejudices) of their owners and designers. Not all roads lead to the perfect cruising yacht, but here are two worthy ones, each with attractions all its own.

BLUEBIRD OF THORNE

THE CONSPICUOUS INNOVATION THAT *Bluebird* exhibits is a pair of bilge keels in place of an orthodox keel or centerboard. Twin keels themselves are no longer a novelty in small boats, of course, but in *Bluebird* they are used on a largish yacht, and, furthermore, the optimum shape for them has been studied with the help of a towing tank. Arthur Robb, *Bluebird*'s talented designer, has provided a number of arguments in favor of twin keels, but most of them depend very critically upon the precise shape and location of the keels. "The border line between poor and high performance is narrow," he says. The following is a summary of these arguments:

1. Higher sailing speeds than an orthodox cruising yacht of similar dimensions but without recourse to multihulls. Part of the reason for this is the relatively small wetted surface, which yields improved light-weather performance and means that proportionately less sail area is required.

2. Avoidance of a centerboard, yet windward efficiency equal to that of the orthodox yacht is achieved on a fixed draft approximately that of an orthodox centerboard yacht. Windward performance in rough water is superior.

3. Lateral-plane appendage efficiency increases with angle of heel, while this efficiency

decreases with angle of heel in an orthodox yacht.

4. Stability is equal to that of an orthodox yacht without recourse to extreme beam, and the righting moment and range of stability are at least equal to those of a well-designed centerboard yacht of relatively deep fixed draft.

5. The primary and secondary wave-flow pattern is reshaped to extend the points of buildup of the forward and after crests and thereby increases the maximum speed of the hull. The reshaping is contributed to by the flow redirected across the upper and lower surfaces of the weather fin, whose lift acts downward; the flow lines are forced to follow the weather fin. The downward lift produces a righting

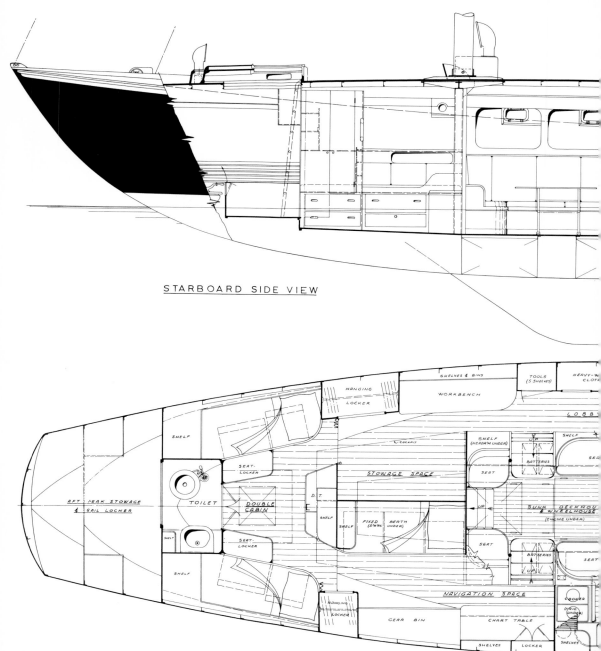

STARBOARD SIDE VIEW

moment that increases stability at the same time.

6. The deep plunging of an orthodox hull is avoided by the stabilizing action of the fins. The fins also provide a certain amount of lift at speed when the hull is upright.

7. The rudder area is smaller and the physical effort of steering is reduced because the lee rudder is nearly vertical, as well as being in the accelerated flow from the lee fin.

8. Directional stability is markedly enhanced by the fins, which is demonstrated both by tank tests and full-size yacht performance.

9. Under power, fuel consumption is reduced and the speed-horsepower ratio is higher than in an orthodox boat due to all-around greater hull

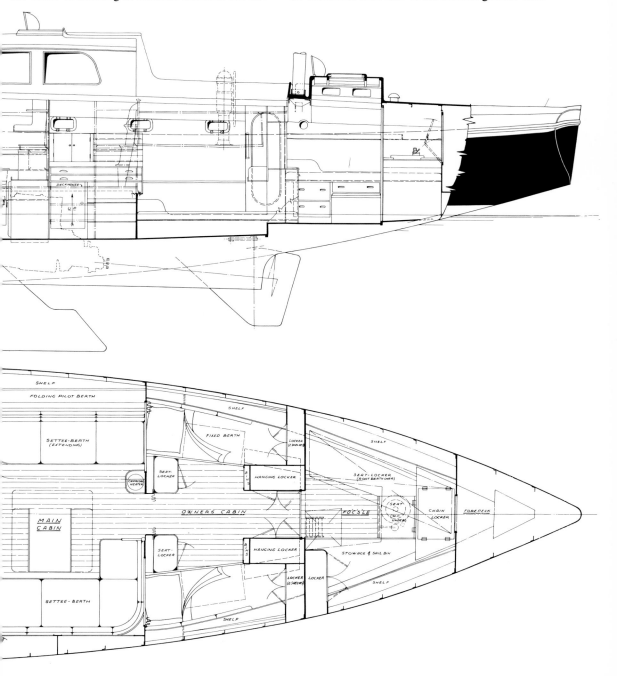

efficiency. The yacht can also be controlled in reverse, which is seldom true of orthodox yachts.

10. General advantages of twin keels include the ability to take the ground in a level position with total stability, so that the yacht can be shipped without the cost and nuisance of a cradle, and in tidal waters it can have its bottom cleaned and painted easily.

If twin keels are all that wonderful, why are there are so few large yachts with them? The answer, according to Robb, is that until now really careful thought and experimentation had not been carried out, but at this time he has

"absolute confidence in this advanced form of the type—so much that I will not be surprised if eventually it predominates where normal comfortable interiors are expected and higher-than-current speeds are desired without structural or heavy-weather performance worries."

Bluebird is a most interesting vessel even apart from her twin keels, as study of her plans will reveal. The topsides have been built up to give a raised deck throughout with a slightly convex sheer, but there is plenty of tumble home and a rubbing strake of conventional sheer as well to prevent an unduly lumpy appearance. The accommodation has been worked out with unusual care, and there are two double

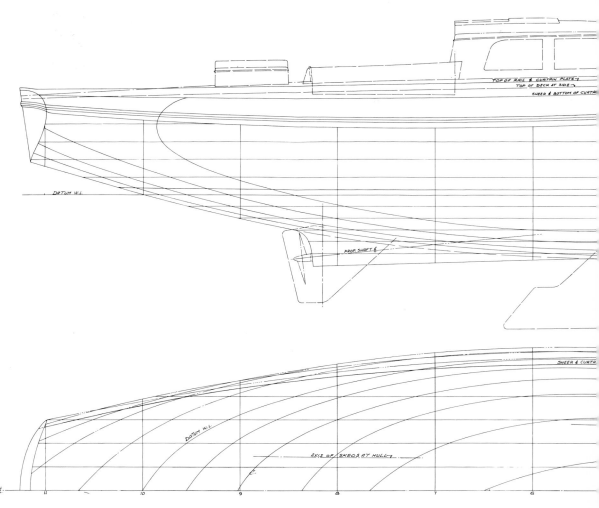

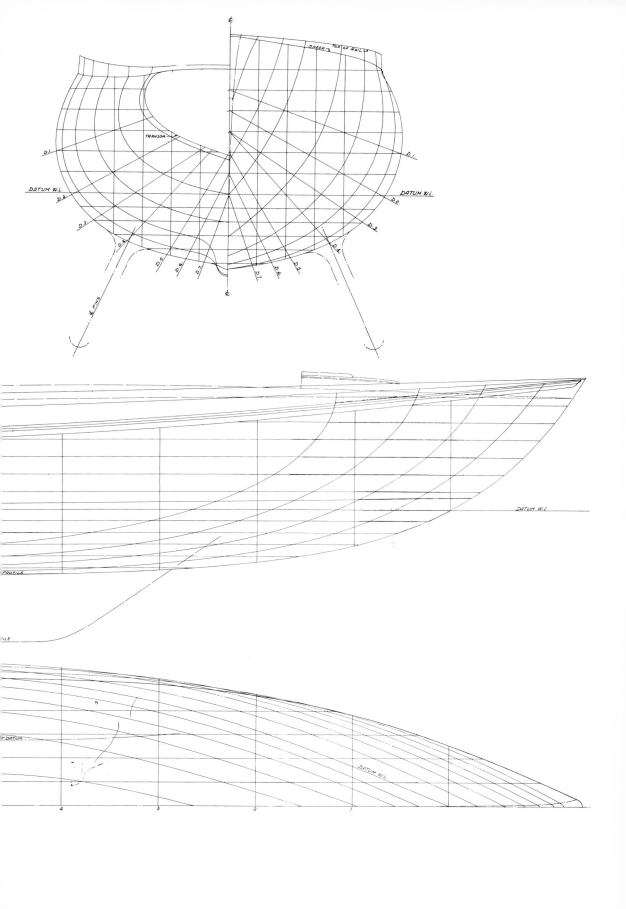

SHEER TOP OF RAIL

TRANSOM

D.1   D.1

DATUM W.L.   DATUM W.L.
D.2   D.2

D.3   D.3

D.4   D.4
        D.5   D.5   D.5
              D.7   D.6   D.6
                       D.7

& FINS

DATUM W.L.

PROFILE

FILE

F DATUM   DATUM W.L.

4   3   2   1

cabins, a forepeak with a Root berth, a main cabin that can sleep three (one on a folding upper berth and two on extension transoms), and a fixed berth near the chart table. The small deckhouse has a duplicate set of controls at its forward end to permit the vessel to be steered from inside. There is a head in the forepeak and one in the after cabin, but the forepeak is accessible only from the deck; most

owners would prefer an additional enclosed toilet room somewhere amidships. However, Bluebird's owner is entirely pleased with his ship after two transatlantic passages in her, and that is what counts.

The sail area of 950 ft² and an engine of 50 hp both seem small for so imposing a yacht, but her hull is easily driven and her displacement of 33,600 lb is modest. A pair of wishbone booms is used in place of a conventional boom for the mainsail, and single wishbones for the mizzen and forestaysail. The lower parts of these sails can take on a natural curve because of the wishbones, but not everyone agrees that the increased efficiency is worth the inconven- ience involved. Two light booms are permanently secured just below the lower spreaders for twin running staysails, and when not in use the booms are secured to the lower shrouds. All in all a carefully thought out rig, one that has proved itself in practice.

BLUEBIRD OF THORNE

DESIGNER *Arthur Robb, 20D New Cavendish Street, London W.1, England*

LOA   50 ft

LWL   40 ft

BEAM   12 ft 2 in.

DRAFT   5 ft 4 in.

DISPLACEMENT   33,600 lb

BALLAST   11,000 lb, half in each keel

SAIL AREA   950 ft²

ENGINE   Gardner 4 LK diesel (50 hp)

CONSTRUCTION   Steel hull, zinc-sprayed inside and out; deck beams of aluminum and deck of two layers of ⅜-in. plywood bonded together

GOUDEN DRAAK

IT IS MY PLEASURE to know the owner of *Gouden Draak,* a gentleman of commanding aspect (especially atop a Moulton bicycle with a daughter aft and his faithful beagle trotting alongside), and I can testify to the thought and care that went into his list of specifications. I had certain doubts as to whether this list could possibly refer to a yacht only 46 ft long overall, but all doubts vanished and were replaced by admiration when I watched *Gouden Draak* sail into Langelinie harbor in Copenhagen. What a lovely boat she is! And her novel but sensible accommodation is a complete success. Goaded by a no doubt difficult client, Philip Rhodes managed to surpass his usual excellent work to produce as fine a medium-sized cruising yacht as any afloat.

The designer describes *Gouden Draak* as follows: *"Gouden Draak* is an all electrically-welded steel vessel with a watertight steel bulkhead (with watertight door) dividing off the forecastle. Her ballast keel is of cast steel so that it can be welded integrally into the hull framing, producing an uncommonly strong ship. She is very ruggedly built and of rather substantial displacement. With her clipper bow she has a relatively fine entrance and smooth easy lines. It will be noted that she is of the raised-deck type where, by using high freeboard, the customary trunk cabin is eliminated. This not only provides a very strong and economical type of construction but also gives unusual deck space and especially generous room for the accommodations below, particularly welcome in respect to upper berths.

"There is a small house aft necessary to get headroom over the after cabin floor which is raised to clear the 2:1 reduction V-drive gear and the centerboard trunk, and also to obtain an unusually wide floor area. In fact the floor widths throughout are wider than usual. The headroom is 6'2" throughout. The trunk also gives protection to the crew in the slightly sunken cockpit. This cockpit is a generous one and of all steel construction. The seats have large watertight lids to extra big storage spaces in the wings. Cushions and teak gratings give this high, self-bailing, watertight cockpit the necessary amiability and comfort. Under one of the cockpit seats there is a watertight scuppered and vented steel box for the stove gas bottles—surely a safer place than on deck where the tubing is often unprotected.

"Other than the mast tabernacles that permit two persons to lower her masts there is nothing unusual about her simple ketch rig. It is modest in area, all inboard and with a masthead single jib fore triangle. The working jib is loose-footed on a boom, the pedestal for which is formed by a ventilator. All three sails are self-tending on travelers. The staying is simplicity itself and the masts have single spreaders.

"The dinghy is carried on the centerline between the mainmast and trunk. While not shown on the plans, there are the customary plastic covered lifelines all around the deck with tubular pulpits forward and aft. The decks are of Burma teak on steel beams.

"The Perkins diesel motor is installed much farther aft than usual, a feature made possible by the use of a V-drive reduction gear. This gets the engine out of the way without placing it too high. It increases the available space for accommodations and leaves the motor unusually accessible. She also has a controllable pitch propeller.

"Gouden Draak's workable galley occupies the port side of the deckhouse and is complete with stainless steel gas stove in gimbals, kerosene refrigerator, double stainless sink, large bins and dish racks. To starboard is a complete layout for the navigator: large chart table with drawer, lockers over and under, and a swing-out seat. A pipe berth is arranged outboard together with miscellaneous stowage areas. Two steps below is the main cabin with a generous corner seat to port and a settee to starboard, both flanked by deep lockers outboard. The toilet is snug but ample with watercloset, folding lavatory, grating, and lockers. There is a large drop-leaf table and a fireplace is worked into the bulkhead which warms the whole boat.

"Forward there is an unusual feature but one that is entirely successful. A longitudinal centerline bulkhead divides the dormitory area into two double cabins with individual fixed berths, thanks again to the raised deck. The port stateroom has a folding lavatory, and both have ample wardrobes forward. The fo'c'sle has a pipe berth, watercloset, and hanging space.

"The 100 gallon fuel tank and the 160 gallon water tank are welded integrally into the hull, and a sump tank is provided for the shower."

The Rhodes-designed ketch GOUDEN DRAAK *under way. Her clipper bow enables a plow anchor to stow with its shank on a roller where it is out of the way yet instantly available when needed.* GOUDEN DRAAK *carries a working jib on a boom and a roller-furling genoa; various sail combinations are thus available with an absolute minimum of labor.* (Beiser)

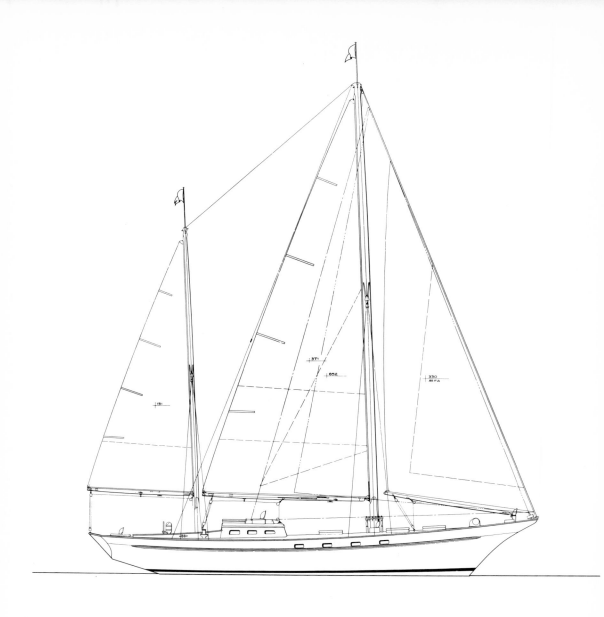

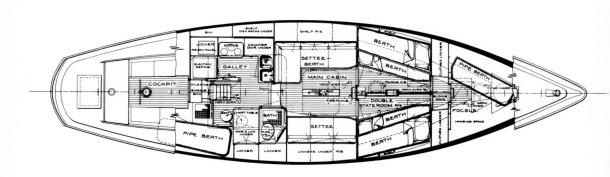

Gouden Draak

DESIGNER *Philip L. Rhodes, 369 Lexington Avenue, New York City*

LOA   46 ft
LWL   32 ft
BEAM   12 ft 10 in.
DRAFT   5 ft centerboard up, 8 ft 1 in. center-
board down
SAIL AREA   852 ft²

ENGINE   Perkins 4-107 (47 hp); variable-pitch
propeller
FUEL   100 gal
WATER   160 gal
CONSTRUCTION   Welded steel with teak decks
and deckhouse; spruce spars

(TEXT CONTINUED FROM PAGE 158)

than anybody would consider for a particular main would still be able to stay together in almost any blow, but instead it is a question of ability to keep the desired shape going to windward in heavy weather. To some extent, the character of the boat is involved here: a tender sloop will need reefing sooner than a stiff ketch and, accordingly, can manage with a lighter main in proportion. Similarly, a roller-reefing main is more likely to be reduced in area when it should be than an orthodox sail, and one can justify the choice of a lighter material on that ground. It is worth remembering that it is you who will be out on deck at 2 A.M. in the pouring rain on a lumpy sea in an icy gale from the northeast dousing the main when everyone else is at the lee rail; and a day or two later, when the wind falls and the sun comes out, it is also you who will be cursing the heavens if the sails are too stiff and heavy for you to take advantage of the cat's-paws about.

An important element in the performance of Dacron sailcloth is the finishing it receives after it is woven. This mystic process, which involves passing the fabric between heated rollers after impregnation with resin, helps to set the fibers and to lock them together, thereby contributing to the imperviousness and surface smoothness of the final product. It also tends to make Dacron sailcloth stiff, slippery, and difficult to handle. I have had a perfectly magnificent mainsail of hard Dacron that set well and did not lose its shape when the wind piped up, but getting it down and furling it was hard work for three men; my new main, of softer cloth, can be stowed by one man, though two make a neater job of it. I was warned that the latter sail would get baggy to windward in a breeze, a serious defect that has not, in fact, materialized. Hence there is a middle ground, and I hope that sailmakers prod the cloth manufacturers to achieve it regularly by applying the same diligence they used in securing the wonderfully efficient cloth now in use. Here again is the old story: winning races brings fame and fortune, while making cruising more pleasant yields no such tangible rewards. It would help if accounts of happy and successful cruises gave credit to the sailmakers who helped make them so, as accounts of racing triumphs usually give sailmakers their just due.

In England it is now possible to obtain Terylene in two finishes, "hard" and "soft," so that some degree of choice is available. This makes it easier to juggle cloth weight and type of finish to obtain good sails that can be coped with easily.

I trust I will not be regarded as a feeble old lady for emphasizing the need for sails that are pleasant to handle. Certainly, Rod Stephens is as stalwart a sailor as anybody, yet he has told me of his horror in discovering that a new jib in hard Dacron could not simply be stuffed into its bag but had to be flaked down on deck and then carefully folded each time it was taken down.

The best cloth weight for a jib depends upon the nature of the boat as well as upon the size of the sail and the wind strength it is planned for. In an under-rigged vessel, it may well be desirable to have three full-size genoas—a real light-weight for drifting, a more substantial one for winds up to perhaps Force 3 or a little over, and a heavy fellow for Force 4 to 5. A boat with a more ample rig need carry only a single light genoa of maximum size, shifting to a smaller, more easily handled one or to double headsails at a wind strength in the neighborhood of Force 3. A masthead sloop needs a fancier array of headsails than a ketch, since the fore-triangle of the former contains a greater proportion of the total sail area. Obviously no general rule can be given, and it is a good idea to talk over the matter with the sailmaker in order to be sure that the purpose of each sail and the style of sailing that is contemplated are clear to him. In all innocence, I once wrote to six leading sailmakers for quotations on a new genoa, enclosing only a copy of the sail plan of the boat, and their recommendations ranged from 5- to 8-oz Dacron—my fault for not having gone into enough detail.

There is no sail that can give as much sheer joy or as much total misery as a spinnaker. In flat water with a steady fair breeze on the quarter and a great cloud of filmy nylon flying ahead, one's pulse beats quicker and each moment is filled with the sense of life being lived to the full. But in a fluky wind or a seaway, excitement can turn to horror as the huge bag loses its veneer of civilization and is metamorphosed into a raging beast with a mind of its own. It is all very well to read a treatise on the care and feeding of spinnakers in an armchair on a winter evening before the fire and to learn how the right move at the right time can tame the most unruly spin, but just what does one do when the damned thing is wrapped tightly around the headstay or when one is knocked down, with the spreaders in the water and no control? Of course, such events should not happen in the best families, but they do just often enough to make one think twice before setting a spinnaker on a shorthanded cruise in a large boat. In a smaller vessel—say, 40 ft or less overall— the spinnaker need not be treated with quite as much respect as in a larger one, and it *is* a lot of fun on occasion. But in a larger boat, where the spinnaker is vast and its gear complicated and expensive, I suspect that the money involved can be spent more wisely elsewhere.

Storm sails are seldom given the thought they require. The essential thing is that such sails be capable of taking the yacht to windward in a genuine gale without being any larger than necessary for this purpose. The windage of spars and rigging is an important factor when the wind blows, and a ketch with two headstays, running as well as standing backstays, and two pairs of spreaders on the mainmast needs more area in its storm sails than an otherwise equivalent masthead sloop with single spreaders. It is unnecessary and, in fact, undesirable for storm sails to be of heavier cloth than the mainsail in most boats, and they may well be an ounce or two lighter in large ones. When there is a forestay as well as a jibstay, a storm forestaysail might be a better bet than a storm jib in those boats that tend to develop a lee helm when under short sail. The same sail can often be set on either stay as circumstances dictate, though their sheet leads will be different; or, of course, one can have separate sails for each stay.

Storm trysails are very rarely used, but when they are needed they are needed badly. There are several schools of thought on trysails, as on practically everything else. One holds, quite rightly, that severe conditions make sail handling difficult and dangerous, so it is only sensible to facilitate using the trysail by fitting it with slides that run on the mainsail track and installing an auxiliary length of track at the foot of the mast with a switch to couple it to the main track when desired. Another school feels, also quite rightly, that it is unwise to rely so completely on the mainsail track, which may be pulled out by too great a strain or may already have been damaged in some way so as not to permit a sail to be hoisted on it, and that a more appropriate scheme is to use lanyards around the mast to secure the trysail. The latter method means that the trysail cannot extend above the lower spreaders, which in some rigs may mean too small a sail to be of any use. Related to this question, then, is the question of how large the trysail should be. If reefing is simple and the

Conceived for extensive cruising, BEYOND *was built of aluminum to designs by Laurent Giles. Her dimensions are LOA 43 ft, LWL 32 ft, beam 10 ft 8 in., draft 7 ft, and sail area about 700 ft².* (Beken)

reefed mainsail sets well, I think one can regard the trysail as strictly an emergency proposition and have it both small and independent of the mainsail track. If the mainsail is not easy to reef and the result is poor, the trysail can be taken more intimately into the family and arranged for frequent use. I suspect that in the latter case a more suitable plan would be to improve the reefing arrangements, if this is possible; in a cruising boat it should not be necessary to use a trysail except in most unusual circumstances.

The great strength of Dacron has led a number of sailmakers to use several layers of Dacron tape on sail luffs in place of rope or wire. The characteristics of the tape and the sail itself are matched in this way, and, on the whole, such sails have worked out well for cruising. I have seen mainsails and mizzens with taped luffs that were still going strong after eight years of use. However, there seem to be stronger arguments in favor of wire luffs for headsails than for rope luffs for mains and mizzens. For one thing, jibs must be set up harder than other sails to be effective, and wire can take excess strain better than Dacron. The best thing is to choose a sailmaker with care and let him do what he feels is best; a good taped sail is better than a poor roped one, and vice versa.

One of the unavoidable consequences of a hard, closely woven sailcloth is that the stitching stands clear of the material instead of sinking into it as in the case of cotton. Not too much chafe is needed to weaken such a seam to the danger point. I have never heard of the fabric of a Dacron sail of the correct weight coming apart, but seams that let go are common enough. The problem of chafe is not too severe in a modern rig, but a gaff mainsail that must contend with topping lifts, lazy jacks, and running backstays can be troublesome. In the latter case a row of hand-sewn stitching to supplement the machine stitching is a good idea, but this is expensive and often spoils the smoothness of the sail—better to sell the boat. The chief menaces to a jib-headed main are the topping lift and the shrouds. The intelligent use of shock cord can completely eliminate chafe due to the former, and the conscientious use of a boom vang when running can minimize chafe due to the latter. Of course, no matter how much care is taken during the season, it is still worthwhile going over every seam periodically and having any weaknesses made good.

In ordering sails, it is usually wise to check the figures on the sail plan against the rig itself. A difference of a few inches here or there is not uncommon, and in the wrong place it can lead to a lot of trouble. An exception is perhaps a stock boat with aluminum spars; but in the case of an existing vessel, a few minutes' work with a long metal tape measure is worth the effort. Or, better, have the sailmaker himself take off the dimensions, so that any illness of fit is clearly his fault.

Dacron cordage is strong, long-lived, and does not shrink or stiffen when wet; it is far superior to Manila, linen, and cotton for running rigging. Nearly as big a further improvement is braided Dacron line, which is stronger, stretches less under load, grips better on a winch drum, and is softer and more flexible than three-strand twisted Dacron line of the same diameter. The last of these attributes makes braid the first choice for applications in which a line must pass through several blocks— for instance, in the case of mainsheets and mizzen sheets. Because most braid is perhaps a bit less tolerant of abrasion than twisted line, it is more of a toss-up between the two for jib sheets. In a large boat the braid still wins, because it is far easier to handle ⅝-in. braid than ¾-in. twisted line, both of which have about the same strength and elasticity. The sole unfortunate aspect of most braided line is that it cannot be spliced, but this is fair enough in exchange for the advantages that are obtained. Samson Cordage Works of Boston does manufacture a type of line consisting of one braid inside another that can be spliced in an elegant manner; I have used it for several years and find it entirely satisfactory.

I have found it advisable to inspect cordage before purchase in order to be sure that it is sufficiently flexible. There seems to be a considerable variation in this important quality, perhaps due to the precise manner in which the primary fibers are made into line, and as a result, to give a specific example, some ½-in. Dacron line can be bent easily in a circle 1 in. in diameter, while similar line of another manufacture can barely be bent in a circle 6 in. in diameter. I have an anchor rode of 1-in. nylon that after four years of use is still supple enough to be cleated and coiled down without much trouble, while a spare rode of the same size but from a different source is so stiff that a fathom of it can be held out horizontally from one end with almost no droop—fine for the Indian rope trick, but virtually useless for anything else. Even good synthetic line tends to lose its pliability in time owing to chemical changes accelerated by sunlight, but this is a different problem and becomes serious only after several years. Sometimes a synthetic line that is beginning to harden can be rejuvenated by soaking it in a concentrated solution of one of the silicone preparations used to soften clothing after laundering by cutting down the friction between adjacent fibers.

A winch makes it possible to apply far greater tension on a line than merely tugging on it can produce, and proper winches permit one man to manage any sheet or halyard on a quite substantial yacht. A medium-sized yawl or ketch equipped for cruising may have a dozen or more winches of several different types and mechanical advantages: reel halyard winches for main and mizzen; direct-action winches for jib, forestaysail, spinnaker, and mizzen-staysail halyards and for the mizzen sheet; geared winches for the mainsheet and jib and forestaysail sheets; and one or two winches each on the main and mizzen booms to make sheeting the jib (or spinnaker) and mizzen staysail to the ends of these booms easier when reaching. My 58-ft ketch has a total of seventeen winches for sheets and halyards, not one of them unnecessary, and if I were to race seriously I would add three or four more. Winches are costly, but it is false economy to install inadequate ones. There are other places to save money on a yacht. I would cheerfully forgo a pressure-water system in order to install a pair of two-speed roller-bearing sheet winches in place of ordinary single-speed ones.

Because winches that are adequate in size and number make it possible for a small crew to sail a boat efficiently without killing themselves in the process, it is important to be sure that they are part of the design and are properly installed. I have never seen a boat yet that came from its builders with enough winches of proper size and type unless the owner himself had stepped in and insisted upon them beforehand. Many stock boats with mainsail areas of 250 to 300 ft^2 are provided with neither main halyard winches nor mainsheet winches, for instance, while some designers are still specifying direct-action winches with a mechanical advantage of 8:1 for use with genoas 500 ft^2 in area. This is ridiculous. Any boat large enough for proper cruising should have winches of sufficient power for every halyard and sheet (except perhaps for such sails as mizzen staysails and spinnaker staysail on smallish vessels), even though some of them may be used only as snubbing winches most of the time. The criterion for a mainsheet winch, for example, should be that one's lady companion be able to trim the mainsail in a moderate wind by herself—that a gorilla could do the job unaided with his little finger is immaterial unless he is one's regular crew. In the absence of enough personal experience to judge for oneself, a good plan is to ask somebody who owns a boat of the same size and type as one is considering what he has replaced his original winches with—or would have if he had had the money. As a rough guide

(TEXT CONTINUED ON PAGE 191)

[X I I]

Three Light Cruiser-Racers:
GLASS SLIPPER, OUTLAW,
& WANDERER

Two of the most distinctive recent additions to the British offshore racing fleet have been *Glass Slipper* and *Outlaw,* both persuasive examples of modern light-displacement design. Even cruising men who do not find these boats wholly satisfactory must admire the originality and meticulous planning that has gone into them, and not much need be changed to turn them into magnificent cruisers. *Wanderer* is a "cruising-racing" boat according to her designer, so that racing considerations were not primary in her conception, and she is, in fact, a fine light-displacement cruising yacht as she is.

GLASS SLIPPER

In *Glass Slipper*, E. G. van de Stadt again demonstrates his mastery of fiberglass design. The plans show a fixed keel with a draft of 6 ft 2 in., but an alternative profile with a draft of 4 ft 11 in. and a centerboard can also be built from the same mold. Since only the hull is in fiberglass, the rig, superstructure, and interior are all optional. In fact, even the manner in which the hull itself is built is not invariant: the first boat from the mold had a sandwich construction with fiberglass on both sides of a 1-in.-thick polyurethene foam core, while the second had a single skin with hollow longitudinal stiffeners running the length of the hull. Thus in *Glass Slipper* the advantages of a fiberglass hull are combined with a remarkable degree of freedom in planning the rest of the yacht.

Glass Slipper is on the light side, though not to an extreme extent, and while the sail plan may seem small for the size of the boat, it is actually adequate. In a smaller boat with the same displacement this rig might be a handful to cope with, but what really counts is the size of the sails relative to the size of the boat, and so *Glass Slipper* should not be too bad in this respect. The aluminum mast is stepped on deck and its thrust is carried to the keel by a steel pillar, which gives another few inches of room in the head, where they are most appreciated.

The layout of the accommodation would be difficult to improve upon. The forward cabin is roomy and has a washbasin and large locker of its own; a small head could readily be fitted in under a removable insert at the intersection of the berths to make a separate unit of this part of the boat. The main head is also adequate in size, and the shower indicated is not the joke it is in smaller vessels. In some climates the thwartship extension of the port settee would be better replaced by a heating stove, which will be able to furnish its cheer from there without being in the way.

The deckhouse represents a brilliant use of the space available. Off by itself to starboard is a fore-and-aft chart table with a permanent seat and a handy locker for instruments and books, an installation that would do credit to a much larger boat. Under the chart table itself is a refrigerator that opens inboard. The galley itself is a snug nook in the best part of the ship yet out of the line of traffic. The ventilator pipe

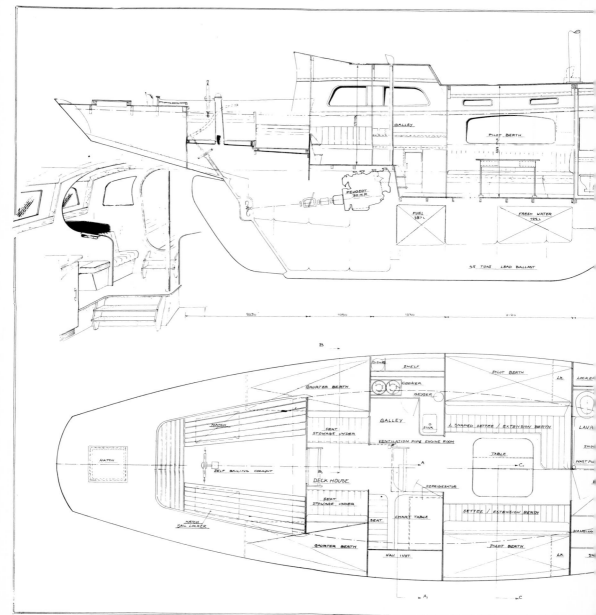

from the engine room is in just the right place to provide security for the cook as well as a handhold for someone negotiating the steps to the raised part of the deckhouse sole. A two-burner stove seems inadequate for a vessel so grand as this, and no doubt a larger one could be made to fit. Adjacent to the companionway is a pair of seats with quarter berths outboard of them. This is a splendid arrangement, since it provides a transition region near the cockpit that can be used for part of the watch on deck to have hot drinks out of the weather, to don and shed oilies, and so on, all without interfering with the use of the quarter berths.

The engine is housed under the deckhouse sole; while a 30-hp Peugeot engine is shown, other boats to this design have had more powerful diesels that provide better performance. The integral tanks shown have capacities of 112 gal of water and 76 gal of fuel, and there is room for additional tankage in the bilge if desired—a big advantage of fiberglass construction.

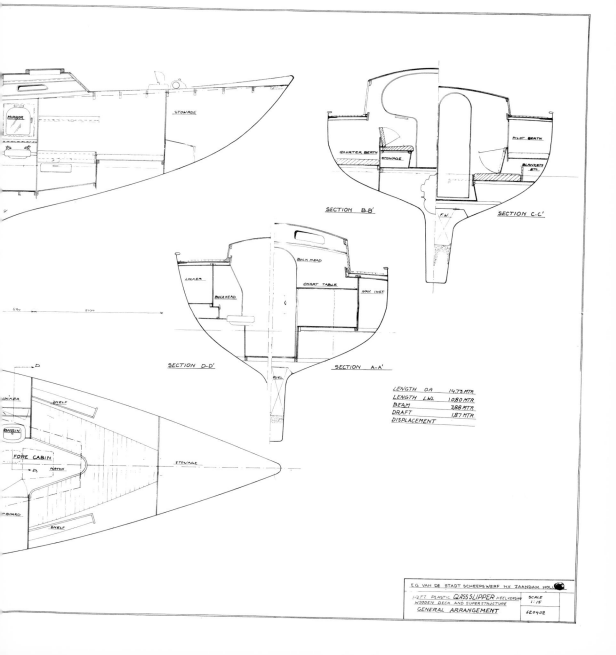

GLASS SLIPPER, *designed by E. G. van de Stadt, is an example of semicustom fiberglass construction in a large boat. Only the hull is invariant, and everything else is at the option of the owner.* (Beken)

The companionway itself is characteristic of E. G. van de Stadt boats, with an oval door in an after bulkhead under a conical bulge in the deckhouse top. One hopes a sea breaking into the cockpit does not enter the cabin and get at the engine; really big clogproof scuppers are a necessity here. The cockpit is on two levels, the after part raised for good visibility from the helm and the forward part lower for more crew comfort and protection.

Because *Glass Slipper* is so outstanding a design, it may seem churlish to criticize two small details; nevertheless, they are not insignificant. First is the absence of an oilskin locker near the companionway so that wet oilies and seaboots need not be carried the length of the main cabin. Second and more important is the matter of access to the engine: how easy will it be in a seaway to clean the fuel filter, to check the ignition, to free a fouled carburetor jet, to fix a jammed clutch linkage? It is unfair to judge from drawings only, but adequate engine access is too important a factor to have any doubt about.

GLASS SLIPPER

DESIGNER *E. G. van de Stadt, Zuiddijk 412, Zaandam, Holland*

LOA 48 ft 9 in.

LWL 35 ft 5 in.

BEAM 12 ft 9 in.

DRAFT 6 ft 2 in. fixed keel, 4 ft 11 in. centerboard up

DISPLACEMENT 29,000 lb

BALLAST 10,000 lb of lead

SAIL AREA 942 ft²

ENGINE Peugeot (30 hp), BMC Commodore diesel (52 hp), or Perkins 4-107 diesel (47 hp)

FUEL 76 gal

WATER 112 gal

CONSTRUCTION Molded fiberglass hull

OUTLAW

Outlaw IS A BRILLIANTLY CONCEIVED light-displacement cutter designed by Illingworth & Primrose for flat-out ocean racing. In her first year she was the Class I RORC champion, which does not mean that she would necessarily make an equally fine cruiser but nevertheless does indicate that her plans and construction are both basically sound. The latter point is not without significance in view of her radical shape and laminated-wood hull and deck, which were made by gluing together eight layers of 3-mm plywood over a mold—probably the lightest way to build a boat of this size consistent with adequate strength and rigidity. Illingworth & Primrose did not alter *Outlaw* by very much in developing a racing-cruising version of her: "We have slightly lengthened the keel to make her even easier to steer, that is to say, steadier on the helm, though even when racing she is not in any way wild. We have also given a more conventional sheer, which, although it will give a little bit more windage, will give appreciated headroom and stowage room in the ends of the boat. The accommodation has been slightly revised so as to give a better W.C. and so on."

The sail plan shows a masthead yawl rig with the three headstays favored by the designers. The boat is so light—32,500 lb on a waterline length of nearly 39 ft—that 992 ft² of sail area is entirely adequate, especially in so efficient an arrangement. The original *Outlaw* was remarkable to windward but not exceptional off the wind; the new version has a potent mizzen staysail three-quarters the size of the main that will perk up her reaching abilities.

The clear flush deck with a low deckhouse is most handsome and a big help in sail handling. The cockpit is divided into three parts to balance the three headstays at the other end of the boat, with the helmsman sitting grandly at the forward end, where the distasteful exertions of the winchmen cannot distract him. Sail and cordage lockers are under the cockpit seats where they belong, and a lazaret offers additional space. These provisions for stowage on deck are valuable here, since there is little room

below for other than domestic and personal gear. The life rafts are secured inside the coamings forward of the cockpit on either side, where they are out of the way yet instantly accessible. There are twin main companionways, an unusual touch that assists traffic flow and is most welcome when the boat is heeled.

The ingenuity of the designers is evident in the accommodation as well as on deck. Thus the chart table is in the after cabin, where the navigator can do his work without interference, and he can communicate directly with the helmsman through two opening portlights in the after bulkhead. A large head compartment to starboard can be entered either from the after cabin or from the main cabin. One hopes that the doors shown just in front of the toilet are sturdy, since all the strain when one is thrown against double doors of this kind comes on the central bolt unless coupled upper and lower bolts are installed. The galley to port is

OUTLAW *under construction.* (Beken)

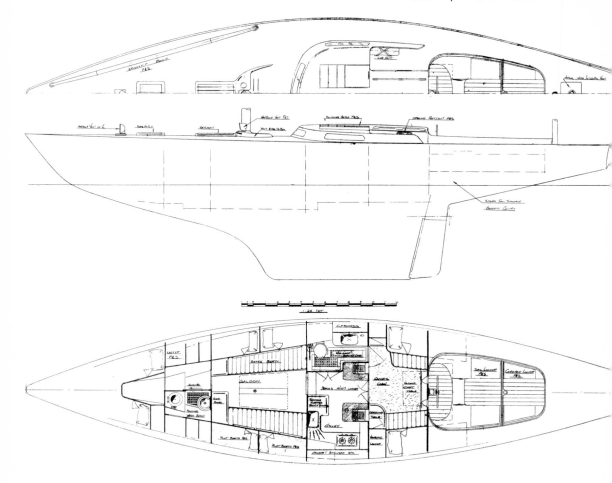

OUTLAW *is a light-displacement cutter designed by Illingworth & Primrose. Among her interesting details are the two companionways, the large steering wheel at the forward end of the cockpit, the concave mainsheet traveler, which reduces the likelihood of the slider's sticking, the winches canted at the best angles for their various functions, and the sheet-blocks secured to the twin backstays for jib topsails whose sheets cannot be trimmed properly to the deck.* (Beken)

OUTLAW *racing off The Needles. Ten men are on deck, but with only minor modifications she could be made into a shorthanded cruiser of exceptional speed and personality.* (Beken)

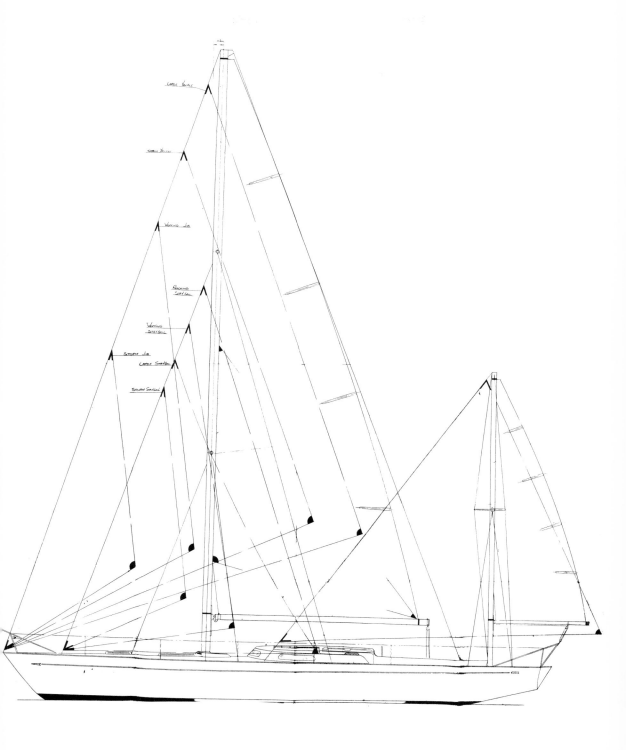

well arranged, and a refrigerator is built under the counter next to the sink. The main cabin has two pilot berths on each side with settees inboard, a practical plan for offshore racing. Forward are another head and a small cabin in the eyes of the ship. It is unlikely that the latter will ever be occupied at sea by anything other than sails, but in port it provides a welcome bit of privacy. In all, there are six berths available without using any seating space, a notable achievement in a boat of this size. The major drawback is a lack of stowage space, which is acceptable for racing but not for cruising. With only one pilot berth on each side of the main cabin, that cabin could be made shorter to bring the forward cabin farther aft and to permit a good deal of additional locker and drawer space throughout.

OUTLAW

DESIGNER *Illingworth & Primrose, 36 North Street, Emsworth, England*

LOA 48 ft 9 in.

LWL 38 ft 9 in.

BEAM 13 ft

DRAFT 8 ft 2½ in.

DISPLACEMENT 32,500 lb

SAIL AREA 992 ft²

ENGINE Perkins 4-107 (47 hp)

CONSTRUCTION Laminated-plywood hull; aluminum spars

WANDERER

CY HAMLIN HAS THE GOOD FORTUNE to live on Mount Desert Island, the heart of the paradise that is the coast of Maine. The special delights of Maine cruising—wooded islands everywhere, snug and lonely anchorages, clean air and water, bright blue skies alternating with dense fog— are not found to such a degree of perfection anywhere else that I know of in the world. The only serious competition is the archipelago that stretches from Stockholm through the Åland Islands and along the southern coast of Finland to the Russian border, an archipelago in which I have spent many happy weeks searching for the equal of Penobscot and Blue Hill Bays, of Somes Sound and Isle au Haut. The search was in vain, if only because *kräftor* can never replace the Maine lobster. I now look at the Northeast Harbor Fleet burgee at *Minots Light*'s masthead with nostalgia, and I look forward to my return to Maine, lily-livered rubber-suited water skiers and all, where not a few of the yachts sailing up Western Way at dusk will bear the clear signs of Cy Hamlin's creative mind.

Wanderer is a Hamlin-designed 48-ft yawl whose relatively conventional appearance conceals a number of most unconventional features. To begin with, her displacement is a mere 23,000 lb, which is phenomenally light for a boat of her size, and is made possible by glued-strip construction that combines strength with minimum weight. With her centerboard up, *Wanderer* draws a mere 4 ft 3 in., again phenomenally little, but her performance under sail is assured despite this by a careful program of tank testing. The ingenious cockpit, more

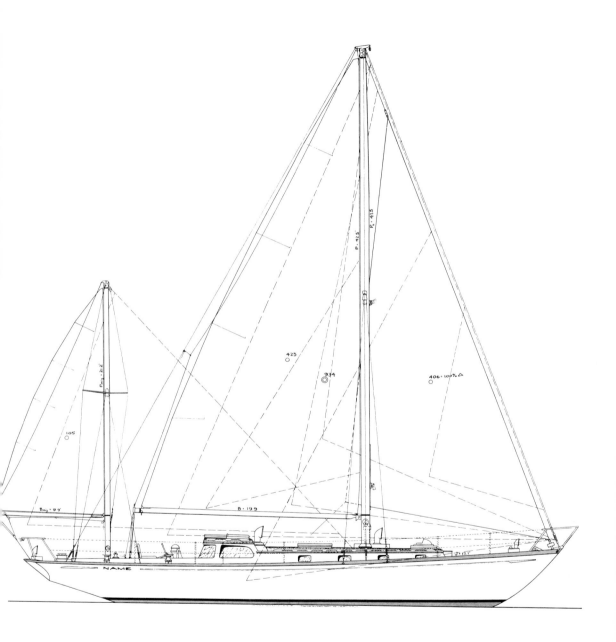

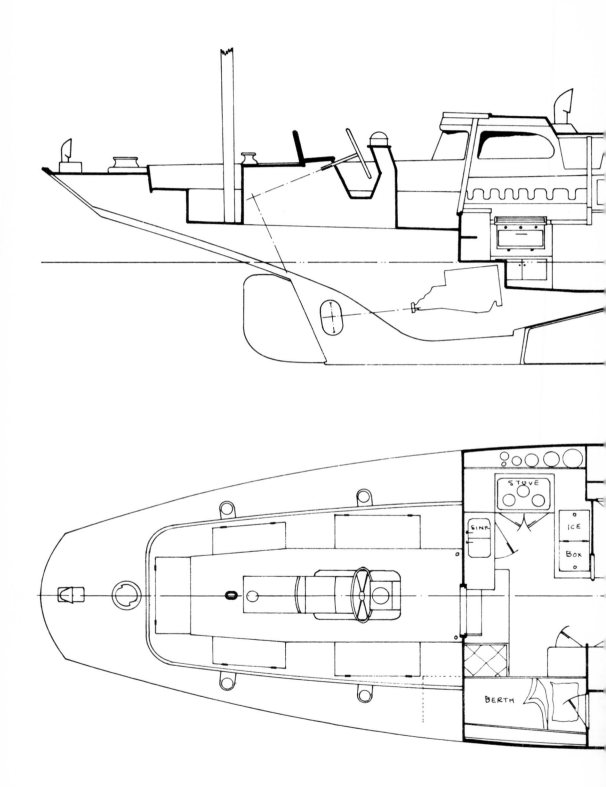

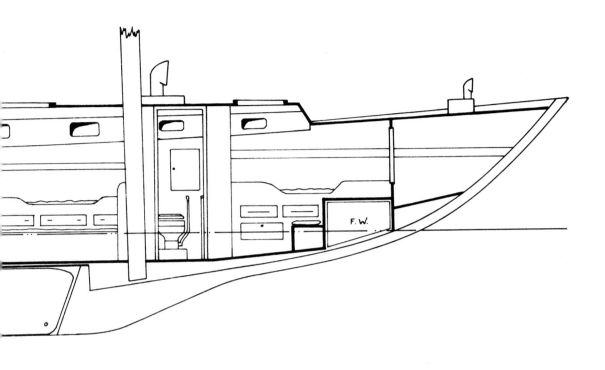

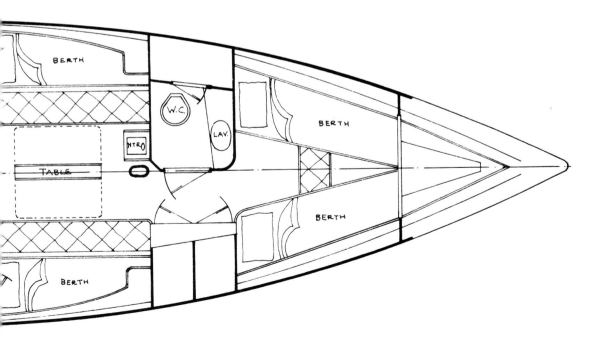

than 12 ft long, makes it possible for the helmsman to give a hand in sail trimming, and his location at the forward end of the cockpit on a central seat means that he is protected by the after end of the deckhouse, with still more protection if a spray hood is fitted. It should be easier to sail *Wanderer* single-handed than most other vessels of her size and speed. The mainsail is a modest 423 ft² in area, and the 108 ft² mizzen is sufficiently large to give *Wanderer* some of the desirable features of a ketch when sail reduction is called for. A 63-hp Gray engine is specified, which will provide plenty of power. Plenty of power, in fact, is the keynote

of the entire design—with her powerful rig, powerful winches, and powerful engine, *Wanderer* should always move along smartly.

The accommodation is straightforward, with no attempt made to squeeze in the maximum number of berths. There are no real quarter berths (the starboard after berth barely extends into the cockpit area), which permits immense cockpit lockers that hold all the sails and deck gear. The berths are a generous 6 ft 8 in. long, and the headroom throughout is 6 ft 4 in. The only improvement one might wish for is another head, and it should be easy enough to fit this into the forward cabin.

WANDERER

DESIGNER *Cyrus Hamlin, Manset, Maine*

LOA   48 ft 3 in.

LWL   34 ft 2 in.

BEAM   12 ft 8 in.

DRAFT   4 ft 3 in. centerboard up

DISPLACEMENT   23,000 lb

BALLAST   6,100 lb of lead

SAIL AREA   934 ft²

ENGINE   Gray 4-162 (63 hp)

FUEL   56 gal

WATER   100 gal

CONSTRUCTION   Planking of 1¼-in. square cedar strips glued and edge-nailed together, with an outer skin of 5/16-in. mahogany; center-line structure of laminated oak; fiberglass-covered plywood decks; mahogany cabin trunk with fiberglassed plywood top; aluminum mainmast, other spars spruce

(TEXT CONTINUED FROM PAGE 174)

to the mechanical advantage required in the case of jib-sheet winches, divide the area of the foretriangle in square feet by 20 and add 5; in the case of mainsheet winches, divide the area of the mainsail in square feet by 30 and add nothing. The figures that come out of these rules of thumb may seem high, but they are based on the assumption of strong winds and weak people, not weak winds and strong people.

A disadvantage of high-power winches is their relative slowness. Speed and power are inversely related: twice as many turns of the handle of a 20:1 winch are needed to crank in a certain length of sheet as is the case with a 10:1 winch. This is seldom a serious matter, since normally a winch is used only to harden in the last few feet of a sheet or a halyard, and a few more turns here or there are unimportant. When mechanical advantages exceed perhaps 30:1, though, a two-speed winch becomes nice to have. In the best of them, the gear ratio is controlled by the direction of motion—say, clockwise for high speed and low power and counterclockwise for low speed and high power. In others, which are less convenient to use, the handle must be shifted to a different socket in the winch head to change the gear ratio. One pulls in the sheet by hand until this begins to resemble work, then cranks away at low power until a similar point is reached, and finally switches to high power for the last foot or two—simple, efficient, and painless. When the foretriangle is modest, single-speed sheet winches are entirely adequate, but when it gets to be 400 ft^2 or so in area, with correspondingly larger genoas, the two-speed winches are a big help. Barient makes what is probably the most splendid line of two-speed winches, with prices to suit, but other manufacturers, such as Gibb and Lewmar in England and Molich in Denmark, do a respectable job also. It is quite essential that the winch drum be capable of freewheeling to permit it to be used as a snubbing winch when one is getting in the bulk of a sheet by hand. Less important but nice if it can be provided is a way to ratchet the winch in its high-power position to make it easier to sweat up that last inch.

Something that is relatively seldom seen yet is perfectly satisfactory if carefully laid out is a single large center-line winch, either at the front or back of the cockpit, as a supplement to a pair of more modest winches beside the cockpit. With a double-head rig or when a spinnaker will be used, two sheet winches should be available on either tack; with a center-line winch, one might be able to have one of these winches more powerful than the other or with a two-speed drive without having to buy and install a matched team. This is an especially worthwhile proposition when one already has a pair of inadequate winches and needs more power on occasion. Whether the forward or after position for a center-line winch is best depends upon the boat: the forward position is more convenient unless the sheets have to go across the cockpit in order to reach the winch. A big winch on the stern is also handy when docking or whenever a stern anchor is used, and if the helmsman is at a wheel he often can tail the sheet more readily if the winch is astern rather than ahead of him.

A two-speed pedestal winch (or "coffee grinder") has a number of advantages in a large boat. It is much easier for one or two men to exert their full strength on a pair of waist-high handles that turn about a horizontal axis than to apply a similar force to a low handle on a vertical axis, which means that a pedestal winch permits both great speed in high gear to wind the bulk of the sheet in and great power in low gear afterward. Another virtue of a coffee grinder is the cleat mounted on the top of its large drum, so that one man can trim a sheet instantly without needing a tailer to free the line and provide tension on it. But the most wonderful thing of all about a coffee grinder is the feeling of utter power and glory one gets by merely sitting on its pedestal top, preferably looking astern at the rest of the fleet—though even in port this position is a powerful ego booster. For this reason, I suspect that the new 12-meter pedestal winches, magnificent though they undoubtedly are, nevertheless will find fewer takers than they might if they were better adapted for sitting on.

Reel winches wind a wire halyard on a drum much like a fishing reel and, since the halyard is automatically stowed, are very convenient. They are too slow to be good for jibs but are ideal for mainsail and mizzens. When a main or mizzen is reefed, using such a winch means that all the strain is taken by wire, with no wire-to-rope splice involved. And there is little danger of a badly coiled halyard fall fouling something when the sail is lowered. The best of these winches use a brake band so installed as to permit the drum to turn only one way when hoisting, while furnishing just enough tension when released to prevent backlashing. In the Merriman and South Coast reel winches, a lever operates the brake, and the winch must be disassembled in order to adjust it. Normally these winches are satisfactory, but every so often one of them slips, and it is not always convenient to drop the sail and take the winch apart. (I have found that a liberal dousing of a slipping brake band with lighter fluid or some other good solvent is at times of help as an emergency measure.) And dirt and salt can gum up the brake, adding friction to the job of hoisting the sail. A better idea is to provide a ratchet as well as a brake—which is done, for instance, by Camper & Nicholson—or, alternatively, to have a brake that is adjustable from the outside, as in Barient reel winches. Despite all the trouble they can cause and their extra cost over ordinary winches of the same power, reel winches still are the only things to have for mains and mizzens on cruising boats. This is particularly so in the case of large mains—say, 400 ft² or more—where otherwise one man would find hoisting the mainsail a strenuous task. When the sail involved is this large or even somewhat smaller, it pays to have a two-speed geared winch, which enables the bulk of the sail to be raised quickly, with power in reserve for the last bit. Of course, a really large mechanical advantage is not necessary, since a downhaul will be used with a sliding gooseneck for the final part of the job, but it is not always easy to raise the boom in the first place to permit this.

CHAPTER SIX

On Deck

THE DECK OF A YACHT forms the arena in which the personal drama of sailing is enacted. Sail handling, steering, anchoring, sunbathing—the deck layout must facilitate these essential activities despite the presence of the cabin house, companionways, hatches, ventilators, and other protrusions so necessary for life belowdecks.

To me a flush deck with a small deckhouse is the ideal because it is inherently strong and provides such a marvelously clear working platform. A flush deck is also cheaper than a trunk cabin and is less likely to develop leaks. Alas, relatively few yachts of moderate size can do without a trunk cabin if serious sacrifices in the accommodation are to be avoided. No matter how large or small a cruising yacht may be, at least 6 ft of headroom must be provided, and unduly high freeboard (a "raised deck") is to be avoided because it raises the center of gravity of the hull, offers considerable windage, and usually looks awful. Perhaps 42 ft of over-all length is the minimum for a flush deck if everything else is favorable, and 45 ft of over-all length is probably a more general lower limit. In boats with shallow bilges, notably centerboarders and ultralight-displacement types, the flush deck might not make sense in crafts up to the largest size two people can handle. Even if a flush deck is possible, not everyone will agree with me about its desirability, and certainly the arguments in its favor have not got the unanswerable quality of those in favor of a jib-headed mainsail, for instance. With a low, narrow trunk cabin that leaves wide decks, one is close to having the best of both worlds, but I still prefer the clean sweep of a flush deck.

One of the most wonderful things about sailing is the feeling of utter voluptuousness as one sinks into one's bunk after a rough watch on deck. And few things about sailing can be as dismal as the discovery that the bunk is wet. A leak over a berth is, to be sure, inexcusable, and I would not mention it except that if a boat is unfortunate enough to develop one, it may be extraordinarily difficult to cure. The trouble is that water entering a crevice on deck—usually at a joint or where a fitting is attached—may travel some distance before emerging into the interior, so that tracing the actual point of entry of the water presents a problem. It is seldom sufficient merely to stop up the inside defect, since the water will then merely travel

A flush deck is of considerable help in handling a large yacht efficiently. Items of interest on STARFIRE's *deck include a removable but husky gallows for the main boom and large cast-aluminum ventilators on Dorade boxes. At the extreme left is a wooden strip to deflect water thrown on the deckhouse top from the cockpit, a small touch worth emulating on other yachts with low houses.* (Beiser)

elsewhere on its inevitable way in. It is therefore imperative to be absolutely sure that a deck leak cannot occur, which means careful supervision of the artisans working on the deck and cabin structure. Nearly all yards are adequately conscientious about the hulls they build, but it is much easier to construct a tight hull than it is to construct a tight trunk cabin or deckhouse that will stay tight. In small and medium-sized boats of orthodox construction, fiberglass-covered plywood makes the best decks and cabin tops; in larger boats, laid teak is as good and looks vastly better—and is more expensive as well, of course. A composite deck made of thin teak laid on plywood is cheaper, lighter, and stronger than an all-teak deck. Canvas-covered plywood is the traditional substitute for teak, and it is normally quite satisfactory and long-lived, but a fiberglass covering is so much stronger, more waterproof, and more durable at a negligible extra cost that it is the logical choice if teak is not used.

Whether or not to have teak decks, if the choice is available, is almost entirely a subjective decision. A fiberglass-covered plywood deck is lighter and cheaper than a teak deck and, if just the right amount of pumice or sand is mixed in the paint, can be as nonskid as teak. Fiberglass does not dry out in the Mediterranean sun and never needs caulking. On the other hand, nobody's soul ever clapped its hands and sang at the sight of fiberglass, however nicely painted; let's face it, a scrubbed teak deck is absolutely gorgeous, one of man's happiest creations, and no cold, factory-made material like fiberglass can ever really replace it. If one is short of either sentiment or money or both, fiberglass over plywood is the answer—though it is perhaps hard to see why anybody not replete with both would want a sailboat in the first place.

These passionate remarks do not apply to the cabin top, where fiberglass-covered plywood is without serious rival. A laid-teak roof adds weight high up, where it can least be accepted, and in practice adds little to the appearance of a boat.

In a fiberglass boat whose deck and cabin are molded in one piece there is, of course, no choice in the matter. Fiberglass-reinforced plastic is not a stiff material, so the deck must be thick, and there would be little point to weighting the boat down further with a top layer of teak. Nonskid surfaces are invariably molded into the deck in such a case, and though there is nothing to be done about them, I might note that some of these molded surfaces are not much fun to live with no matter how skidproof. The worst of them are actually abrasive and will take the skin right off one's knees and knuckles for the first season or two (until the sharp edges are worn down). And these same decks are the devil to clean, so the blood shed on them is likely to become a permanent warning. A more wafflelike pattern is reasonably nonskid, while showing no special affinity for human skin and being a bit easier to keep clean—or, more accurately, less impossible to keep clean. (The best cleanser for a molded-fiberglass deck is a good gale.)

An all-fiberglass boat is not immune to deck leaks, contrary to what the manufacturers say. Fiberglass-reinforced plastic is a hard, unyielding material, and all fittings attached to it must be carefully bedded down with a permanently weather-tight compound. My wife's pleasure at the ease of maintaining the fiberglass sloop *Petrouchka* we once owned was considerably diminished by her damp berth, a failing not remedied until I had removed and properly bedded down every single fitting on deck. Of course, a fiberglass cabin house cannot rot, but that is hardly a reason to build it sloppily.

What to do about a dinghy must be settled at an early stage. In some waters—for instance, the tideless Baltic, where yachts almost invariably tie up to a quay or (most delightfully) directly to the shore—a dinghy is just a nuisance, and few boats bother with them. Elsewhere, however, a dinghy is essential as a means of getting to land, either because of shoaling at the water's edge or because a large tidal range means that docking lines would have to be constantly adjusted. Furthermore, a dinghy extends the possibilities of a cruiser to include anchoring off a strange coast and going in to explore, to picnic, to swim—all perhaps in blessed isolation. So, all in all, a proper cruising boat should at least be able to carry a dinghy conveniently, even if she may leave it behind or tow it on occasion.

Why not always tow the dinghy? The trouble is that a boat too small to carry a dinghy is also too small to be able to afford the drag of towing one, which is not inconsiderable. Further, in bad weather a towed dinghy is prone to ship water, which may increase the stresses on it, its painter, and the point of attachment on the mother vessel to the extent that something may break. It is all very well in any boat to be lazy and tow the dinghy on a casual afternoon's sail from one harbor to the next, but the point is that this should not have to be the *only* way to transport it.

There are, then, three major possibilities. First, a folding or an inflatable dinghy, the latter not to be confused with a self-inflating life raft. For occasional use, and perhaps as a second dinghy in a larger boat, these contrivances are not bad, but having tried both, I cannot say I am very fond of them. (It is only fair to note that some people swear by as well as at them.) Despite the advice of the experts, who counsel 8 ft as the minimum size for a dinghy, I have had 6-ft dinghies in two boats and found them adequate for two reasonably sober adults if intelligently used; one was a plywood pram and the other a double-ender of molded plywood, and both replaced inflatable rubber dinghies. The new Avon rubber dinghies, however, are a big improvement over the ones that gave me trouble, and they are very widely used in England.

Possibility two is the usual expedient of carrying a dinghy on the cabin house just abaft the mainmast. For most boats large enough (say, more than 35 ft overall) to be otherwise good cruisers, this is the best place—out of the way yet immediately accessible. If inverted, the dinghy can enclose an inflatable life raft and usually blends nicely with the yacht's profile. If right side up, it is easy to launch and hoist aboard with the main halyard and is a most convenient repository for sails, skin-diving gear, fenders, and docking lines, children, onions, and other items for which stowage space may be in short supply. The argument that an upright dinghy is bad because it can be filled with junk and so will be unavailable as a lifeboat is not impressive, since an inflatable life raft should be carried anyway; moreover, dinghies make very inadequate lifeboats. In boats under perhaps 45 ft overall, an upright dinghy is a bit ungainly and offers a bit more windage than is always acceptable. A nice rig in such a case is a set of chocks that will permit the dinghy to be carried either upright for coastwise cruising or inverted for photographs, racing, and deep-sea passages. (But be sure that it will fit under the main boom when upright before having the chocks made!) It is worth having the dinghy in mind when deciding whether or not to have a raised deckhouse and, if so, how big it will be, since a dinghy carried with one end propped way up on a deckhouse looks simply awful. On the other hand, a dinghy that just fits between mast and deckhouse often looks quite neat.

The third alternative is to carry the dinghy inverted forward of the mast over the forward hatch. I have done this in two boats—in a sloop 32-ft overall, whose cabin house was too short even for a 6-ft dinghy, and in a ketch 58-ft overall, with a small dinghy for my children, since the main dinghy is too big for them to handle. In the sloop, we carried the dinghy this way during a cruise in the Bahamas, an offshore passage from Miami to New York, and some hundreds of miles of New England cruising; and in the ketch, we carried the second dinghy for a thousand miles or so of cruising in the Baltic. In neither case was the dinghy in the way to an excessive extent; in fact, I would say that being able to leave the forward hatch open in all weathers made up for part of the inconvenience of having the dinghy on deck. Of course, this is not an ideal arrangement, but it works and is much better than having no dinghy or having to tow one. Carrying a dinghy on the foredeck is not uncommon in Europe, but it seems quite rare in American waters for some reason.

The purpose of a cockpit is to provide a comfortable place to recline at sea, the better to enjoy a warm sun or a starry night sky while the wake hisses past the quarter and the scuppers gurgle below. It should also be a place where one can commune with one's soul, pipe in mouth and rum in hand, as one watches the sun set behind Moorea and listens to the vahines singing across the bay.

Alas, a cockpit is also handy to set a wheel or tiller in and winches around, so that it is easy to lose sight of its primary functions and to consider it, wrongly, as no more than a necessary evil, to be endured despite the space it "wastes." An hour in a bad cockpit, back aching, legs cramped, and with no protection from the weather, is no fun at all, and yet such abominations are still being built. I vividly remember a bad night in a so-called modern yawl: while I steered, the mainsheet-block support dug into the small of my back as I sat behind the wheel in the only place from which the compass was visible, my knees far apart to avoid the spokes; and when I was not steering, the wide deck-level seats with low coamings were both uncomfortable and gave a pronounced feeling of insecurity. I also recall crossing the Gulf Stream in a young gale snug on the lee seat of a proper cockpit, the same cockpit in which, two days later, I stretched out under a brilliant blue sky while the yacht sailed herself across the Bahama banks toward Nassau.

A deep cockpit is safer as well as more comfortable than a shallow one. It is a fact that more people have been lost overboard from modern deep-sea yachts by having been washed out of the cockpit than by having fallen from the foredeck. Of course, nobody wants a cockpit so large that the vessel would be in jeopardy if a breaking sea should fill it; in fact, the current CCA rules contain a provision against oversize cockpits. However, there is nothing to prevent having a coaming with a slot in it down the deck on each side to permit the rapid draining of enough water to eliminate any real hazard before the scuppers take care of the rest. A decent cockpit should provide its occupants with safety, protection from the weather, and something to lean against, three things that a shallow cockpit with deck-level seats and low coamings does not furnish. A further bonus of a deep cockpit is that the weight of its occupants is lower, enhancing the stability of the boat, and their windage is reduced. The disadvantages of a sunken cockpit—extra cost and reduced stowage space—are too minor in magnitude to swing the balance against it.

In boats whose beam is carried well aft, there is enough space for cockpit lockers of substantial size. Access to these lockers can be by means of either hinged seats or opening panels in the sides of the cockpit well. The advantage of the former is that access is much better, so that the entire available volume can be used, and also the larger opening permits stowing bulky objects such as sails. The disadvantage is that some care is needed to keep water out, though a deep groove in the rim of the opening, a rubber gasket, and adequate latches usually do the trick. A perfectly astonishing amount of gear can be stowed in the cockpit lockers of a beamy boat. The lockers in a 32-ft sloop of mine held four jibs and a spinnaker, together with their sheets and guys, an anchor and its nylon cable, fenders and docking lines, snatch blocks and winch handles, and much miscellaneous junk besides. Quite properly, all the gear for working the ship stayed out of the living quarters, and the boat was fat enough aft so that the stowage there did not upset the trim—again, quite properly.

Vessels with fine lines aft generally have little room outboard of and below the cockpit, so it is out of the question to stow much more than a few sheets and some blocks there. However, in such boats it is especially important to have every available corner accessible, and some thought should be given to the placement of the openings and to having lips or partial bulkheads to prevent items from sliding out of reach forever. Even when excess weight cannot be tolerated in the counter, a few fenders will make no difference, and it is nice to have a handy place for them where a little mess does not matter.

A midships cockpit is sometimes seen, and it makes especially good sense when there is a large engine installation that would otherwise impose so high a deckhouse as to eliminate visibility from a cockpit aft. Really good engine access can often be arranged in this way without encroaching on the accommodation. A central cockpit is well protected, especially from following seas, and it can be full of people without causing the boat to squat in the water. Further, the resulting separation of the after cabin from the rest of the accommodation is very convenient under some circumstances, since it can serve as independent guest cabin or as a place of refuge when the rest of the boat is full of children and dogs.

There are three major objections to a midships cockpit that have to be set against its advantages. First, it takes up a lot of space in the middle of the ship that could more profitably be used for the accommodation, space that, moreover, is of no special help to the activities that take place in the cockpit. Second, splitting up the accommodation in this way has the psychological effect of shrinking the boat; instead of being a floating palace, it may more resemble a collection of yurts on a steppe. A passageway to the after cabin removes this objection, but it can be managed only on a large vessel. Third, except in the case of light-displacement boats with reverse sheer that look terrible anyway, a midships cockpit occasionally seems to add a lumpy note to a vessel's appearance. To be fair, sometimes such a cockpit has the more welcome effect of giving an impression of sturdiness and power to a hull that, though perhaps able enough, could never be graceful regardless of the arrangement of the upperworks.

While every design must be examined separately, I think it is correct to say that the conventional cockpit aft normally is best, and only in yachts over 50 ft overall is any alternative scheme likely to be competitive.

A spray hood over the main companionway is an unqualified blessing, and if it can be made big enough to shield the forward part of the cockpit, the unpleasantness of bad weather at sea can be considerably mitigated. These hoods are ordinarily

(TEXT CONTINUED ON PAGE 209)

[X I I I]

The Great Cabin Aft:
MAHANUI & RENOWN

IN CENTURIES PAST EVERY SHIP HAD A GREAT cabin in the poop, and while the salt horse and cat-o'-nine-tails of the same period are not likely to be revived, there is much to be said even today for a cabin with windows all around in the extreme stern of a yacht. What a grand place for a drink, a pipe, and a gam! And what better spot than the raised poop deck overhead for a sunbath as the ship rolls down the trades to Barbados? In *Mahanui* and *Renown,* two skilled British designers have tried their hands at cruising yachts featuring great cabins aft, and it would not be surprising to see more and more vessels of this type in years to come.

MAHANUI

IT IS HARD TO THINK OF ANY YACHT architect whose seagoing experience has been as extensive and varied as that of Colin Mudie. His first notable voyage was with Patrick Ellam in the 19-ft long *Sopranino* from England to America, and his most recent exploit was another transatlantic crossing, part aloft and part afloat, in the balloon *Small World,* whose dual-purpose gondola he designed. Mudie's output is also remarkably varied, from the brilliant catamaran *Rehu Moana,* in which David Lewis made the first long catamaran passage to windward (in the 1964 Single-Handed Transatlantic Race), through any number of more orthodox sailboats and motor cruisers (including one for King Baudouin of the Belgians) to high-speed powerboats for racing at sea. I like to think that the pecan-pie recipe my wife gave his wife some years ago has helped nourish his creative gifts: whenever I spy one of his swift, elegantly proportioned craft, I always see him in my mind's eye drawing its lines with one hand while with the help of the other he steadily consumes pecan pie to keep his inspiration at white heat.

In *Mahanui* (Maori for "great pleasure"), Colin Mudie has taken the concept of the great cabin aft and developed it to produce an exciting, rakish vessel with none of the dumpy, topheavy looks that are an ever-present danger in a moderate-sized craft of this kind. *Mahanui* is rigged as a staysail schooner. Why? "She is a schooner because for a modest displacement the size of the sails is not out of proportion, and because windward ability is not of prime importance for a long distance cruiser with a good engine. She is also a schooner because for comfortable cruising the biggest sail should be in the most convenient place to handle it, which is aft. Furthermore, the schooner rig looks nice." While I personally am convinced that the best place for the biggest sail is amidships, I fully agree that schooners look more splendid than ketches, and I would be the last to denounce anyone for accepting a certain amount of inconvenience in order to achieve his idea of beauty—provided, of course, that he knows

exactly what he is doing. In the plans of *Mahanui* the extreme end of the bow is omitted, presumably because the precise nature of the figurehead was not yet decided upon—another plus for the schooner, since a figurehead with any other rig usually looks silly.

Mahanui's accommodation follows a more open pattern than is possible with a conventional layout. Pilot berths flank the U-shaped settee in the stern, an area flooded with light

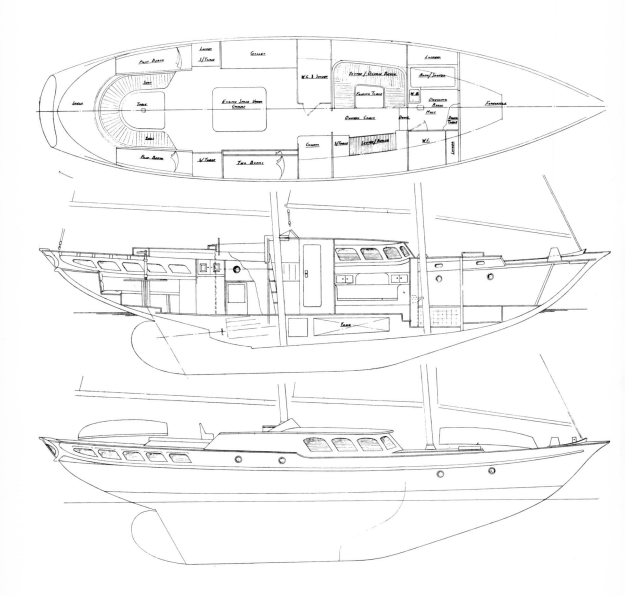

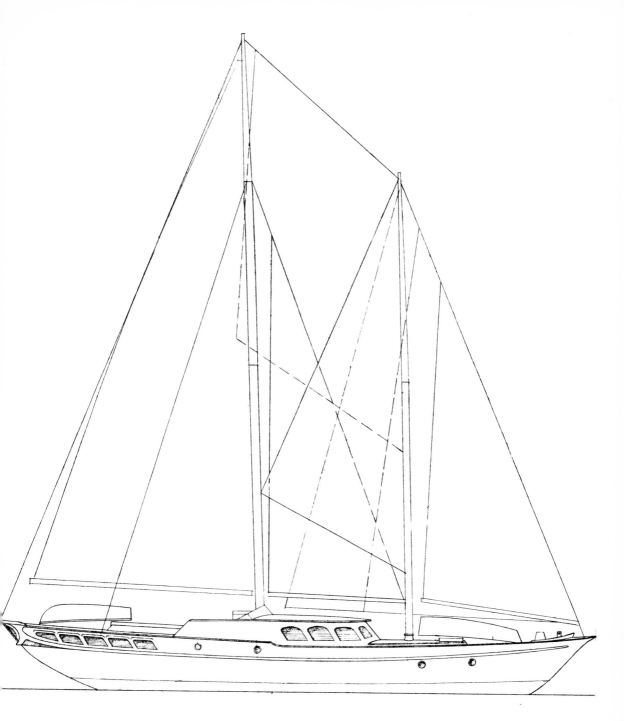

during the day and offering a view of the stars at night. Next forward are the galley to port and two berths, one above the other, to starboard. The owner's quarters are nothing short board. The owner's quarters are nothing short of glorious for a sailboat only 36 ft long on the waterline; note especially the dinette to port (perhaps for a private champagne supper when the passage is over), which appropriately converts to a double berth. Adjoining the cabin is a dressing room the width of the ship that sports an enclosed head, a dressing table, and a bath-shower. The forepeak, which is reached from the deck, can accommodate two more berths, but its primary function is to provide stowage space.

M A H A N U I

DESIGNER *Colin Mudie, 5 Catherine House, 25–27 Catherine Place, London S.W.1, England*

LOA 51 ft
LWL 36 ft
BEAM 13 ft
DRAFT 6 ft 7½ in.
DISPLACEMENT 42,500 lb
BALLAST 17,000 lb

SAIL AREA 1,012 ft^2
ENGINE Ford diesel (65 hp)
FUEL 150 gal
WATER 200 gal
CONSTRUCTION Conventional wooden, with carvel planking on steamed frames

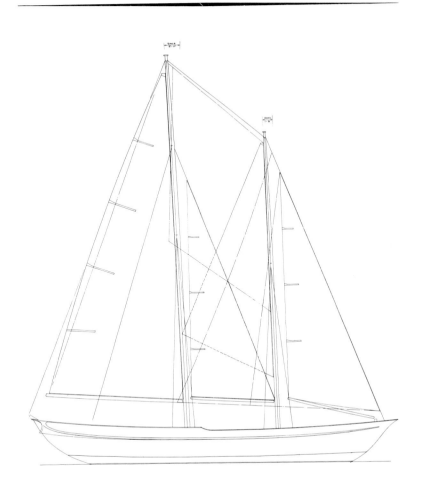

RENOWN

ACCORDING TO HER DESIGNER, Arthur Robb, *Renown* "combines, with the greatest care in avoiding any whimsical and imitation traditional ship characteristics, the fast modern cruising hull form with a clipper bow and a low raised deck and stern windows in the transom. Its special interest probably lies in the layout where the saloon is in the extreme stern. On a waterline of only 37 feet, this yacht has a saloon line-of-sight of nearly 14 feet with a galley at the forward end of it. The owner's double cabin is the full breadth of the yacht under a flush deck, and it has its own toilet and shower. Above the owner's cabin is an on-deck cockpit with wheel steering, and next forward is a deck saloon large enough for the crew to have afternoon tea. A 'Nanny's cabin' for one is to port next to this saloon, or that space is available for an owner's other special needs. Farther forward is in effect the space normally occupied by the saloon in the average yacht and which could be used as either a second saloon with built-in berths each side or as a large double cabin or to provide two single cabins. The forecastle is large and provides for one or two professionals if required or, as in the case of one yacht now building, [can be used] as a workshop and store."

As is the case with all of Arthur Robb's designs, *Renown* has been planned meticulously to take advantage of every cubic inch of space, and *Renown* has no less than twelve berths all together. I suspect that if twelve adults were ever aboard for a cruise, they would find it hard to find stowage for their gear and enough food to last, say, a week. A pleasanter and more convenient accommodation would, to my mind, have fewer berths and more lockers. But this is a mere quibble, since interior details are always largely at the whim of the owner, and in terms of his primary responsibility of providing a noble hull and rig, the designer has come up with a superior yacht.

RENOWN

DESIGNER   *Arthur Robb, 20D New Cavendish Street, London W.1, England*

LOA   48 ft

LWL   37 ft

BEAM   12 ft 11 in.

DRAFT   7 ft 6 in.

DISPLACEMENT   36,400 lb

BALLAST   13,200 lb of lead

SAIL AREA   1,033 ft^2

ENGINE   B.M.C. Commander diesel (50 hp)

FUEL   600-mile range at 7 knots

WATER   186 gal

CONSTRUCTION   Conventional wooden, with carvel planking on steamed frames

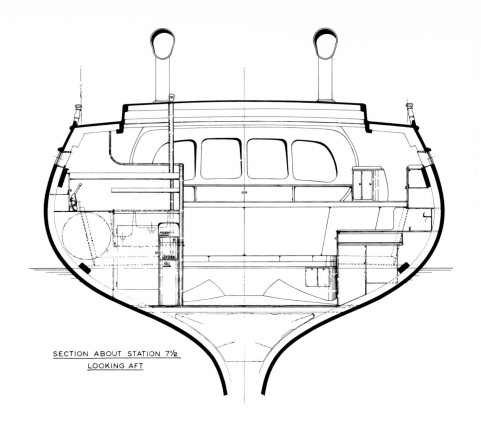

SECTION ABOUT STATION 7½
LOOKING AFT

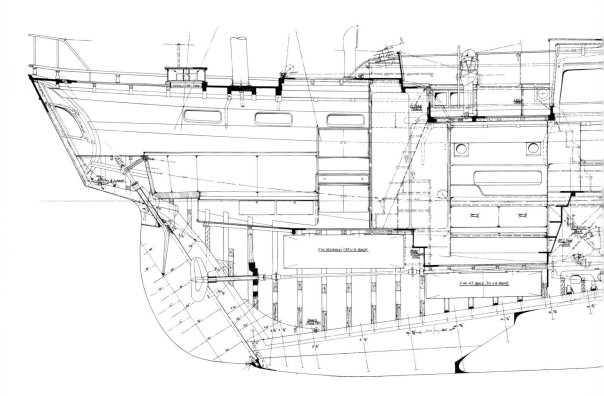

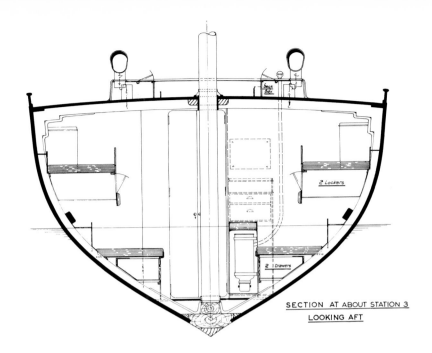

SECTION AT ABOUT STATION 3
LOOKING AFT

2 Lockers

2 Drawers

Bench
Bdkr

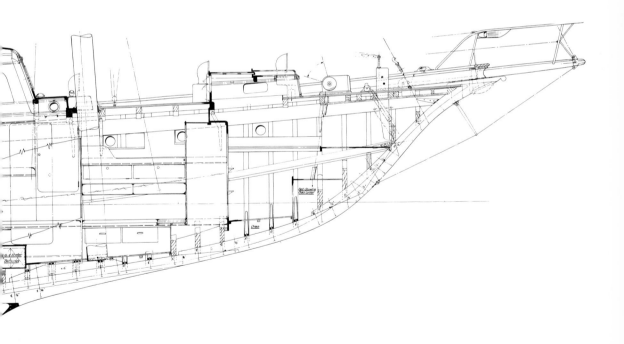

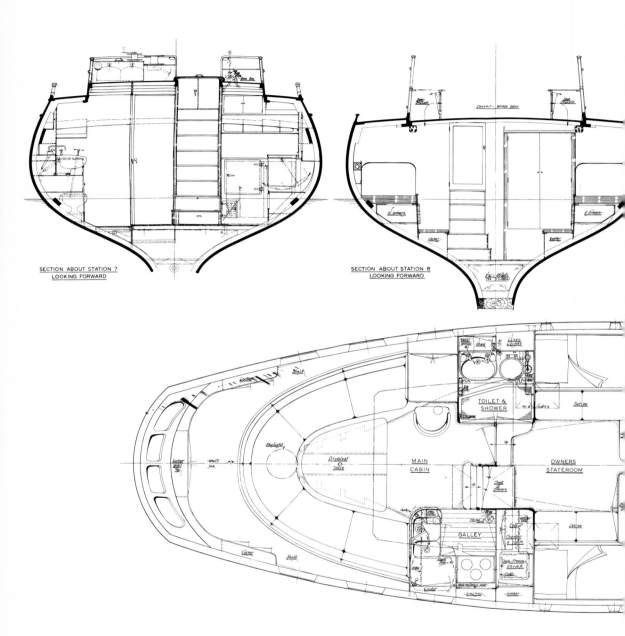

SECTION ABOUT STATION 7
LOOKING FORWARD

SECTION ABOUT STATION 6
LOOKING FORWARD

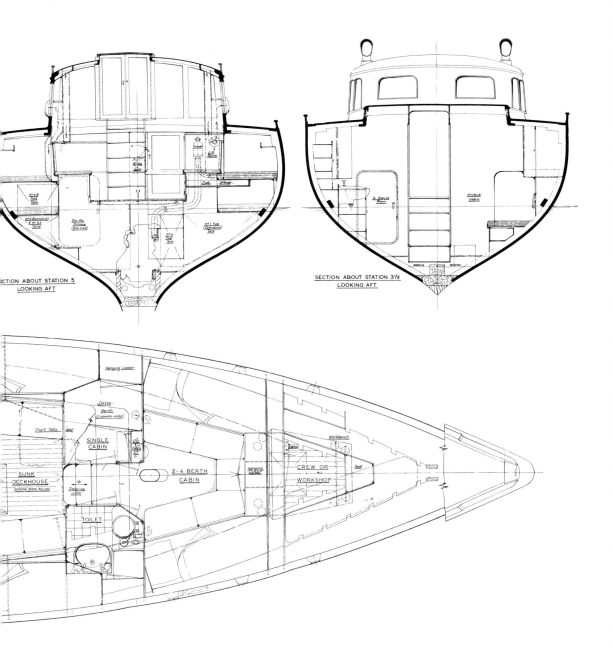

SECTION ABOUT STATION 5
LOOKING AFT

SECTION ABOUT STATION 3½
LOOKING AFT

(TEXT CONTINUED FROM PAGE 198)

framed with bronze or stainless-steel tubing so arranged as to permit them to be folded out of the way, and windows of transparent plastic are often sewn into the front and sides. The latter in time become brittle and hard to see through, but they can be readily replaced if the rest of the cloth is still good. If the companion slide does not house in a watertight box, the forward part of the hood can be extended to cover the entire assembly and thereby neutralize an otherwise tiresome source of water below. The after end of the hood should go back somewhat past the vertical if it is to be fully effective and can be held there by shock cord to permit its being tilted forward when one is using the companionway. A high hood that obstructs the helmsman's vision is a bad idea, and the use of shock cord in this way makes a fairly low one acceptable. The plastic windows seldom seem to be much use to the helmsman, and they are of primary benefit to somebody standing in the companionway who wants to look around without getting wet—a not ignoble purpose. A good big one that extends across the entire trunk cabin should have curved hoops rather than rectangular ones to make it stronger and easier to see around without reducing the protection it affords, and the cloth should preferably be secured in a beading that runs around the entire foot to keep driven spray out. So nice is some form of cockpit protection that I regard the impracticability of fitting either a permanent or a temporary shelter over the forward end of the cockpit of a ketch as an argument of some force against this rig. A ketch can sometimes fit a hood wholly within the cockpit aft of the mizzenmast, as I have seen aboard the 46-ft *Gouden Draak* and the 72-ft *Ticonderoga,* but in my own ketch the watch on deck has thus far had to be content with good oilies. Of course, a midships cockpit in a ketch makes the problem easy to deal with.

Steering with a tiller is fun in a fast, well-balanced, craft, but for serious cruising a wheel is normally a better idea. A wheel means less work, and it is more comfortable to sit for hours behind a wheel in line with the lubber lines of a compass that is right there in full view. A wheel makes it possible for the helmsman to sit on the lee side when on the wind, allowing a full view of the jib, without his arm coming off at the shoulder after a while. Also, an automatic pilot is much easier to install with a wheel steering system—a good thing, since it is easier to fall asleep at a wheel than at a tiller. And life in the cockpit, including handling sheets as well as taking naps and sunbaths, is pleasanter with a wheel. As far as safety goes, while it is true that steering cables and quadrants break more often than they should, it is not hard to arrange matters so that an emergency tiller can be installed quickly if need be; and the excellent Edson worm steerers are wholly reliable. So tillers probably have no place in proper cruising boats—which is really a pity, since under the best of circumstances there is nothing half so thrilling as the feel of a live tiller in the hand.

Though one must pause to regret the passing of the tiller, it is still a good idea to make the transition to a wheel a wholehearted one and have a wheel with a continuous metal rim instead of bare spokes. Spokes look terribly romantic and all that, but the romance fades when one tries to stop a spinning spoked wheel or fractures a rib falling on a spoke. And steering with one hand is easy with a continuous rim, difficult with spokes. True, a shiny stainless-steel or chromed "destroyer" wheel is not quite to everybody's taste, but a metal rim screwed to the ends of the spokes of an orthodox mahogany or teak wheel works well and does not offend anybody's eye. After a good prod by one of the spokes of the wheel on my boat, I had a rim of bronze tubing fitted to it, and everyone who saw it before and after agreed that it looked the better for the change. Now one can steer with one hand while sitting on the cockpit coaming or standing on the cockpit seat, which was not feasible before but which is helpful in a big boat with a deckhouse that partially obstructs the view ahead from the helmsman's usual seat.

Any yacht meant for shorthanded cruising should have some means of automatic steering to permit the helm to be left unattended. Automatic steering means that whoever is on watch is not chained to the wheel but can take care of all sorts of chores—adjusting sheets, taking a sight or a bearing, cooking a meal—without rousing anyone out from below. It is difficult to exaggerate the benefits of an automatic helmsman; they include less fatigue and greater effectiveness for the watch on deck, longer periods of sleep with fewer interruptions for the watch below, and fewer crew needed for long passages. And how nice it is to come in out of the rain for a while, and for the entire crew to have dinner together.

There are two possibilities, either a conventional compass-controlled automatic pilot or a wind-controlled self-steering device. The former has the virtue of being independent of wind direction or strength, and it can be used to avoid the excruciating boredom of long stretches under power in a calm. However, automatic pilots have several disadvantages. The first is power consumption, which, though not very great, means charging the batteries at regular intervals. Second, from a technical point of view, the electronics of most automatic pilots for yachts are back in the Stone Age and are not nearly as reliable and maintenance-free as they could be. With a certain amount of luck, a conventional automatic pilot may well be satisfactory, but to make sure that luck is on one's side, it is wise to inquire into the experience of others. Finally, since the pilot follows the compass and not the wind, some sort of periodic lookout is necessary to keep track of wind direction.

Wind-controlled self-steering received its greatest impetus from the single-handed transatlantic races of 1960 and 1964, in which each of the competitors had such a device fitted. The most successful scheme was that worked out by H. G. Hasler. A wind vane was used to adjust the angle of attack of a swiveled fin in the water aft of the boat's counter. Depending upon the deviation from the set angle with the wind, the fin is turned to port or to starboard about a vertical axis by the vane. The pressure of the water due to the boat's motion then swings the fin upward toward the side the fin was rotated to, and it is this hydrodynamic force that is coupled to the rudder. Hasler's inspiration was to use the force of the water to turn the rudder, with the force of the wind on the vane serving merely to orient the fin. M. S. Gibb Ltd. in England manufactures a version of the Hasler gear that seems reasonably satisfactory. The chief disadvantage of wind-controlled automatic steering is that it works only when there is a certain amount of wind present. Also, the gear cannot be used with certain rigs and steering systems. If a new boat is involved, the Hasler gear, or a modified version of it, can usually be worked into the plans somehow if it is thought of in time. A difficulty with all wind-controlled systems is that since the boat follows the wind in its vicissitudes, navigation requires more attention than in the case of a compass-controlled pilot, where all course changes can be noted when made.

Because compass- and wind-controlled steering systems so neatly complement each other, the ideal thing is to have both fitted. If this seems too big a chunk to bite off at first, either system is vastly better than none, and which is to be preferred depends almost entirely on the kind of cruising that is contemplated.

The only kind of compass that is really satisfactory is one with a spherical liquid-filled top and internal gimbals. With the entire compass immersed in liquid, damping is very effective and the card remains steady in rough weather. In addition, the liquid-filled dome of the compass magnifies the card so that the graduations are visible a considerable distance away—no more hunching over the compass in the rain to see where one is going. Lighting may be through a bulb on the back of the dome or through the base; in either case, a red filter is necessary. The Danforth-White (formerly Kelvin-White) Constellation spherical compasses are the best known and are very fine instruments; several other firms manufacture similar ones. As with any other compass, in time the liquid filling will need replacement, and eventually the jeweled bearings may wear and the card will tend to stick on certain headings. At the first sign of difficulty, and none may appear for ten years or even more, it is worth bringing the instrument to a competent repair agency for complete overhaul.

A card marked in points exudes tradition, but as far as I am concerned it belongs safely in the past with salt horse and the cat-o'-nine-tails. A black card with white marks every 5° and numerals every 30° combines maximum legibility with maximum intelligibility and has my vote every time. Some cards are marked off in points with tiny degree inscriptions around the rim, which I don't recommend. The dominant consideration is that the helmsman be able to see clearly what course he is on from some distance away from the compass. Thwartship as well as fore-and-aft lubber lines make taking bearings easier and are worth having.

When wheel steering is fitted, the almost invariable practice is to install the compass on the wheel pedestal. This keeps the compass out of the way and is satisfactory when provision is made for the helmsman to sit behind the wheel—or perhaps I should say to chock himself to sit behind the wheel. When the helmsman is off to one side—say, sitting to leeward on the cockpit coaming—the pedestal mounting is not very convenient. And when a tiller is fitted, unless the cockpit is a long one indeed, a pedestal-mounted compass is seldom a good idea. What to do here? Often the compass can be mounted on the forward end of the cockpit, where it is far enough away from the tiller for the helmsman to be able to glance at it without having to swing his body around. In the old days a compass would often be installed inside the cabin with a little window to permit viewing it from the cockpit, and this might be the answer in the case of a short cockpit. In a few boats, I have seen dual compasses, one on each side of the forward end of the cockpit. The 12-meters use this scheme because it keeps the compass just below the helmsman's line of sight as he watches both the sails and where he is going. Two compasses must be several feet apart (the exact separation depends upon the strength of their magnets) if they are not to interact, but in a small vessel one can use a portable compass with a mounting bracket and a watertight electrical outlet on either side. Danforth-White makes a portable model of their Constellation with a robust bracket and built-in compensators that I have used and found satisfactory except for the tendency of stray lines to snag on it; a curved guardrail would probably eliminate the problem.

Any boat setting off out of sight of land should have a spare compass. There is no reason why it need be the twin of the main compass, though for a long passage the spare should be such that it can be installed as a replacement in case the main one is damaged or its pedestal gets carried away. A second compass may have a function of its own. Thus a good one mounted near the direction finder is a big help in taking radio bearings, since it saves shouting back and forth to the helmsman, who may not always be able to hold the boat steady enough. Some skippers like a compass below, perhaps visible from their bunks, so that they can keep track of what the monkeys on deck are up to. I have doubts as to how good a hand bearing compass is as a spare, since it must be held up to one's eye to make out the reading, and it is not easy to do this and steer at the same time. What I like is a first-class spherical compass, permanently mounted so as to be capable of taking bearings in all directions and also acting as a standard compass for checking the steering compass. The top of a deckhouse is sometimes a suitable place for this, as is a pedestal aft of the cockpit if there are no winches there. In the latter case, a fairly low pedestal is all right, since the steering compass is fine for bearings close to the direction in which the boat is headed.

Any measure that reduces the chance of falling overboard is worth taking, which is why every proper cruising boat should have lifelines and both fore and aft pulpits. Actually, sailing efficiency as well as safety is involved. A pulpit makes changing headsails less of a project than otherwise, since Lucky Pierre on the foredeck can brace himself forward of the headstay and use both hands to pull down the existing jib and unhank it. The lifelines and their stanchions keep sails on their way up or down from slipping over the side and are handy to secure sails to before or after their use. An after pulpit means that the stern light can be installed so as to have greater range than if it were on the counter, and in a yawl the mizzen sheet can lead to a block on a suitably reinforced pulpit instead of to a projecting boomkin. On the debit side is the occasional interference with various sheets, as well as the considerable expense—both minor considerations compared with the security offered by a good fence.

There is no need to have the appearance of a boat suffer because of pulpits and lifelines. In fact, by extending the ends of a boat, appropriate pulpits can even add a certain elegance to its looks, though it must be admitted that some pulpit styles are more grotesque than anything else. If polished stainless steel adds an unpleasant note to a deck otherwise devoid of it, bronze pulpits and stanchions can be specified, and no law prohibits painting them to make them look more presentable. In the latter case, galvanized steel will save a good bit of money; and if the galvanizing is done properly and the paint kept up, the fittings should last many years before regalvanizing is required. My own lifeline stanchions and after pulpit are galvanized steel painted dado brown, which goes well with the black topsides, tan cabin top, mahogany cabin sides and trim, and teak deck. The forward pulpit is, alas, in stainless steel because of the wear it receives. I have seen a number of other boats with painted stanchions and pulpits, and when the color was right, they looked fine—and the saving can be considerable.

Rubber-coated stainless-steel wire is best for the upper lifeline, since it is kind to the hands and the increased diameter means less chance of injury if one is hurled against it. The lower lifeline looks vastly better in less conspicuous bare wire, which is acceptable there, and it also can be of somewhat lighter gauge than the upper lifeline.

The Achilles' heel of most lifeline installations is the stanchion sockets. These *must* be large and bolted down; a flagpole socket that is merely screwed in place is rather easily pulled out by the roots. The best arrangement is to attach the stanchions to the rail as well as to the covering board, but this is not possible when the stanchions are set inboard amidships to stay clear of the jib sheets. My experience is that every dock has an idiot who will try to fend a vessel off by pushing on the lifelines instead of on the shrouds, being afraid of breaking the latter, so the stanchions should be installed to withstand inboard as well as outboard stresses. Transverse pressure on a lifeline is transformed into a tension of greater magnitude, and the lifeline ends must therefore be secured to take a considerable pull. The tighter the lifeline, the higher the multiplying factor becomes, while a taut lifeline confers no advantage in safety over one just a trifle slack; so there is no point to tightening the lifeline turnbuckles too much. It is a good idea to have braces on pulpit uprights and gate stanchions that serve as anchors for lifelines, especially since it seems rather hard to discourage people from sitting on lifelines. I always try to restrict my crews to those who have studied vector analysis, but I have found it expedient to add another pair of braces to each of my pulpits.

Double lifelines and a pulpit are very much in the way when it comes to getting an anchor aboard, but using pelican hooks to secure the forward ends of the lifelines to the pulpit solves the problem completely. At the right moment, upper and lower lifelines are released, the anchor is hauled over the rail just aft of the pulpit (metal chafing strips are in order here), and the lifelines are secured again. For an offshore passage, it is only a few minutes' work to mouse the pelican hooks.

A gate amidships is practically a necessity when double lifelines are fitted, not only as a convenience when getting on and off the boat but as a safety measure to make it possible to recover someone who has fallen overboard. At sea I always secure a line across the middle of the gate that can be readily cut if necessary. With the pelican-hook arrangement for releasing the lifelines, of course, a gate is largely a matter of taste: it is perhaps as much in the way as helpful in a medium-sized boat, more helpful than not in a larger one.

Safety measures do not end with lifelines: safety belts and life jackets for every member of the crew, a pair of horseshoe life rings with electronic-flash water lights, and rescue quoits with floating lines are all necessary, and a flagged, ballasted buoyant pole is a good idea offshore. A self-inflating rubber life raft is the best way —indeed, the only way—to provide for the ultimate disaster of a sinking ship, since dinghies are worthless at sea. The value of these rafts has been proved in scores of fishing-boat accidents in European waters, where they are mandatory equipment on fishing and commercial vessels, and the Royal Ocean Racing Club now requires them to be carried on all competing boats in the races they sponsor. The best of these rafts (and why have less than the best?) meet the standards of the 1958 International Convention on the Safety of Life at Sea, and they have canopies that erect automatically when the raft is inflated. The canopy is a valuable feature, since it keeps the sea and the weather out and the people and their warmth in. Approved rafts have paddles, flares, a hand pump and repair kit, a bailer and sponge, water and concentrated food, a calibrated drinking vessel, and so on. A canopy that catches rainwater and leads it inside via a tube is worthwhile, as is a built-in light that gets its power from a battery that is immersed in seawater. The raft, which comes sealed in a waterproof bag, is kept on deck, and a pull on its painter releases

(TEXT CONTINUED ON PAGE 216)

The William Tripp-designed and Henry Hinckley-built Bermuda 40 fiberglass yawls are among the very finest stock boats ever built. Hull, deck, and cabin trunk constitute a strong, monolithic shell that requires little maintenance, while the accommodation is nicely finished in wood. The winch bases are hollow and are handy places to keep winch handles, sunglasses, and beer. These four photographs were taken of the Bermuda 40 GOLDEN EAGLE. (Rosenfeld)

(TEXT CONTINUED FROM PAGE 213)

the carbon dioxide that inflates it. When the raft is brought in for its annual check, it is both fun and most reassuring to tug the painter and watch it burst free from its bag and inflate.

The time to consider where to keep the life raft is before the boat is built. They are not so small that they can go just anywhere: a typical fully-equipped eight-man raft is 3 ft long and 16 in. in diameter packed in its bag. Possible locations are under an inverted dinghy, on the counter, or in a lazaret whose hatch is large enough for access. The raft should, of course, be lashed in place securely, and if this is done with the help of pelican hooks, the raft can be cast loose in a moment.

The weight of ground tackle is often cited as one of the two ultimate limiting factors on the size of a proper cruising boat, the other being the area of the main-sail. Though these factors are certainly important, neither imposes a really sharp cutoff on size. While a 500-ft^2 main may be a handful in a sloop, it should present no great problem in a ketch; similarly, while a 60-lb anchor on $\frac{1}{2}$-in. chain is distressing to contemplate pulling in by hand, a power windlass removes most of the curse. In fact, the best of the latter are so reliable and easy to live with that I am sure any crew able to handle a certain boat under sail need have no trouble with the ground tackle of that boat.

The three most reliable types of anchors are the fisherman (or yachtsman's), the plow (or CQR), and the Danforth. For the same holding power in a good mud bottom, a much heavier fisherman is needed than either a plow or a Danforth, but there are some bottoms in which only a fisherman will hold at all. Experienced sailors can be found who strongly favor each of these types of anchors: in the magnificent 70-ft brigantine *Varua*, William Albert Robinson carries four 200-lb Danforths; Eric Hiscock sailed his 30-ft *Wanderer* twice around the world with two 35-lb plows; and every harbor has a dozen shellbacks who will have nothing but fisherman anchors. I have anchored hundreds of times with a Danforth, and the only times it dragged, the fault was mine for not having enough scope out. I invariably put a healthy strain on the anchor with the engine in reverse even when I have sailed in, and if it just won't hold after a few tries, I get out a heavy fisherman. If there is still no luck, I go elsewhere.

While it is essential to have large enough anchors, there is no simple way to determine what large enough is, since the required holding power depends upon so many different factors—for instance, displacement, total windage, mast height, and draft. Tables giving anchor weights in terms of over-all length or Thames tonnage are almost meaningless for this reason. If one does not have enough experience, the best advice is to find someone who has a boat of a similar size and type and get his advice—or, better, that of several people. If the boat is a stock boat, a good guide is to replace the anchor that comes as standard equipment with the next heaviest one of that type for the working anchor, and obtain a still heavier one for the storm anchor.

The working anchor belongs on the forward deck if it is too heavy to carry around easily, but otherwise it is better to have it out of the way—for instance, on the cabin house or in a cockpit sail locker. In a boat of moderate size the storm anchor will probably not be too much of a monster, and it can also be stowed off the foredeck. When the anchors are big fellows, they can be kept in chocks on the forward deck, but sited so as not to snag lines or trip people. Here the Danforth stock is often troublesome, and the only real way to cope with the problem is to fit wooden chocks under its ends.

The exact design of a particular type of anchor is quite critical. With the expiration of the original plow and Danforth patents, a number of imitations have appeared on the market, and some are decidedly inferior to the originals. And despite the antiquity of the fisherman anchor, not all designs are equally effective. The only safe thing to do is to stick to the originals in the case of plows and Danforths and to a reputable manufacturer in the case of a fisherman.

Opinion is divided on the necessity for a chain anchor cable. Natural cordage leaves much to be desired for this purpose, since it is relatively weak, inelastic, and prone to rot, and past practice dictated chain on cruising boats of all sizes. But nylon has none of these defects and is kind to the hands, weighs very little, and comes up clean—virtues that make it superior to chain in boats under perhaps 40 ft overall. It is no great strain to haul aboard by hand nylon line up to ¾ in. in diameter, and several hundred feet of such line can be coiled on deck without much trouble and stowed wherever convenient. Of course, a rocky bottom or the presence of coral may make it wise to have a few fathoms of chain next to the anchor to prevent chafing the nylon, and an all-chain cable is still required in certain cruising grounds, characterized perhaps by insufficient swinging room in the anchorages or the presence of strong tidal currents or poor protection from the sea and the weather. But, generally speaking, chain is not as necessary in small cruising boats as it was once thought to be.

In large vessels, though, chain has certain advantages. A few hundred pounds of chain is not a serious matter in a boat more than 45 ft long overall, and since such a boat should have a power windlass anyway if it is to be handled with a small crew, the unpleasantness of heaving in chain by hand does not arise. While light nylon is easy to coil and stow, heavy nylon is not so cooperative, and even when it is possible to coil it directly into a suitable locker or deck box, the box must be disproportionately large if the coiling is not to be a frustrating and time-consuming chore. Chain, on the other hand, is self-stowing, is always ready for immediate use, and occupies surprisingly little space. The weight of chain means that the angle it makes with the bottom is smaller than that made by a nylon cable even with more scope on the nylon, so that there is greater security and perhaps a somewhat lighter anchor can be used. This last consideration, again, has meaning only for larger boats, where the use of chain may mean that one man can cope with the anchor instead of two.

Since every cruising boat should have at least two anchors and the cables for them, it makes sense to have one of the cables in chain and the other in nylon if the chain can be carried without penalizing performance. The dividing line comes, to my mind, between 40 and 50 ft, though I respect the thinking that places the line between 30 and 40 ft. In any case, it is a snare and a delusion to have chain of too light a weight. Chain with links of $\frac{5}{16}$-in.-diameter galvanized steel is perhaps the minimum that has sufficient strength and is heavy enough to provide a decent catenary in even the smallest cruising boat, and still larger chain is better. Once a chain cable has straightened out, it transmits the shock of snubbing directly to the anchor (not to mention the back teeth of the crew), which tends to break out the anchor as well as to break out whatever fitting on deck the chain is held by. Nylon is nice and springy by contrast, and in a real blow I would prefer nylon if there was room for enough scope to be paid out.

If chain is wanted, a suitable locker for it, together with a fairlead to that locker, is best established in the design stage. Since 200 ft of ⅜-in. BBB chain for use with a windlass weighs 350 lb, the effect of such weight on the boat's trim and stability must be considered early in the game. Similar thought must also be given to the anchor windlass, which may get in the way of the forestaysail boom if one is fitted or catch the foot of the genoa when coming about or otherwise be a nuisance unless sited carefully.

Any boat except the very smallest that regularly uses chain will benefit from a windlass of some kind, but a manual one is adequate for over-all lengths of up to perhaps 45 ft. An able man can cope with a nylon cable in such vessels also, though help from the engine or sails may be needed. Beyond 45 ft the desirability of power becomes overwhelming if one wants to be able to manage the boat shorthanded, and I myself would fit a power windlass in a 40-ft boat even though I might not always use it with a nylon cable. In a smaller boat I would have a vertical capstan whose motor and gearbox are under the deck, thereby taking up less deck space and lowering the center of gravity. In a larger one I would prefer the whole works in a waterproof enclosure on deck, a wildcat for line on one side and a gypsy for chain on the other. How powerful a motor to have depends upon what is going to be pulled up. As a rough guide, I would say to use a windlass capable of 350 lb of line pull for ⁵⁄₁₆-in. chain, 500 lb of line pull for ⅜-in. chain, and 1,000 lb of line pull for ½-in. chain. Even more roughly, this means, in the same order, vessels from 30 to 40 ft overall, from 40 to 50 ft overall, and from 50 to 60 ft overall. It is impossible to have too powerful a windlass, but the power should not come at the sacrifice of too much speed; 25 ft per minute at the rated line pull is about the minimum, and 40 is better.

I think it is worth making structural provision for a windlass in any new boat more than 40 ft long overall, so that even if one is not installed immediately, it can be done later without having to rebuild the boat. Windlasses are heavy and can exert considerable stresses on the deck when in use, and just bolting them down is asking for trouble unless the deck is suitably reinforced to distribute these stresses.

A windlass can be powered by its own electric motor or hydraulically from a pump belted on the main engine. I have an electric windlass and have had no trouble with it at all, so I personally see no reason to go in for the complexity and slow operation of a hydraulic installation. In a really big vessel the latter permits a smaller and lighter deck unit than does a comparable electric windlass, but I would estimate that this applies to boats at least 60 ft long overall. Excessive drain on the battery can be reduced by merely running the engine while using the windlass, which has to be done in any case with a hydraulic rig.

It is worth laying out the foredeck so that line can be led fair from either bow to the windlass wildcat. Then one can let the windlass do the work of pulling the boat up to a dock against the wind or hauling it off a shoal regardless of orientation. I find a windlass of immense help in canalling; it is difficult to keep the bow of a large yacht in position in the ascending locks without it. And a jib or spinnaker halyard can be led to the windlass to haul a man aloft quickly and easily.

CHAPTER SEVEN

Engines
and Related Troubles

INSTALLING AN ENGINE in a sailboat is vandalism, no question about it. But there are degrees of vandalism, and it is not impossible to work in an engine in such a way that its virtues are not swamped by its essential vulgarity. Engines are bulky, heavy, dirty, smelly, unreliable when needed most, and dangerous. A small, handy sailboat can readily dispense with one, to the enhanced pleasure of its crew. But in a big vessel an engine is mandatory if it is to be at all self-sufficient. The late George Roosevelt prided himself on doing without an engine in the 60-ft schooner *Mistress,* but he also had a large power tender to do the dirty work. An engine means that two people can bring a boat the size of *Mistress* to a dock and tie her up by themselves, that the boat can negotiate narrow channels and canals, that it can get through the entrance to a lagoon in the Pacific in the teeth of the trades, that a dragging anchor in a bad spot need not mean disaster, and so on and on.

Further, there is the matter of electricity. In a small boat, the power drain is likely to be so small that dry cells are adequate, or a storage battery by itself can be taken ashore periodically to be charged. In a larger boat, too much current is needed just for lighting for this to be possible on anything but the briefest cruise, and when one starts to install such aids to the good life as power windlasses, refrigerators, automatic pilots, electric pumps, and radiotelephones, the need for a generator becomes overwhelming. To have an engine to drive a generator but not for propulsion seems to me absurd—even the smallest engine is just as noisy and dangerous and smelly and as much bother as a larger one adequate to push the ship when desired. So the question in most cruising boats more than, say, 30 ft long overall and in all cruising boats more than 40 ft long overall is not whether to have an engine but instead how the nasty beast can be tamed and put to best use.

Diesel engines are heavier and more expensive than their gasoline-powered rivals, but diesel oil cannot explode, while gasoline can. As far as I am concerned, this factor by itself is enough to settle the matter. Diesels offer two other major advantages as well: they are more reliable, and they use less fuel. The reliability is partly because no ignition system is involved and partly because the engines themselves are robustly built and fairly simple mechanically. The General Motors diesel engine I have in my boat is now fifteen years old, but it has never failed to start and deliver the goods whenever called upon to do so. (But there is a price to pay for this: when I acquired the boat, the cost of putting the neglected engine in top shape was more than $3,000. I am still happy with the engine, though not pleased with the previous owner.)

My other boats have had gasoline engines of various makes and ages, but all shared an ability to perform beautifully in flat calms on sunny days and a disinclination to stir whenever the going got rough. I still vividly remember trying to beat into Chesapeake Bay in a northwesterly gale with a nasty sea running on a certain November night some years ago. After a while, it got to be a bit of a bore, so we decided to use the engine to help out. The engine was new that year and had been checked out two days earlier, just before we left New York, but it still took an hour of working head down to clear the carburetor jets and cause the spark plugs to spark properly. This same engine was subsequently to stop abruptly as a current bore the boat down on a closed lift bridge in the Intracoastal Waterway; only quick work with the anchor saved the day. Such failures are typical of the behavior of gasoline engines on sailboats. Other sailors I know have had worse experiences, still others have never had the slightest trouble. I am sure that these difficulties could be remedied if the manufacturers cared to do something about them; there is no reason to expect that engines designed for automobiles or tractors should be ideal in so very different an environment as that of a sailboat without improvements in the quality of certain critical components.

The fuel consumption of diesels is strikingly less than that of gasoline engines, being only about half as great for the same power output. This means twice the cruising range for the same tankage. Diesel oil is also roughly half the price of marine gasoline, so the fuel cost per mile is only a quarter as much. However, while this is a major consideration for high-powered motor yachts, few auxiliaries are under power long enough for the reduced fuel expense to make up for the higher initial price of a diesel engine. The primary reason to have a diesel engine in a sailboat is self-preservation, with reliability a close second.

This does not mean that gasoline engines do not have good features apart from their low cost. For all their inclination to failure, they are usually easy to fix, and mechanics and spare parts can be found almost anywhere. They are also lighter in weight than diesels, which means that they permit that much more lead in the keel and so a stiffer boat; and they are more compact, so they take up less space in the best part of the boat, namely, the middle. However, I think it is fallacious to argue that a boat to be used for racing cannot afford the weight of a diesel, because stability is now measured directly in deriving a CCA rating, while the RORC partly takes into account engine weight in computing the stability allowance. And, anyway, if one feels that strongly about engine weight, one can simply get a small diesel. Diesels are more conservatively rated than gasoline engines, so a 10- to 15-hp diesel may well deliver just as much power to the propeller at cruising speed as a 25-hp gasoline engine and may be not much if at all heavier.

Some marine engines, gasoline or diesel, are light and compact, scarcely larger than the batteries needed to start them, while others of the same power are monstrous affairs that seem to date from the early days of the Industrial Revolution. The basic difference between them is that the former develop their power at high speeds, the latter at low speeds. At first glance, a high-speed engine seems like a good idea, since it can conveniently be tucked away in the bilge, while the weight saved can go into the keel, but a closer look is less encouraging. An engine running at, say, 3,600 rpm not only has twice as many operating cycles per hour as an engine running at 1,800 rpm, but the thermal and mechanical stresses it experiences are greater in magnitude. Furthermore, owing to the high speeds, all moving parts must be lightly built to minimize inertial loads. Faced with this triple whammy, it is not surprising that fast engines are, on the whole, less reliable than slower ones, which are both easier on themselves and more robustly built. The basic question is the kind of service the engine is expected to provide. If it is truly an auxiliary and meant only to get the boat home on a windless Sunday afternoon, a small, fast-turning (say, 3,000 to 3,600 rpm) engine is fine; but if one would like to be able to spend long periods under power—say, in canals or during calms at sea—or would like to be able to rely on the engine in a tight spot of some kind, a low-speed (say, 1,500 to 2,000 rpm) engine is the best choice.

How powerful should the engine be? There are many variables here, but, generally speaking, about 1 hp of engine rating per 1,000 lb of displacement is the minimum that will deliver enough propulsion to make the installation worthwhile; 1½ hp per 1,000 lb will give good performance under power for sustained periods; and 2 hp per 1,000 lb is about as much as a sailboat hull can ever make use of. Too large an engine is to be avoided because fuel consumption will be high even when the engine is run slowly as well as because of its size and weight. For most boats, 1½ hp per 1,000 lb makes a good preliminary figure, to be decreased a little in the case of a narrow, easily driven hull and to be increased for a bulky one. Of course, there are not that many reliable engines to choose from, and considerations of available space may be important, so no flat advice is ever possible. But basing power on displacement seems to be more sensible in practice than trying to take specific hull characteristics into account in an involved formula.

A disproportionate share of the difficulties experienced by marine engines is due to dirt and water in the fuel. Usually the filter that comes with the engine is both inaccessible without dismantling the boat and also is so small that the filth stirred up in the tanks in a seaway is enough to choke it—unless it is of the type that simply passes on the excess to the carburetor jets or the injectors. Some experienced people prefer to have two additional filters between tanks and engine, so arranged that the feed can be switched from one to the other in the event of fouling. These filters can be placed where they can easily be reached, and the disconnected one can be cleaned and its paper or cloth element changed while fuel flows to the engine through the other—a simple and inexpensive precaution, but one that is seldom taken on new boats, though not uncommon on older vessels.

A built-in carbon dioxide fire-extinguishing system is a comforting thing to have aboard, particularly when a gasoline engine or generator is present. Such a system consists of a cylinder of liquid carbon dioxide with pipes leading to strategically placed discharge nozzles in the compartment being protected. A manual actuating line is led to some convenient spot, normally in the cockpit, and typically terminates in one of those little boxes with the reassuring inscription, "In case of fire, break glass and pull lever down." Sometimes an automatic actuator is also installed; it releases the carbon dioxide when the temperature at the sensor becomes too high or rises at too rapid a rate. Used in time, a system of this kind is most effective, and the harmless nature of the carbon dioxide means that the extinguishing process makes no mess of its own. A carbon dioxide system is not particularly cheap: the basic price for a 10-lb system, the smallest, is more than $300, to which must be added the cost of the piping and installation. A 10-lb system will protect a maximum volume of perhaps 150 ft³, and proportionately larger ones are needed when the compartment involved exceeds this volume. In the absence of watertight bulkheads that isolate the engine and tank spaces, the volume to be protected must include the entire bilge; fortunately, carbon dioxide is a heavy gas and will flood the bilge when released.

But fire, horrible as it can be, is still not as bad as explosion, and carbon dioxide systems, like other fire extinguishers, can do nothing about an explosion. Care and vigilance, or the exclusion of bottled gas and gasoline, represent the only methods of ensuring against blowing up.

The propellers used in most auxiliary-powered sailboats are solid ones whose diameter, number of blades, and the pitch and width of the blades are chosen to suit the "average" condition in which the engine will be used. Thus a boat whose engine is used almost exclusively to get in and out of harbors and in dead calms will have a narrow two-bladed propeller that can extract a relatively slow speed through the water from a small engine. At the other extreme is the virtual motor sailer, which will, more often than not, be run at a fairly high speed under power and so will have a larger, probably three-bladed propeller. The latter type of propeller offers more resistance when the boat is under sail but is more efficient; in the former case, efficiency is unimportant, but minimum resistance is vital.

What about the man who wants everything: to sail without unnecessary underwater drag, to have an extended cruising radius under power at a moderate speed, and to be able to make a fast passage of shorter length? Sometimes, especially in a vessel of moderate size, a compromise two-bladed propeller with a fairly large blade area is satisfactory, but in larger boats a variable-pitch propeller whose blades can be feathered is the near-perfect solution. The changeable pitch means that engine speed and boat speed can be matched to give maximum efficiency under all conditions, whether in calm water, in moderate winds with the engine helping the sails, or to windward in severe weather. The feathering ability means that the blades can be lined up fore and aft to give the least possible resistance (and, incidentally, make a shaft brake unnecessary). Many variable-pitch propellers are also reversible, eliminating the need for a heavy, expensive reverse-reduction gear—although there are times when an instantaneous reverse is welcome.

Variable-pitch propellers are not especially common in the United States, but they are almost universally used by Scandinavian fishermen, who find the flexibility they confer to be especially valuable. I have been aboard a number of European cruising sailboats that have such propellers, and the owners seem delighted with them.

Experiments have been conducted to determine the actual drag of propellers at various sailing speeds. Typical results with a two-bladed propeller of 12-in. diameter and 8-in. pitch showed a resistance of 43 lb with the propeller locked horizontally, 27 lb with it locked vertically in line with the deadwood, and only 1.5 lb with the blades feathered. Also, a freewheeling propeller produces more drag than one locked vertically in the deadwood. In small and medium-sized boats, the reverse gear can do this locking, but hydraulically operated gearboxes cannot, and a robust auxiliary device is needed. A good scheme is to use an automobile

(TEXT CONTINUED ON PAGE 238)

[X I V]

Three Fine Yawls:

GIRALDA, MARGAREE,

& MANUKAI

THE CLASSIC STYLE OF YACHT DESIGN IS UN-questionably one of the glories of Western culture, and three especially splendid representatives of this style are *Giralda, Margaree,* and *Manukai.* In these vessels the only straight lines are the spars; everywhere else are curves that sing, here with vigor, there with sweetness, but always harmoniously. Large enough to be swift and steady under way, small enough to be enjoyed by small crews, and, above all, handsome, these three yawls are very close to ideal. Not the least of their attractions, perhaps, is the minute gap that separates each of them from perfection, so that one can still dream of

the absolutely perfect cruising yacht without the feeling that it has quite been done before. If *Giralda*'s bow were not snubbed so abruptly (a condition for successful racing under the RORC rule, a rating formula that is the pride of the contemporary conspiracy that tries to force everything to be as ugly as possible), if *Margaree* and *Manukai* could somehow have managed flush decks despite their shoal draft— if, if, if. . . . But a good argument can be made out for letting well enough alone, since changes in plans mean delay, and who would want to put off possessing such lovelies as these?

GIRALDA

THE FIRST THING ABOUT *Giralda* that caught my eye when I saw her sailing into the harbor of Cascais was her clear flush deck, the dinghy nestled low between a nicely shaped deckhouse and the mast with the spinnaker poles chocked underneath near the center line. Next perhaps one becomes conscious of her simple, efficient masthead rig with single spreaders on main and mizzen. The forestay and running backstays are

detachable and are meant to be set up to permit double headsails when the wind gets up to Force 5 or 6. She has a roller-reefing main boom, and its sheet leads to a traveler on a track that bisects the cockpit just forward of the helmsman. The deckhouse vent so conspicuous on the drawings is less prominent in the flesh because of the adjacent main-companionway spray hood, whose height is the same.

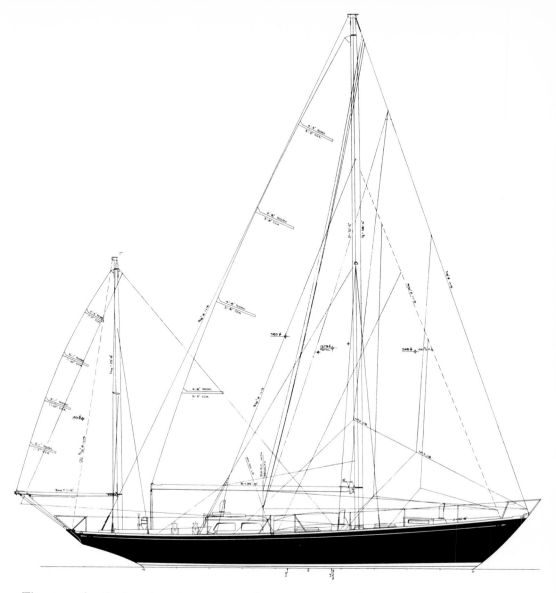

The same air of calm, elegant competence is evident below. On port side of the deckhouse is the galley, while to starboard is a chart table nearly 3 ft square with chart and instrument stowage below and a quarter berth outboard. Aft of the quarter berth is a sail locker. Oilskin stowage is not indicated, but it should be easy enough to arrange, perhaps behind the companion ladder. Underneath the deckhouse is the engine, a 47-hp Perkins diesel, which is unusually easy of access, not only through flush hatches in the deckhouse sole but also from forward through the hinged staircase that leads down to the main cabin. Just under the foot of this staircase is a reliable and large-capacity Edson diaphragm bilge pump; it is always good to see such a pump as part of a design from the very start, not just as an afterthought.

In hard weather a double-head rig is worth having. Here the lovely yawl GIRALDA, *a Sparkman & Stephens design, takes a nasty windward turn in her stride.* (Beken)

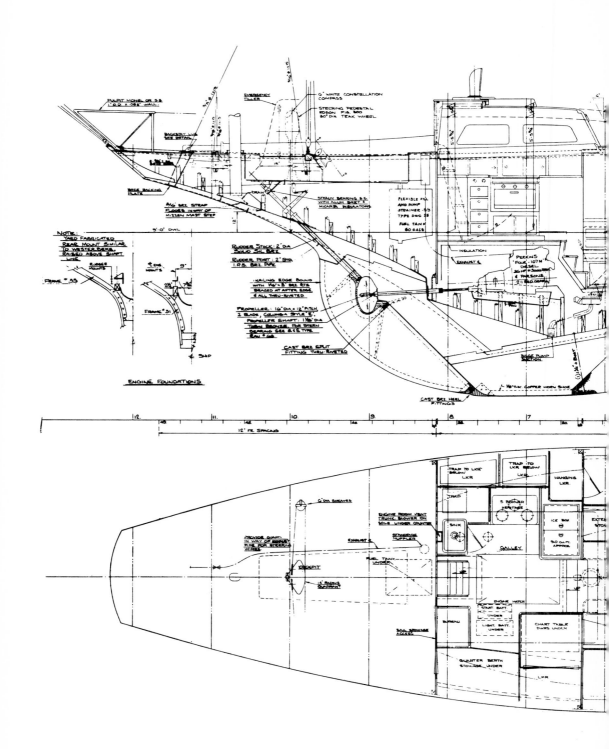

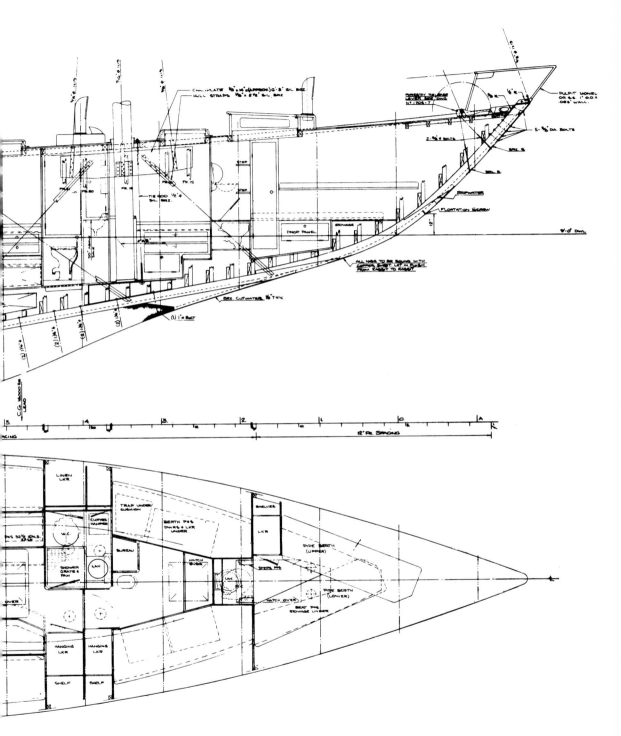

The main cabin itself is conventional, with pilot berths and extension transoms on either side of a swinging table. Forward to port is a head, and forward to starboard is a hanging locker. Then comes a comfortable double cabin with adequate stowage and a convenient seat at its forward end. As in the case of the main cabin, a Dorade vent with a transparent plastic top to its box supplements a plastic-topped hatch in furnishing light and air. Sliding curtains are fitted under both hatches to permit privacy when desired. The two-berth forepeak is isolated from the rest of the ship and can be reached only through its own companionway. The toilet facilities for the forepeak are set in a recess that projects into the double cabin, a neat arangement that adds to the habitability of the former without detracting from the spaciousness of the latter.

Giralda is a trifle heavy for her size, but her nicely shaped hull and adequate sail plan have made her Spanish owners "completely satisfied with her performance; she more than held her own when alongside other competitors [in the 1963 Fastnet], and her behavior under stress of severe weather conditions was excellent." I am certain of the latter, having seen her take a Mediterranean gale in her stride. The engine is small for a boat of this size, but not too small in view of the reduction gear, which permits a larger, more efficient propeller, the slippery hull, her handiness under sail, the additional range under power, and the accessibility of the installation. The fuel tank holds 70 gal, and the three water tanks hold a total of 175 gal, both adequate.

Giralda's accommodation is not the only one possible in such a vessel. *Jan Pott III*, a near-sister of *Giralda* in hull and rig, has a very different interior arrangement that her owner finds more to his taste. In *Jan Pott III* the deckhouse contains two extension transoms well inboard, and just forward is a small stateroom the width of the ship with quarter berths on each side that extend aft into caves outboard of the deckhouse transoms. Next are a head to port and a galley to starboard, followed by the main cabin. The hull is too narrow here for more than a single pilot berth, and by being near the middle of this cabin the mast is rather in the way. Farther forward is a small double cabin with its own head, and in the forepeak a single pipe berth just fits. *Jan Pott III* thus manages to sleep ten in five different locations, as compared with *Giralda*'s nine berths in four locations, but the additional cabin carries the price of a claustrophobic layout—worthwhile to some, not worthwhile to others.

GIRALDA

DESIGNER *Sparkman & Stephens, Inc., 79 Madison Avenue, New York City*

LOA   51 ft 11 in.

LWL   37 ft

BEAM   12 ft 6 in.

DRAFT   7 ft 10 in.

DISPLACEMENT   42,000 lb

BALLAST   17,000 lb of lead

SAIL AREA   1,279 ft^2

ENGINE   Perkins 4-107 diesel (47 hp)

FUEL   70 gal

WATER   175 gal

CONSTRUCTION   Mahogany planking on laminated-oak frames, with teak and oak centerline structure; fiberglass-covered plywood deck; spruce spars

MARGAREE

YACHTS DESIGNED BY JOHN ALDEN have always been noted for the controlled boldness of their bows, and this tradition has been carried on by his successors in the firm of John G. Alden & Co., Inc. *Margaree*'s bow is a good example: can anyone but a clod look at it without his pulse beating faster? Not every boat can live up to a bow like this, and it is a tribute to *Margaree* that the rest of her does not suffer by comparison. *Margaree* has the full, shallow hull typical of centerboarders, and a trunk cabin permits her to avoid the aesthetic disaster in

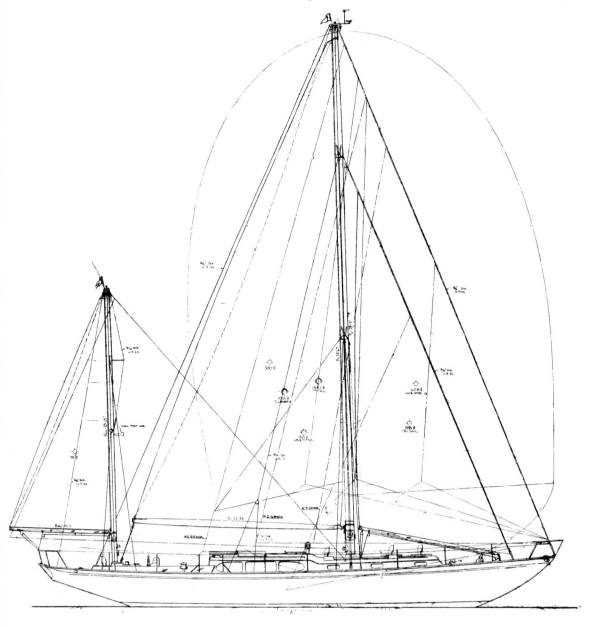

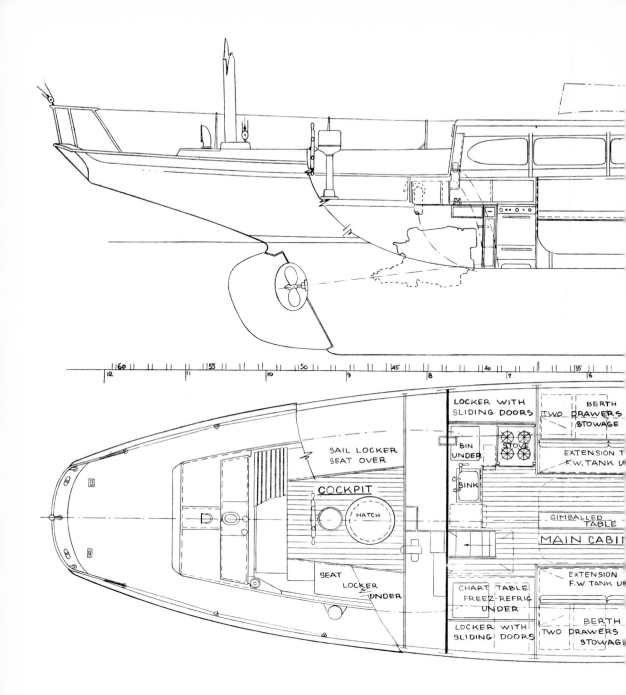

this type of hull of having sufficiently high freeboard to permit a flush deck. The slightly raised deckhouse is just right in length and position to suit the character of the boat, and it adds a touch of visual interest in place of the monotony of a long, straight cabin house. The raked masts also help *Margaree*'s looks, and the net result is a vessel that has an air of excitement about her even in repose.

The chief virtue of a centerboard is that it permits shoal draft, and *Margaree* draws only 5 ft 3 in. with her board up—about 2½ ft less

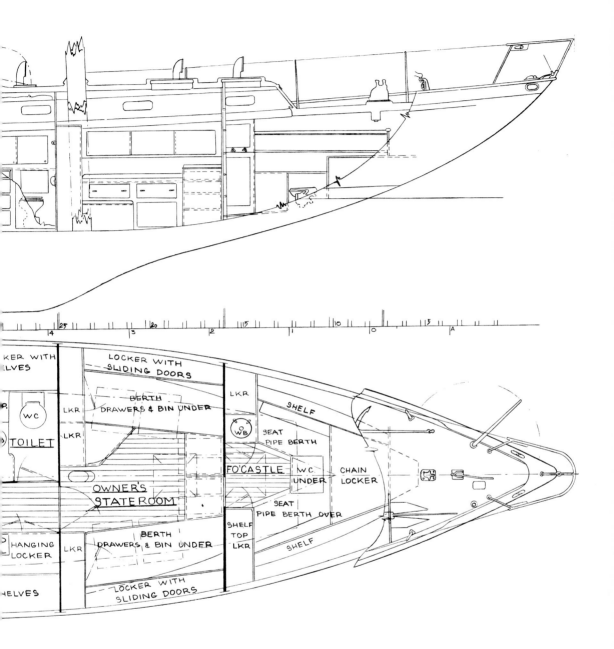

than *Giralda*, whose dimensions are otherwise comparable. *Margaree* is based in Chesapeake Bay, where a modest draft is mandatory. Such a hull is harder to push through the water than the narrower one of a deep-keel boat, and *Margaree* accordingly has a greater proportion of her sail area in the foretriangle, where it will do more good—and be harder to handle—than elsewhere. The pedestal winch on her stern is not just for decoration. As a by-product of the mainmast location, the mainsheet can lead to the after end of the cockpit without the necessity

MARGAREE *is a masthead centerboard yawl designed by John G. Alden & Co., Inc., for fast cruising. The exuberance of spirit embodied in her lines brings joy to the beholder and pain to the formulators of rating formulas for racing.* (Brignolo)

of dividing the cockpit. *Margaree* has more than enough power in the form of a 120-hp General Motors diesel, and her fuel capacity of 150 gal is not excessive for such an engine.

The accommodation, like the hull, is easy and relaxed with no sense of strain. The squalid cubbyholes of the racing boat are absent, and everybody goes first class. Aft the galley extends across the width of the boat, with the top of the refrigerator-freezer serving as a chart table. The stove has four burners on top and a large oven and broiler below; it is not gimbaled, which is hardly necessary in so stiff a vessel. The main cabin is on the same level, so the effect is of a single chamber a full 10 ft long. Pilot berths and extensions transoms flank the central table. The head is to port, with lockers across the passage from it, and forward is a luxurious double cabin. A double berth, permanent or otherwise, could readily replace the single one on the port side if desired. A solid bulkhead separates this cabin from the forepeak, which contains quarters for two men and is reached through a hatch on the cabin house.

Margaree's equipment is quite complete: pressure hot and cold water, electric head, mechanical refrigeration, automatic pilot, electric anchor windlass, radiotelephone, and so on. An Onan 3-kilowatt diesel generator is accordingly squeezed in to supplement a generator belted on the main engine. The engine and generator are housed under the cockpit, which is inevitable in a hull of this kind, and access is via a manhole in the cockpit sole. How adequate the access is cannot be told from the drawings, but it does not seem that cleaning the fuel filters or checking the oil will be especially pleasurable tasks—a slightly sour note, though it is hard to see how it could be avoided.

M A R G A R E E

DESIGNER *John G. Alden & Co., Inc., 131 State Street, Boston, Massachusetts*

LOA 54 ft 6 in.	FUEL 150 gal
LWL 36 ft 6 in.	WATER 200 gal
BEAM 13 ft 2 in.	CONSTRUCTION Honduras-mahogany-over-
DRAFT 5 ft 3 in.	cedar double planking on white-oak frames
DISPLACEMENT 42,700 lb	and center-line structure; teak decks and teak
SAIL AREA 1,340 ft^2	and mahogany deckworks; spruce spars
ENGINE General Motors 4-53 diesel (120 hp)	

MANUKAI

A VISITOR TO ENGLAND is at once struck by the absence of beauty in so many of the yachts there, a depressing sight to anyone who has seen the fleets of graceful craft to be found in America or Scandinavia. Almost alone until recently among British naval architects in his ability to draw a bold sheer, proper overhangs, sensible beam, and unobtrusive deck structures, in addition to realizing the superiority of stainless-steel and bronze fittings over rusty iron ones, Arthur Robb has many an elegant vessel to his credit. Add a passion for detail, so that

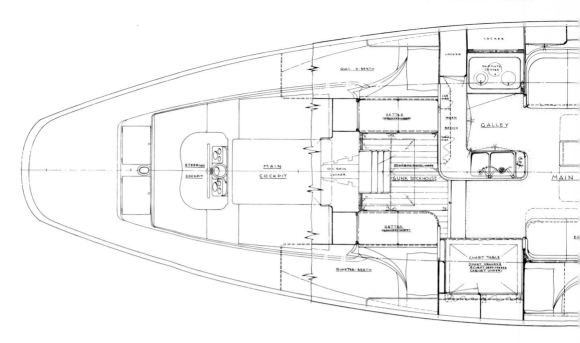

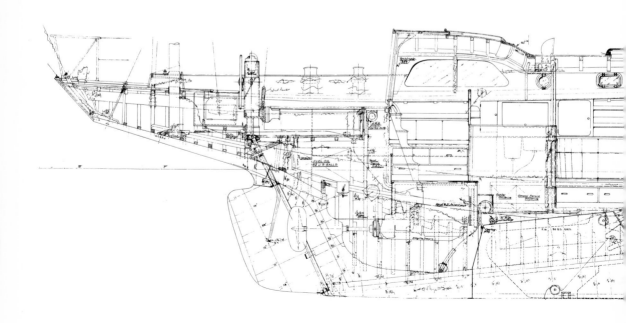

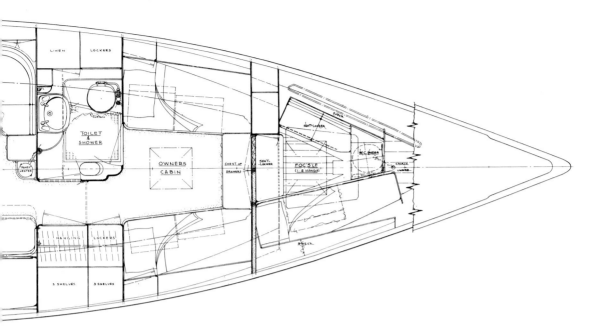

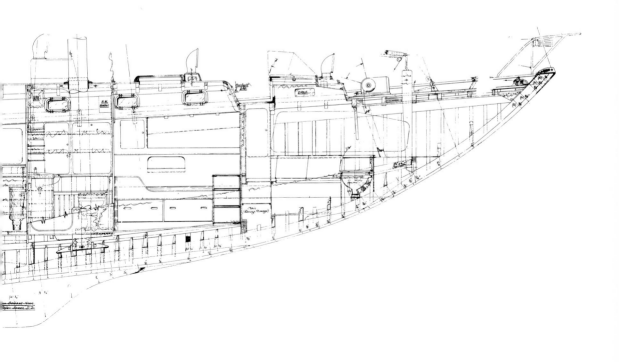

no element of a design is left to chance (or, worse, to the discretion of a landlubber builder), and it is not surprising that so distinguished a yacht as *Manukai* should have come from his drawing board.

Manukai has more than her appearance to offer: there is also a slippery hull that has benefited from her designer's tank-testing experience, a centerboard that holds her hull draft to 5 ft 6 in., a generous sail plan disposed for reasonably easy handling, an intelligent (if cramped) mechanical installation, and a comfortable and practical accommodation. The rig is high as well as large for more efficiency, and the removable forestay makes it easy to change to or from a double-headsail rig. Racing considerations are evident (though secondary) in various places, for instance in the small size and extreme aft position of the mizzen—or, as another way to look at it, the artificially short main boom. The diesel engine is fitted with a 3:1 reduction gear to permit efficient propulsion, and a cruising speed of more than 7 knots is coupled with an estimated range of 480 miles. An auxiliary shaft belted to the engine drives a generator, the pump for the hydraulic anchor windlass, the deepfreeze compressor, and bilge and deck-wash pumps, all of which have individual clutches.

The designer has referred to the accommodation as "orthodox," and while this is true in the strictest sense, it is still unusual in the careful utilization of the space available. Drawers and lockers are present in profusion; there are five fixed berths in the middle of ship that do not take up any seating space (and a grand total of ten, including a Root berth over the port main-cabin settee), a freezer of 8 ft³ capacity, and so on. The only obvious fault is the single chart drawer; surely the possession of *Manukai* will produce such hubris in her owner that she will be sailed to the ends of the earth, and more space for charts will be needed.

MANUKAI

DESIGNER *Arthur Robb, 20D New Cavendish Street, London W.1, England*

LOA 50 ft

LWL 35 ft

BEAM 13 ft 4 in.

DRAFT 5 ft 6 in. board up, 8 ft 9 in. board down

DISPLACEMENT 36,400 lb

BALLAST 8,840 lb of lead

SAIL AREA 1,212 ft²

ENGINE B.M.C. Commander diesel (50 hp)

FUEL 62 gal

WATER 170 gal

CONSTRUCTION Iroko planking on acacia frames (every fourth frame laminated), with iroko center-line structure; floors, fastenings, centerboard and case, and other metal structural elements of Everdur, Superston, or stainless steel; teak deck and trim; aluminum masts and spruce booms

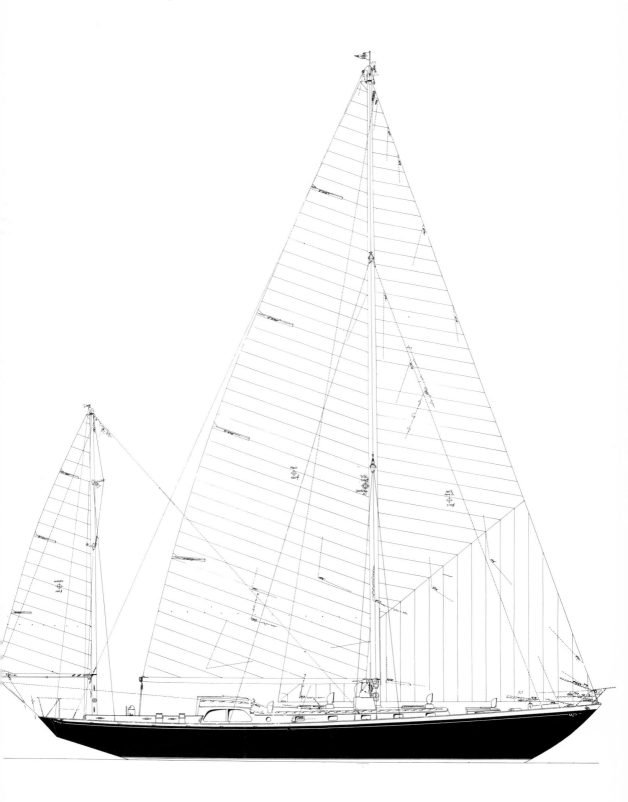

(TEXT CONTINUED FROM PAGE 222)

brakeband assembly attached to the drive shaft, which permits the shaft to be brought to a gradual stop. This can be a bother to set up and release, however, unless fitted with remote controls. I have had poor luck with such controls and have been reduced to adjusting the band directly with a miniature block-and-tackle system. A promising idea is to couple a spring-loaded brake-cylinder assembly to the oil-pressure system of the reverse gear so that starting the engine will automatically release the normally set shaft brake; but it remains to be seen how foolproof this will be in practice.

It is virtually impossible to have too much water and fuel capacity provided that the location of the tanks does not cut down the living space or stability of the boat unduly. There is no need to use all the tanks at all times, so one can enjoy the livelier performance of a lighter boat when cruising coastwise and still be able to make more ambitious voyages. With care, ½ gal of fresh water per person per day is adequate, especially if seawater is used for cooking and dishwashing. Of course, 1 gal per person per day is more comfortable, especially on long passages, when personal washing is likely to be more important than on brief trips—dishes don't mind salt water, but skin does. I cannot see a proper cruising boat without, as an absolute minimum, the ability to be self-sufficient for at least a week. This means 7 gal of water tankage per berth, and if one adds almost half that again as a reserve, the figure is 10 gal per berth. Anything less makes no sense. Actually, one can establish quite a good case for much more capacity than 10 gal per berth, a case whose merit increases with the size of the boat. I have tankage for 235 gal of water, nearly a ton, and certainly far more than I normally need. But "normally" means nothing, since one must plan for extreme situations. Seven of us used about 100 gal in crossing the Atlantic, and we were grateful for the rest afterward, even apart from its reserve aspect, because the dockside water in Scotland was a rich dark brown. The Scots said it was due to peat in the hills and was perfectly all right, but all *they* ever drank was whisky. We were still on New York water two weeks later, when we found a clear spring at Crinan.

Perhaps a better basis than number of berths for water capacity is displacement. A small boat with many berths crowded in is unlikely actually to take that many people on a cruise, while a big boat may well spend extended periods away from convenient water sources with every bunk occupied. A reasonable figure might be 8 gal per ton of displacement. Of course, if larger capacity can be built in down low, which is often possible in metal and fiberglass hulls, so much the better.

Multiple tanks are a good idea for a number of reasons. Most obvious is that in case of a failure, one has not lost all of one's fuel or water; and in any case, there is an automatic check on the rate of consumption. Also, if one must take aboard doubtful water, it can be kept separate from water of known potability; the same is true of fuel suspected of being dirty. Another advantage is that one tank at a time can be used, with the others either full or empty to minimize the free-liquid surface and so to improve the boat's stability. (In a partially full tank, the contents always move to the lee side of the boat, tending to heel it further, while the position of the center of gravity of a full tank does not change.) For the latter reason, narrow, deep tanks are preferable to broad, shallow ones—an argument in favor of keelboats, whose tanks can go in the bilge under the cabin floor.

Monel and stainless steel are the best materials for tanks. I have heard arguments favoring each over the other, but nobody questions their joint superiority. At the same time, it is worth keeping in mind that the more traditional tinned copper and galvanized steel make quite acceptable alternatives, though one has to rely to a greater extent upon the workmanship and integrity of the maker. Tinned copper is particularly good when a small tank must be fitted into an irregular space, since copper is easy to work and its relative lack of strength and stiffness is no handicap in this case. Steel tanks galvanized after fabrication may well last the life of the boat and are cheaper than Monel and stainless steel, but any flaw may have unpleasant consequences. On balance, I would say either of the latter is to be preferred in new construction, but a secondhand boat with galvanized or tinned-copper tanks in perfect condition need not be downgraded on that score.

Now that the disadvantages of the early fiberglass tanks (for instance, their inflammability and the taste they often imparted to drinking water) can be largely overcome, they may be worth considering as an alternative to metal tanks. The major point in their favor is the relative ease with which a complex form can be constructed, which permits a tank to be made to fit any vacant space in the hull. The tankage can even be integral with a fiberglass hull, and the tank walls then provide additional stiffening for the boat's structure. In such a hull, tanks can be built in along the bottom of the bilge, which adds to stability and makes use of otherwise wasted space. There is some uncertainty, though, as to how desirable integral gasoline tanks are, since there is always some possibility of rupture in the event of severe hull strain, as might occur during a grounding—a possibility that is rather remote for tanks in the bilge of a sailboat, to be sure, owing to the great strength of the hull in that region and the keel and deadwood underneath.

The unpleasant taste of water that has been stored in many fiberglass tanks is due to improper curing of the resin employed, but, one is told, this can be remedied by circulating live steam in the tank for several hours. In a boat of conventional construction, I think I would still prefer metal tanks; but in a fiberglass one, integral water and diesel-fuel tanks should be a good bet.

Regardless of the material it is made from, a tank must be strongly built with adequate baffles to prevent surging. All connections should be made through the top, and the vent pipe should be large enough to permit water or fuel to enter the tank as fast as it can be directed into the fill. Some sort of provision is necessary to check the level within; a straightforward sounding stick is perfectly good, and it should be possible to use one even if a remote-reading gauge is installed in case the latter should fail. It is good to be able to get at the interior of a tank to clean it out if necessary; fuel tanks do get full of crud at times, and water tanks sometimes have been filled with fuel. In the latter situation, merely pumping the fuel out again and flushing the tank with water is seldom adequate, especially in the unfortunate situation where the fuel is diesel oil. I blush to admit that I once put several gallons of diesel oil in a water tank, and though there were extenuating circumstances, the miserable stuff still had to be gotten out. The procedure that finally worked was to unbolt the cover plate (it seated on a rubber gasket) and wipe the tank interior out with clean cloths. In case anybody is interested, we ran out of clean cloths and finished the job with paper towels, shreds of which later clogged the check valves in the water piping. Without a removable cover plate, I suspect that the tank would have been unusable for drinking water without really heroic measures.

Another point worth keeping in mind is that all tanks should be removable

without having to rip the boat apart. There can be no guarantee that a tank, no matter how well it seems to be designed and built, will never develop a defect, so it is prudent to see that the boat is constructed so as to permit taking out each tank without having to blast.

Compact evaporators are now manufactured for yacht service that convert seawater to fresh water. The source of heat is the engine's cooling water, and the engine must be a fairly large one to furnish enough water at a high enough temperature. The key element in the evaporator is a vacuum pump that reduces the pressure in the raw-water chamber until the boiling point is in the neighborhood of only 125°F. The vapor is then separated from any water droplets to assure purity and is condensed. The smallest evaporator weighs about 55 lb, costs about $1,500 for DC operation, and yields 9 gal of water per hour. While it can hardly replace adequate tankage—there are too many links of uncertain reliability in the chain—an evaporator may well have value in a supplementary role in a boat whose crew is accustomed to the lavish use of water, which has a large engine in regular operation, and whose owner has nothing better to do with his money.

Once upon a time, electricity in a sailboat was looked upon with suspicion, and only the most foolhardy would fit, for example, electric running lights. After many a night of vainly trying to keep lit kerosene running lights that were carried, according to the approved practice of not so long ago, on boards clamped to the shrouds, I cannot understand why electric running lights were not joyously welcomed a couple of generations back. But, then, so many things remain mysterious, such as the aversion to winches as opposed to tackles that one sometimes still finds. At any rate, even the humblest sailboat today employs electrical equipment of various kinds, and the only problem for discussion is exactly where the power should come from.

Any vessel large enough to have a permanent auxiliary engine should have two independent batteries, one exclusively for starting the engine and the other for everything else. A voltmeter for indicating the degree of charge of each battery is also highly desirable. I myself use Chargicators, but other kinds are also good. Then one always knows the state of one's batteries and whether they are being properly charged when the engine is on. Of course, a hydrometer reveals the former information, and an ammeter reveals the latter—but how often is one likely to use a hydrometer, and how is it possible to tell from an ammeter only whether the charging rate at any time is inadequate or excessive? My Chargicators are located in a conspicuous place in the deckhouse, so I always know the condition of my batteries without having to think about the matter consciously.

Another imperative is a big master switch for each battery. If both batteries have the same voltage, a switch can be used that is able to transfer the starting load to the other battery if this should be necessary, but a pair of heavy cables with spring clips on their ends (most automobile supply houses have them) is adequate for the rare occasions when such a transfer is required. The master switches should

[OPPOSITE] *The 46=ft Sparkman & Stephens-designed centerboard ketch* ANTILLES *has a small cabin tucked away in the stern without spoiling her appearance. A roomy, solidly built ship,* ANTILLES *has made many offshore passages in safety and comfort.* (Rosenfeld)

be near the companionway, since they will be the first things turned on when coming aboard and the last turned off when leaving.

On a small boat the generator supplied with the engine is adequate for both batteries, being used in turn to charge them as they need it. Past an over-all boat length of 35 ft or so, however, the load due to the additional lights and electrical accessories that inevitably accumulate makes another generator desirable. An excellent system is to use the ordinary small engine generator for the starting battery and to belt on an alternator for the other battery. The virtue of an alternator is that its power output is approximately independent of engine speed, so one can get a healthy charging rate with the engine idling. These days, alternators are in wide use on cars, which has brought their price down to a reasonable level.

The problems of a boat that is equipped with such power eaters as electric windlasses, pressure-water systems, and refrigerators are less easy to solve. A large enough generator can always go on the main engine—and, indeed, it should—but it is not much fun to run the engine, even at an idle, for an hour or two every day when living aboard at anchor or at a dock that does not have electricity for a shore charger. And the fuel consumption becomes no joke on a long cruise in remote waters (which is where long cruises should take place). In sailboats under perhaps 45 ft long overall, there is seldom room for a separate charging plant; and if one insists on a water-cooled diesel plant, the minimum length of the boat jumps to, say, 55 ft overall. Of course, how much of a problem is involved depends upon how the boat is used; certainly a coastwise cruiser is likely to use its engine in calms and to get in and out of harbors often enough to keep the batteries charged. I myself now have a very nice Petter air-cooled diesel generator that fits easily in my 58-ft ketch, but it is noisy even with a water-cooled exhaust.

Another possibility with attractive features is a small portable gasoline generator that would be used only in emergencies. Drained of fuel, the generator could be safely stored below, though it would have to be used on deck. I once had a 750-watt generator of this kind that was small and light and quite reliable, but it was a noisy beast and had to be bolted down on an asbestos pad because of its, vibration and high operating temperature. With a muffler and a robust removable base, I think such a portable generator might be an interesting proposition as an auxiliary.

Sooner or later, some water will find its way into the bilge of every boat, even if it is merely rainwater blown into the companionway or a dollop of spray coming in through an open portlight. A few strokes on the bilge pump and all is well for another week or two. But sometimes the volume of water to be dealt with is not so trifling. Even if the hull remains tight, a loose hose in the engine's cooling system or a broken deckhouse window in a severe storm can lead to a lot of water that must be pumped out quickly. Situations can occur in which an efficient pump means the difference between losing and saving the vessel, and the toys that one sees at boat shows, for all their chrome plating and elegant styling, just do not belong on a seagoing boat. There is simply no substitute for a large-capacity manual diaphragm pump, such as those made by Edson, by Munser, Sims, and by Henderson, which not only requires less effort to lift a given amount of water but also is virtually clogproof. Such a pump should be bolted down in an accessible place and should exhaust through a sea cock—perhaps one through which a cockpit scupper already

(TEXT CONTINUED ON PAGE 257)

[X V]

Two Large Cutters:

ANGANTYR & PAZIENZA

AGREAT DEAL OF THOUGHT HAS GONE INTO each of these two yachts, and while both owners felt that the answer to their needs lay in flush-deck cutters 45 ft on the waterline and 60 ft overall, with sail areas of somewhat more than 1,600 ft², the resulting vessels are quite different from each other. From a glance at their respective plans, it will come as no surprise that *Angantyr* is meant for world cruising, including rounding Cape Horn, while *Pazienza* is intended for service mainly in the Mediterranean. Because *Angantyr* and *Pazienza* represent specific design concepts carried to their logical conclusions, with attention to comfort and convenience but without cost being a major factor, they are exceptionally interesting vessels, and much can be learned from them of value in planning more modest craft.

ANGANTYR

Angantyr WAS DESIGNED by MacLear & Harris for James W. Crawford, an experienced yachtsman who had already circumnavigated the world in the 60-ft Alden gaff schooner *Dirigo II*. With her mast amidships, *Angantyr* is with justice referred to by her owner as a "one-masted schooner." The designers have been kind enough to provide a complete description of *Angantyr*: "The mast was stepped aft for several reasons. First, to reduce the size of the mainsail and provide a divided rig in a craft with only one mast. Secondly, midships is near the widest point of the vessel and therefore the mast can be more easily stayed. Thirdly, a mast stepped this far aft is in a drier and quieter portion of the craft, where there is less pitching motion and where halyards can be handled more easily.

"The tandem centerboards permit the boat to be given zero helm, weather helm or lee helm. They can be trimmed to balance under various sail arrangements and on various points of sailing. With the forward board down and the after board up, the craft is expected to be able to tack with the staysail alone. The reason for the balanced rudder is that it will give a greater steering force with less effort from the helmsman, and will permit the craft to heave to under power without any forward motion. The large propeller driven through a 2½:1 gear will provide a large flow of water over this relatively larger rudder, thus keeping the vessel's stern such that the bow will remain head to wind, again with the help of the forward board in a down position.

"Another unusual feature of this design is that the two centerboards are extremely strong, being made of two-inch steel plate. The centerboard trunk is also of two-inch steel plate. While this is four to eight times thicker than the

trunks will permit the craft to anchor in shallow, sheltered water by simply lowering the boards onto the bottom. This will probably be more of a stunt than of practical value. Since the craft only draws five feet six inches, the heavy boards in the lowered position will also have a stabilizing effect and stiffen the boat.

"Still another unusual feature is that *Angan-*

A model of ANGANTYR's *hull. In the past, most boats were designed by first shaping a model and then taking the lines from it. Even today, models are useful for appraising hull form both by eye and, with greater accuracy (and expense), by towing with proper instrumentation in a tank.*

customary thickness of centerboard trunks, it was deemed worth while since it would permit the vessel to be grounded rather severely without doing damage to either the trunk or the boards. Furthermore, the craft needs ballast down low and the weight of steel replaces the weight that would have to be there in the form of lead otherwise. Incidentally, the enormous strength in the centerboards and centerboard

tyr's flush deck is carried right aft, there being no cockpit for the helmsman or the afterguard. This provides an unobstructed working platform and excellent visibility for the helmsman. Clamp down seating will be provided by the owner after the boat is built. The navigating area is very accessible from the deck, being only three steps down and to starboard in a navigator's tweendeck. The skipper or navigator

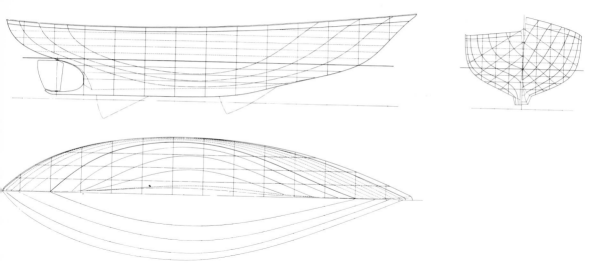

can sleep on the starboard bunk in the navigating area with his legs under the chart table, and can sit up and look at the chart when he so desires.

"One feature about which Mr. Crawford is adamant is centerline hatches. He does not believe that any hatch on a craft going offshore should be far from the centerline because of the possibility of knockdowns and flooding. For this reason, all deck openings are near the centerline.

"Below decks, we note a long gimbaled table, which does not obstruct passage fore and aft. On the port side is a powerful 150 watt two-way radio in a special radio nook. The owner's stateroom, aft, has ample privacy. The athwartship double berth was requested by the owner, who favors this arrangement and points out that Irving Johnson with his tremendous experience off shore also used this arrangement in his personal yacht, the newest *Yankee*. There is a vanity for the skipper's wife and the bathroom

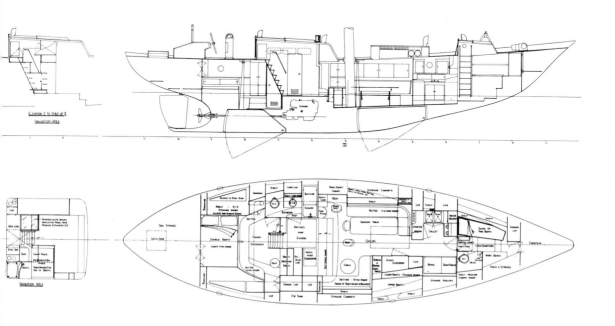

has both a bathtub and shower. The forepeak has a work bench as well as a washing machine and a single pipe berth. The guest stateroom on the starboard side provides privacy and has an upper and lower bunk.

"The cutter's cruising range under power is over 3,000 miles and the water tank is generous. Three independent water catchments can be used. When underway the mainsail drains into a groove on the upper side of the boom which carries the water forward to the tack where a threaded hole through the boom can be attached to a hose which leads into one of the water tanks. Another catchment area is the top of the doghouse which has a rail built around it and drainage at the forward corners. The third catchment area is the full deck of the vessel, which can trap water that drains directly into the catchment tank. With these three catchments, and tankage for 623 gallons in three separate tanks, the craft should be fairly independent from shore facilities when this is required. The owner states that in areas where he cruises, the rainfall is usually adequate.

"*Angantyr*'s rig differs somewhat from the average modern ocean racer and cruiser in that she will not carry large overlapping genoas, her overlapping sails being primarily for reaching. Since she will never be strapped down with these overlapping headsails, the chain plate breadth is very wide and the spreaders were made somewhat larger than is customary. The large jumpers were provided to obviate the use of running backstays on a craft which will often be sailed long distances, shorthanded. Rungs are provided on both sides of the mast so that a man can readily go aloft to the lower spreaders. The climbing position is straddling the mast while facing aft.

"The staysail has a deep set of reef points so that as the wind freshens, one does not have to drag up a new smaller sail and take off the one that is hanked on, but, rather, simply lower the staysail and tie in a reef. This operation will be relatively easy because the headsail is further aft than is customary where the craft is widest.

"Since the passages which Crawford usually takes are done in the same direction as prevailing winds, much thought was given to the handy downwind rig. For this reason, a downwind sail plan was drawn which depicts all sails which can be used off the wind. This includes two strong downwind staysails, which hoist on their own stays. These stays are set up once the craft is in steady winds, such as the North East Trades. The sails are hanked on these stays and outhauled to the poles that are set out on their own topping lift, fore guy, and after guy. Thus when it is necessary to shorten down in a following squall, the sail can be dropped and inhauled by one man without touching the spinnaker poles. When the squall has passed the sail can be hoisted and the clew outhauled to the pole end by one man.

"In a downward passage, if the wind becomes too light for the two downwind staysails, one increases sail area by dropping the leeward staysail and in its stead hoists a larger headsail on the head stay. Such a sail can be sheeted to either the end of the main boom or to the spinnaker poles. These poles, as can be noted from the sail plan, are housed topped up along the mast most of the time, and thus do not need to be picked up off the deck and placed in their sockets, but, rather, simply lowered and a fore and after guy rigged. In a long passage to windward these could of course be unshipped from the mast and housed on the deck. The owner, however, states that he seldom takes passages that require much windward work, but would rather follow the winds of the world, as he often has done in the past. When the designers discussed tacking with the owner, he pointed out that on the trips that he takes, he only tacks once every three days.

"The two dories forward are nested to con-

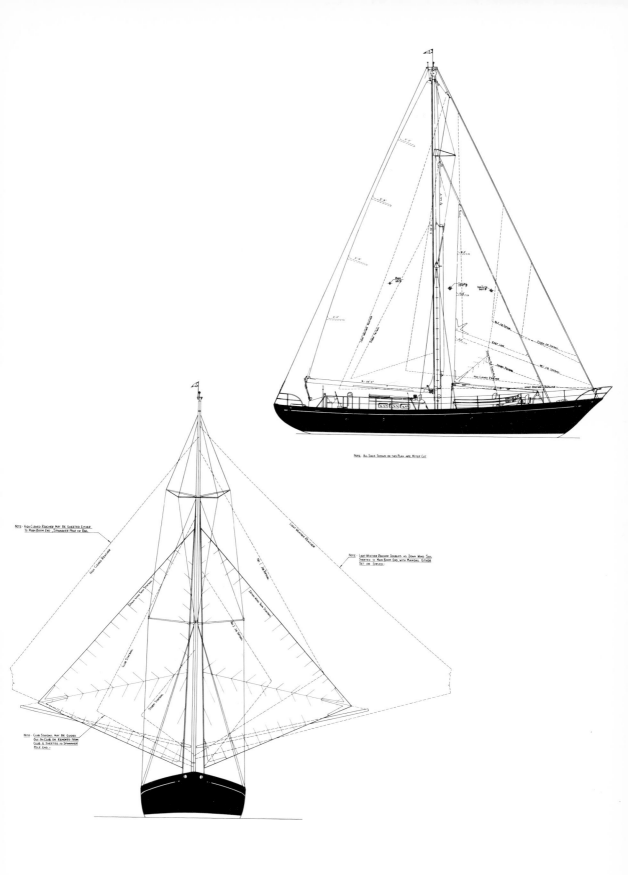

NOTE: All Sails Shown on this Plan are Mitre Cut

NOTE: High Clewed Reacher may be Sheeted either to Main Boom End, Spinnaker Pole or Rail.

NOTE: Light Weather Reacher Doubles as Down Wind Sail Sheeted to Main Boom End, with Mainsail either Set or Girled.

NOTE: Club Staysail may be Guided Out on Club or Removed from Club & Sheeted to Spinnaker Pole End.

ANGANTYR *being launched. The product of much experience and thought, this 60-ft MacLear & Harris-designed cutter has many splendid features. Immediately apparent is the fact that she is no toy: the high bulwarks, pulpits and gallows of large-diameter tubing, heavy anchors, stout roller for the anchor chain, and massive forestaysail-boom pedestal leave no doubt on this score. But for all* ANGANTYR's *robust gear and construction, she is still a graceful boat, proof that flimsiness is not essential for beauty in a yacht.*

serve space. This form of craft was chosen because both the owner and the designers have found that the dory is the best craft for going through the surf in areas where no docks exist.

The small dory on top will be fitted with a centerboard as a sailing dory, while the larger dory will be fitted with an outboard and oars.

"Another way in which this craft differs from

the average ocean racer or ocean cruiser which is intended for local waters and occasional ocean races is that *Angantyr* has heavier ground tackle than is customary. While nylon is very convenient for the use of 99 percent of all yachts, in the case of *Angantyr,* which will be lived on all year round, and have to spend much of her time lying to her own anchor rather than to a mooring, stout chain and heavy ground tackle become far more important. For this reason the craft shall have two anchors of 212 pounds each as well as the usual light Danforths and lunch hooks. The owner required that the capstan be strong enough to pull up 30 fathoms of chain, hanging straight down.

"The craft has a canoe stern because double enders can heave to stern to the wind better than transom stern vessels. Also they tend to be better steerers off the wind and in quartering seas. The balanced rudder, aside from having the advantages already listed, has a further point in its favor. While on a boat of this size, the turns of the wheel, hard over to hard to over, might normally be three turns, on the *Angantyr,* they are only two. This could normally cause a very stiff wheel that is hard to turn because of the large force and poor mechanical advantage afforded the helmsman, but in the case of the balanced rudder, the forward part of the rudder assists the helmsman put the rudder over because of the counterbalancing forward rudder area. It was estimated that with two turns hard over to hard over, and assistance from the water force, a helmsman could keep the craft on course more easily without turning the wheel so far. In other words, one or two spokes of the wheel would give the boat considerably more rudder angle than is customary on a craft of this size.

"The larger aperture for the propeller has several purposes: one is that a boat with as long a lateral plane as *Angantyr* has, and with two centerboards placed far apart, would tend to remain on a straight course, be slow in stays, and have a large turning radius. The cutaway skeg relieves these tendencies because the open area aft permits the stern to swing freely in answer to rudder commands. Another reason for the larger aperture is that a propeller operates more efficiently with free unobstructed water and no obstruction before or aft of it. Since *Angantyr* will go on long voyages and will sometimes cross calm portions of the ocean and will always want to maintain a speed of over 5 knots, it is anticipated that she will use her engine for extended periods of time. It is desired to increase the efficiency of the propeller by first making it large and secondly permitting it to operate in free water. The relatively large reduction gear of $2\frac{1}{2}$:1 makes possible a large propeller which is efficient under power. A custom built Hyde type propeller (folding) with three blades will feather under sail."

ANGANTYR

DESIGNER   *MacLear & Harris, 366 Madison Avenue, New York City*

LOA   60 ft 8 in.

LWL   45 ft

BEAM   17 ft 3 in.

DRAFT   5 ft 4 in. board up, 7 ft 10 in. board down

DISPLACEMENT   70,000 lb

SAIL AREA   1,647 ft²

ENGINE   Caterpillar D311 diesel (75 hp)

FUEL   1,120 gal

WATER   623 gal

CONSTRUCTION   Steel hull

PAZIENZA

WITH CAP FERRAT INSTEAD OF CAPE HORN IN mind, *Pazienza* is rather different from *Angantyr,* but no less care has gone into her planning. According to Laurent Giles & Partners, her designers, *Pazienza* is a "good example of a comfortable shorthanded cruising boat with a first class performance under power yet able to take part successfully in ocean races." *Pazienza* has a tall, efficient rig, its area almost equally divided between foretriangle and main-

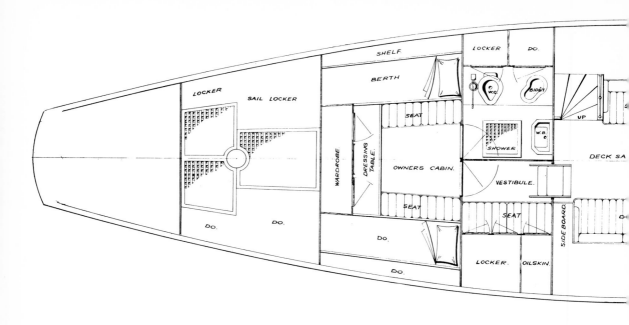

LOCKER

SAIL LOCKER

DO.

DO.

DO.

DO.

SHELF

BERTH

WARDROBE

DRESSING TABLE

SEAT

OWNERS CABIN.

SEAT

DO.

LOCKER

DO.

W.C.

BIDET

SHOWER

W.B.

VESTIBULE.

UP

DECK SA

SIDE BOARD

SEAT

LOCKER.

OILSKIN

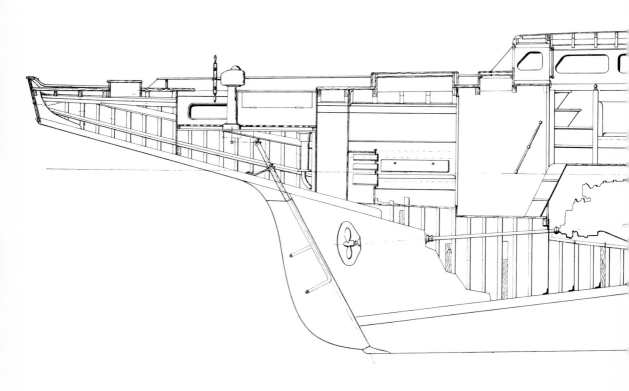

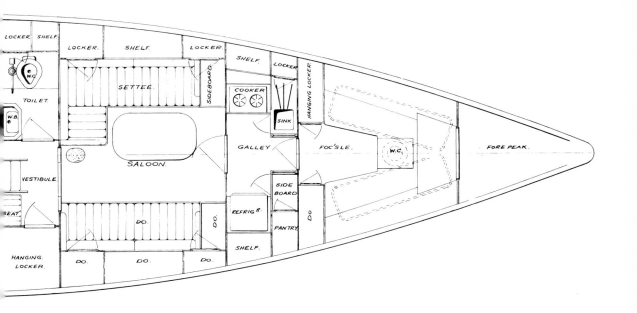

LOCKER. SHELF.   LOCKER.   SHELF.   LOCKER.   SHELF.   LOCKER.   FORE PEAK.

W.C.

TOILET.

W.B.

SIDEBOARD

COOKER

SINK

HANGING LOCKER

SETTEE

SALOON.

GALLEY

FOC'SLE.

W.C.

VESTIBULE.

SEAT.

DO.

DO.

REFRIG.

SIDE BOARD

DO.

HANGING. LOCKER.

DO.

DO.

DO.

SHELF.

PANTRY

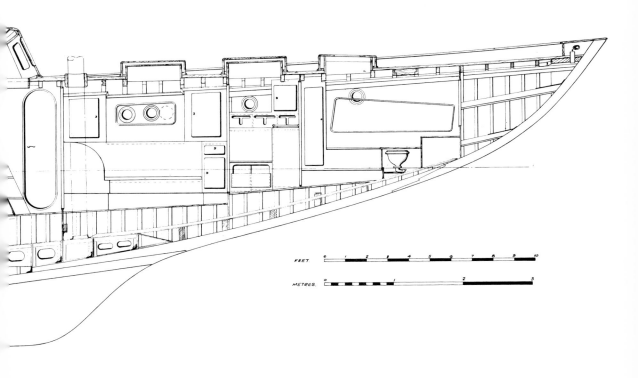

FEET. 0 1 2 3 4 5 6 7 8 9 10

METRES. 0 1 2 3

sail, and with her moderate beam and displacement, she should be a fast boat on and off the wind—and an easy one to handle as well, thanks to the clear foredeck and generous gap betwen jibstay and forestay.

No attempt has been made in *Pazienza* to crowd in as many berths as could possibly fit, and in consequence the accommodation abounds in stowage space and features that contribute to the good life afloat. One descends from the deck via a curved stairway, a welcome touch of elegance that also avoids cutting into the after head and vestibule, to find oneself in a compact deckhouse with visibility in all directions. Aft to starboard is a short passage with a seat and lockers behind it, just right for wrestling with oilskins and seaboots—or cloaks and pumps. To port is a roomy head that includes a shower and a bidet, and farther aft is the owner's cabin—though any such quarters

with separate seats should really be called a stateroom. Forward of the deckhouse is another little vestibule, also with a convenient seat and lockers, and there is a head to port. The main cabin is unconventional for a boat of this size in that pilot berths are absent; an occasional pair of guests can be taken care of, but no more. The galley is small, as is usual in Mediterranean boats, and there is a forward cabin for two hands with its own head. Ports in the hull as well as skylights help to keep the interior light and airy.

Told that so imposing a vessel as *Pazienza* basically accommodates two, most people would no doubt react with a certain degree of horror, which is all the more tribute to her owner and designers for declining to compromise the quite correct dictionary definition of a yacht as a "sailing vessel for private pleasure."

PAZIENZA

DESIGNER *Laurent Giles & Partners, Ltd., 4 Quay Hill, Lymington, England*

LOA   59 ft 2 in.
LWL   44 ft 10 in.
BEAM   13 ft 11 in.
DRAFT   8 ft 10 in.
DISPLACEMENT   58,000 lb
SAIL AREA   1,670 ft²

ENGINE   Scripps six-cylinder diesel
FUEL   125 gal
WATER   310 gal
CONSTRUCTION   Teak planking on acacia frames, with oak center-line structure; teak deck and deckworks; spruce spars

(TEXT CONTINUED FROM PAGE 242)

drains, in order to minimize through-hull fittings. The intake should be via a hose, so that the strainer at the end can be lifted out in case it is blocked.

Two pumps are desirable, and the prudent man will supplement his diaphragm pump with a mechanical pump belted on his main engine. Rubber impellers disintegrate rapidly when they turn in the absence of water, which means either a clutch on the pump or a small auxiliary intake so that there is always a little seawater passing through it. Both schemes work, but the former has the advantage that one can more readily keep track of how much water the boat is making.

What about an electric bilge pump? A small one seems to me worthless, since it cannot do much about a serious influx of water, while the manual pump that must be aboard anyway can cope with minor accumulations. It is just something else to give trouble—without being all that wonderful at its chosen job. A large-capacity electric pump is fine provided that its load is not too great for the batteries; if one must run the engine to provide power for the pump, it makes more sense to belt a still larger pump onto the engine directly. I think an electric pump is perfectly splendid when it can also be used to furnish seawater under pressure for such tasks as washing down the deck and getting the mud off the anchor and chain as they come aboard. In fact, even with adequate bilge pumps, I would fit an electric deck-wash pump if there is a chain anchor rode, because the amount of mess that chain can bring aboard is truly remarkable.

CHAPTER EIGHT

The Accommodation

WHAT YACHTSMAN HAS NEVER seen a wet, tired, hungry, and generally bedraggled party stagger ashore, barely able to reach the club bar yet full of praise for their staunch vessel? What they really mean is that they are grateful to have made port alive and that nothing could get them back aboard until they have restored themselves to human condition on dry land. In a proper cruising boat, such a state of affairs need never develop. Such a boat is kind enough to its crew so that they arrive wherever they are going in good shape and, second but no less important, is able to take care of their needs after the passage as well as during it. I have not called this chapter "The Cabin" because the noun has a cold, utilitarian sound to me, which is reinforced by its formal definition: "small rude dwelling; room or compartment in a ship for sleeping or eating in." I prefer the warmer, softer word "accommodation," which my dictionary defines with such terms as "convenience," "compromise," and "adaptation of anything to a purpose." One can hardly expect more of a cabin than that it keep the rain out, but an accommodation should provide much more: warmth, comfort, food, dry clothing, privacy; a fireplace and a liquor locker; books and chessmen, fiddles and flutes.

[OPPOSITE] BELMORE *was designed by Aero Marine of Emsworth, England, for offshore racing under both American and British rating rules, and perhaps for this reason is a sturdy, wholesome craft with character as well as speed. Her dimensions are LOA 36 ft 4 in., LWL 26 ft 6 in., beam 9 ft 6 in., and draft 5 ft 11½ in., and her sail area is a trifle over 600 ft². Below,* BELMORE *is conventionally arranged, with a double cabin forward, an enclosed head, pilot berths on both sides of the main cabin, a quarter berth aft to starboard with a chart table over and the galley to port. All this seems a lot in a 36-footer, but* BELMORE *has a transom stern, which means that she is, in effect, a larger boat than her overall length indicates, and there is no bridge deck between cockpit and cabin house, thereby enlarging the available space in the accommodation. (Beken)*

The fact that much—probably most—serious cruising is done in boats with inadequate accommodations for the purpose is simultaneously a tribute to the joys of cruising and a reminder that one cannot wholly delegate the responsibility for planning a boat if one is to get what one wants. The manner in which a boat is to be cruised is the basic factor in establishing the most suitable accommodation scheme. However, to make the point once more, what should count most here is the vision in one's heart, not the vulgar reality of the moment. A splendid hull fitted out as a housewife's delight but incapable of sustaining its crew on a night at sea is a pathetic thing, a bad joke that represents the symbolic emasculation of its owner. Far better to have the kind of vessel that needs only two hours spent at the grocery before one sets out on a passage beyond the horizon; everything good in this world has its start in a dream, and a proper cruising yacht is no exception.

Perhaps the first aspect of the accommodation to consider is the type and placement of the berths. Harbor berths and sea berths have different requirements: roominess and privacy are important in port; at sea, security and minimum motion take precedence. It is seldom possible to arrange matters so that every berth is comfortable (or even tenable) both in a norther in the Gulf Stream and tied up at Nassau Yacht Haven later on, but it *is* possible to have berths uncomfortable in both situations, and care is needed to prevent the latter.

The conflict between one's needs at sea and in port is most difficult to resolve in smaller boats. In a boat 30 to 35 ft long overall, the usual scheme is to have two berths in a tiny forward cabin, with the galley nestling under a bridge deck aft; the main cabin and an enclosed head are in the middle of the boat. This represents the most that can be done for harbor convenience in a boat of that size, since two separate compartments are provided. Under way, however, the two berths forward can be absolute hell, and I have always preferred to bed down on the main-cabin sole rather than face that particular imitation of tumbling over Niagara Falls in a barrel. Another possibility is to have two quarter berths flanking the companion-way, next forward the galley, then the two settees that constitute the "main cabin," and finally an enclosed forepeak that contains the head. Here, provided that the quarter berths are properly protected from spray, all four berths can be used in the worst weather, but there is little privacy.

I think no decent compromise is possible in boats under perhaps 35 ft long overall, which is one of the reasons why I do not regard such boats as "proper" for cruising in the sense in which I have been using the word. A 35-footer normally has enough beam (say, 9 ft) to allow a permanent "pilot" berth outboard of a settee in the main cabin, which means that two people can sack out there and still leave room for others to sit down. And it is beginning to be large enough so that at times the forward berths can be occupied under way. Few boats of this size can afford pilot berths on both sides without being cramped, and the illusion of spaciousness is worth having.

In a boat somewhere between 38 and 42 ft long overall and with a beam of at least 10½ ft, two permanent pilot berths can be fitted in reasonably well, which makes life at sea much pleasanter. Also, perhaps by accepting a smaller galley or a smaller forward cabin, a quarter berth can be squeezed in. I feel that this is worth doing if it does not mean the sacrifice of a decent oilskin locker, which a vessel of this size deserves. The chart table can hinge down over the forward end of the berth or can even be permanently installed there if there is enough space left to get into the berth. If the main companionway is offset toward the quarter berth, the galley will be large enough; in fact, the cook may well benefit from having a compact domain independent of the navigator (and vice versa). The skipper who stands out of watch will find such a quarter berth just what he needs; it is convenient to the cockpit and is a comfortable hole of his own that he can climb in and out of without disturbing the off watch.

The usual—and usually justified—argument against quarter berths is that they are difficult to keep dry. While the difficulty is certainly there, I do not think that it is an impossible goal, and I would not give up the idea of one or two quarter berths on that ground. The simplest expedient is to install a heavy waterproof curtain to keep the spray out. It may be necessary virtually to seal off the side of the berth with such a curtain, in which case the bulkhead at the forward end of the berth should be cut away for ventilation. A better argument against quarter berths is that they may prevent having cockpit sail lockers of adequate size. Such lockers are valuable, and if two quarter berths would mean minute lockers, it might be better to compromise and have only one quarter berth plus one big locker.

A possibility sometimes worth considering is a pair of fixed pilot berths with narrow settees below them that do not extend and are not meant for sleeping on. A settee not much over 1 ft wide can be comfortable to sit and lounge on if it is tipped up inboard at just the right angle and if the panel behind is tilted outboard at a smaller but also fairly critical angle. In this way a vessel whose beam is only 9 to 10 ft can have two really good berths in the best part of the ship, and these berths can be used without the occupants getting in the way. The penalty, of course, may be claustrophobia, but a clever color scheme and enough light can sometimes make the arrangement acceptable.

A different scheme is to have a full-sized settee on one or both sides as the senior partner and a fold-out pilot berth above it. The latter is often hardly more than an upper berth set a trifle outboard, and since it must overlap the settee, neither provides much headroom, and the settee will be uncomfortable for sitting when the upper is in place. One sees this bastard arrangement in many stock boats; it permits their makers to claim an ability to sleep six or eight or forty people in boats that should have been laid out for two or three, but if carefully worked out they may be satisfactory.

When the waterline of the yacht is perhaps 32 ft or more, a good deal of flexibility is possible in planning the interior. One can have a separate after cabin, or quarter berths and an especially splendid galley and navigation nook, or an elongated main cabin with two pilot berths end to end on each side, or a decent double cabin forward of the main cabin and a small but habitable compartment still further forward, and so on. With a beam of 13 to 14 ft, one can even divide the ship longitudinally with separate compartments on each side of the ship. The problem here—and a delightful one it is—is how best to use all this volume.

Two extreme positions on layout are sometimes espoused—the open layout and what I can only call the tourist-class layout. In the open layout, the vessel is one big chamber with, at most, only partial bulkheads from one end to the other. I have sailed in an old 12-meter that was completely open below except for the head, an arrangement adopted, of course, to make the hull as light as possible and, as a secondary benefit, to permit stopping up headsails rapidly down below. It was very pleasant for racing and made the gloom produced by a flush deck without ports in deck or hull quite bearable, but the almost total lack of privacy and the inability to shut oneself away from the world for a quick snooze were decided drawbacks. I doubt that anybody would ever build so extreme an interior in a cruising boat, but some pretty close approximations do exist. The feeling of spaciousness is very nice, but, after all, merely going on deck once in a while should moderate any feelings of being trapped.

At the opposite end of the spectrum is an accommodation set up to provide the greatest possible number of separate cabins. It is surprising how many of these can be worked in if full advantage is taken of sliding doors and the various overlaps possible. In Visby Harbor I once visited a 57-ft Polish yawl owned by a Stettin sailing club that sported seven separate enclosed double cabins—with a pair of settees left over. The galley, head, and chart table were not skimped, either. So it can be done, and I trust that the boat's designer got whatever reward is given for exceeding his assigned norm, but I doubt that the requirements of a club yacht and that of a personal cruising yacht are closely related.

When a third full cabin becomes possible, the principal choice is between an after cabin and a deckhouse. Each is very nice in its own way, but while one can have either in a vessel that is 32 ft on the waterline, a much larger craft is needed for both. The big advantage of an after cabin is that it is isolated from the rest of the ship: nobody eats there, navigates there, walks through it, or dumps wet jibs down its hatch. It is an oasis of peace and quiet and comfort and privacy. Some sailors I know disapprove of after cabins on the grounds that they "waste" space by having only one function, but to me this is their great virtue. It is usually possible to have a head and washbasin in the smallest after cabin, even if not in a separate compartment of their own, and they are well worth having.

The criterion for a proper deckhouse, as opposed to what is merely the raised after end of the cabin trunk, is the presence of at least one permanent seat—or, better, a pair of them. These need not be long enough to serve as berths, particularly if they are inboard of quarter berths, but should be wide enough to seat at least two people—say, 3 ft as a minimum. A proper deckhouse is also where the chart table, chart drawers, radiotelephone, direction finder, and stowage space for sextant, chronometer, and navigation books all belong; where one can go for a respite from the wet and cold outside without disturbing the watch below; where true sailors have their rum while the martini crowd swills its poison in the main cabin. In some boats a deckhouse is the logical solution to a big engine, which can be housed in comfort and, one hopes, accessibility beneath large soundproof and smellproof hatches. A deckhouse that is just forward of the cockpit is especially desirable, since one can extend its top and sides aft to shelter the forward end of the cockpit as well as to protect the companionway.

In the case of a boat with a flush deck, some sort of deckhouse projecting above it is most desirable. In such a design an after cabin almost never makes sense, but doing without one is a reasonable price to pay for a flush deck. A double cabin can be set between the deckhouse and the main cabin, but this is perhaps a waste of space on the widest part of the ship, and no matter how many auxiliary companionways are built, the natural flow of traffic will be right through the cabin. A better idea is to have a double cabin forward of the main cabin, where there is still adequate room and where it can be made into a dead end by using a solid bulkhead to separate it from the forward cabin. If there is not quite enough space for a full-

(TEXT CONTINUED ON PAGE 273)

[X V I]

Two Large Double-Ended Ketches:
ASKOY II & MERGANSER

JUST AS THERE ARE PEOPLE WHO PREFER A castle to a ranch house, so there are sailors who prefer a ship to a mere sailboat. *Askoy II* and *Merganser* are both ships, big, strong, able vessels with plenty of power and spacious accommodations, clearly craft for voyages rather than passages. This impression is reinforced by the intelligent engine rooms that have been provided: engine access is possible even under way, and one need not be a midget or human skeleton to clear a fuel filter or check the dipstick. In both boats the helmsman has been well taken care of, with central cockpits that furnish both protection and visibility. The navigator too is coddled, since *Askoy II* and *Merganser* have centerboards.

But a price has to be paid for all this splendor, and neither *Askoy II* nor *Merganser* is at her best to windward under sail. Their respective designers, Hugo van Kuyck and Colin Mudie, are men of character, and they have in each case pressed forward to the only logical solution to the difficulty of windward performance in a large, shoal-draft vessel meant for a small crew: use the damn engine. So *Askoy II* and *Merganser* are over the line that separates the true sailing yacht with auxiliary power from the motor sailer whose engine is a necessary rather than an optional feature—they are boys, not men; goats, not sheep. However, they are still capable of being sailed properly off the wind, and most cruising, in real life, is done with a fair wind. Boats like these, when well designed (as these are), are easy on their crews, and a man who is no longer as robust as he once was, or who is rather lazier than he should be, can enjoy a shorthanded voyage in one of them that he might not be able even to endure in a more exciting craft.

ASKOY II

SO MANY NICE THINGS HAPPENED TO ME IN Denmark that I always think of that pretty land with affection. One of these nice things was meeting Hugo van Kuyck, the Belgian architect and yacht designer, and seeing his ketch, *Askoy II*. Early in September, 1963, I sailed *Minots Light* to Copenhagen, and as we entered the yacht harbor at Langelinie, a racing shell appeared dead ahead with a crew of lightly clad, robust blonde young ladies. Being

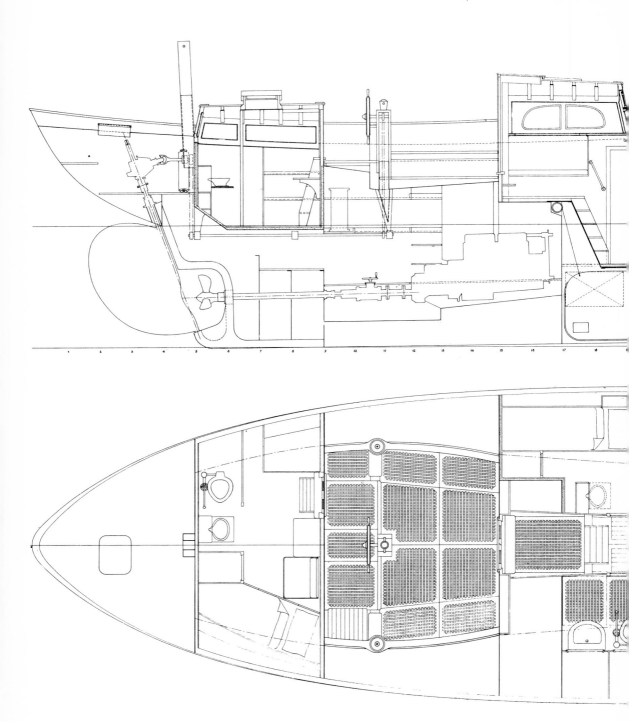

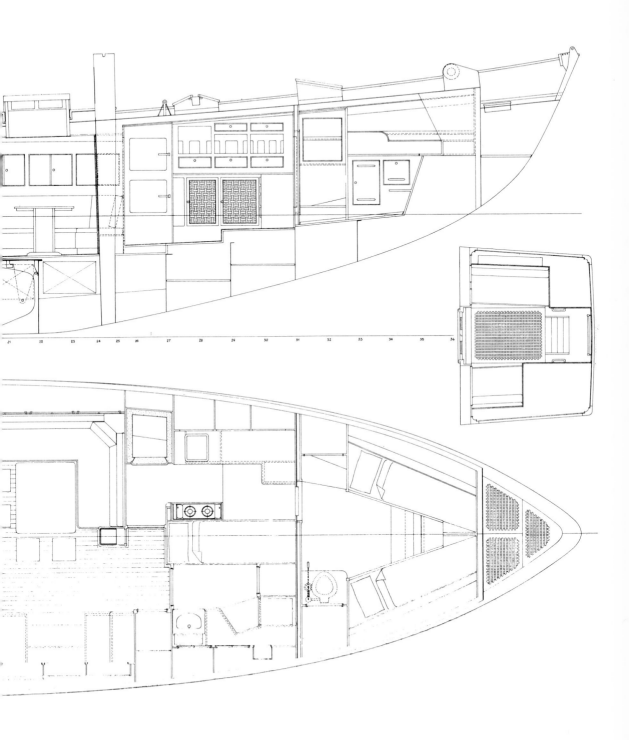

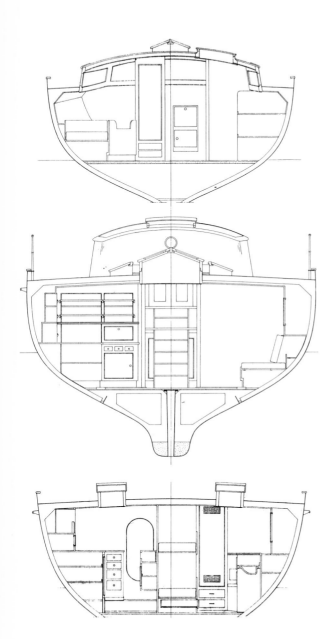

an admirer of good design, I found it hard to take my eyes from them, and when I finally did it was, remarkably enough, only to see before me an almost equally splendid sight, the ketch *Askoy II*. We tied up alongside her, and in due course I became acquainted with her cordial designer and owner, Hugo van Kuyck. Man and boat radiate competence, and I knew that this impression was not mistaken when I had the opportunity to look around the vessel.

Askoy II is solidly built of steel, and her deck, cockpit, and cabin houses are in steel also. The work was so beautifully done that the result is good looking as well as immensely strong and watertight. The cockpit is located well forward of the mizzenmast, and its occupants are protected by high coamings, the after cabin house, and a deckhouse forward; the helmsman has a raised platform to provide him with clear visibility all around. The rig is simple and sturdy, with both masts in tabernacles to permit them to be lowered for inland-waterway cruising. Stowing the dinghy on the forward deck under the boomed forestaysail works out well on a yacht this large, since there is enough room on both sides to get around it.

The main engine, a 100-hp Gardner, is located aft of the centerboard in a roomy compartment reached through a hatch on the starboard side of the cockpit. The engine drives a Hundested three-bladed variable-pitch propeller, a combination of especial value in a boat that is often driven under both sail and power since it makes possible maximum engine efficiency at all times.

The after cabin is fitted out for *Askoy*'s owner with a single berth, a head and folding washbasin, and commodious stowage space. The deckhouse itself is small, but it has seats on either side and a large chart table. A single cabin to port and an enclosed head to starboard are just forward of the deckhouse, and farther forward is a most comfortable main cabin. No

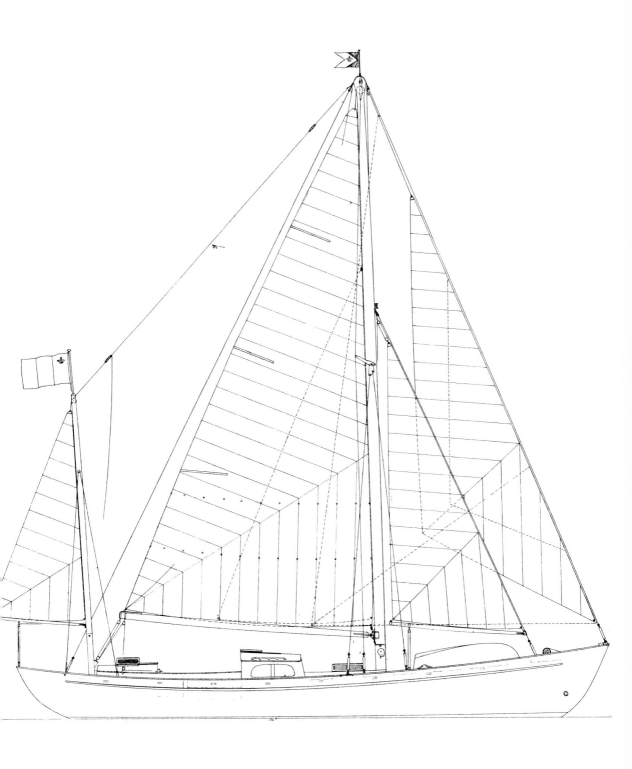

attempt was made to make a dormitory of this cabin, and its spacious air makes it a pleasant place indeed. Forward of the main cabin are a single cabin to starboard and the galley to port; the vertical doors to the refrigerator suggest the designer's faith in *Askoy*'s stability, a faith that has turned out to be justified. The forward cabin has two berths and a head. All together there are five permanent berths, as opposed to the dozen or so that could have been worked in—the proper way to lay out the proper cruising yacht.

ASKOY II

DESIGNER *Hugo van Kuyck, 25 Rue des Capucines, Antwerp, Belgium*

LOA 61 ft 4 in.

LWL 49 ft 3 in.

BEAM 16 ft 2 in.

DRAFT 6 ft 3 in. centerboard up

DISPLACEMENT 80,000 lb

SAIL AREA 1,530 ft²

ENGINE Gardner diesel (100 hp); variable-pitch propeller

CONSTRUCTION All welded steel; spruce spars

MERGANSER

IN *Merganser*, COLIN MUDIE HAS TRIED TO produce a luxury cruiser with high all-weather performance. With fair winds, the snug ketch rig, augmented if need be by a genoa and a whopping mizzen staysail, can send *Merganser* along at a good pace, while in light airs or in a hurry to get to windward, the twin engines come into use. Though *Merganser* is not exactly over-canvased, her hull is easily driven, and an all-inboard rig with a permanent mizzen backstay is well worth some sacrifice in area in a vessel like this. Neither running backstays nor jumper stays are specified, and the upper part of the mast itself is meant to transfer the horizontal component of the headstay load to the permanent backstay at the masthead.

On good days the helmsman sits grandly up high behind the deckhouse, while on bad days he can operate the ship from a steering position in the deckhouse. The twin engines are located in the stern, and their torque is transmitted to the propellers by V-drive units. This arrangement has several advantages to offset the added complexity of the V drives: the engines are up where they can be worked on readily, their noise and smell and fire hazard are effectively contained behind a solid bulkhead, the space they occupy would otherwise be largely wasted, and they permit a lower profile than if located under the deckhouse sole.

The after cabin has a double berth to starboard and a settee to port that converts to a single berth. An enclosed head opens into this cabin, and its top forms the chart table in the deckhouse. The galley is divided into two sections—a "cold galley" to port, with a refrigerator, a double sink, and stowage and working space; and a "hot galley" to starboard, with a stove, a separate oven, and another sink. Two single cabins are forward of the galley, and then comes a pair of enclosed heads, the one to starboard for the guest cabins and the one to

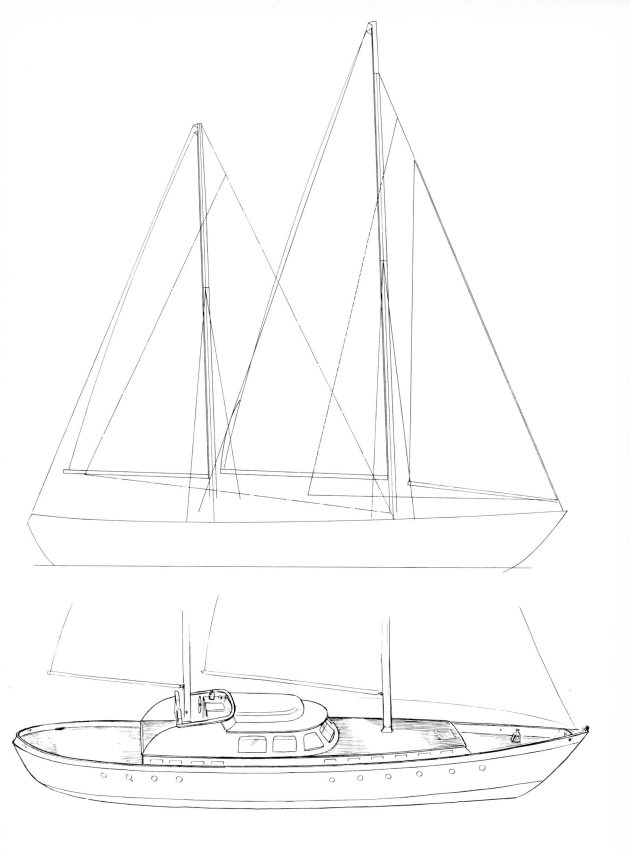

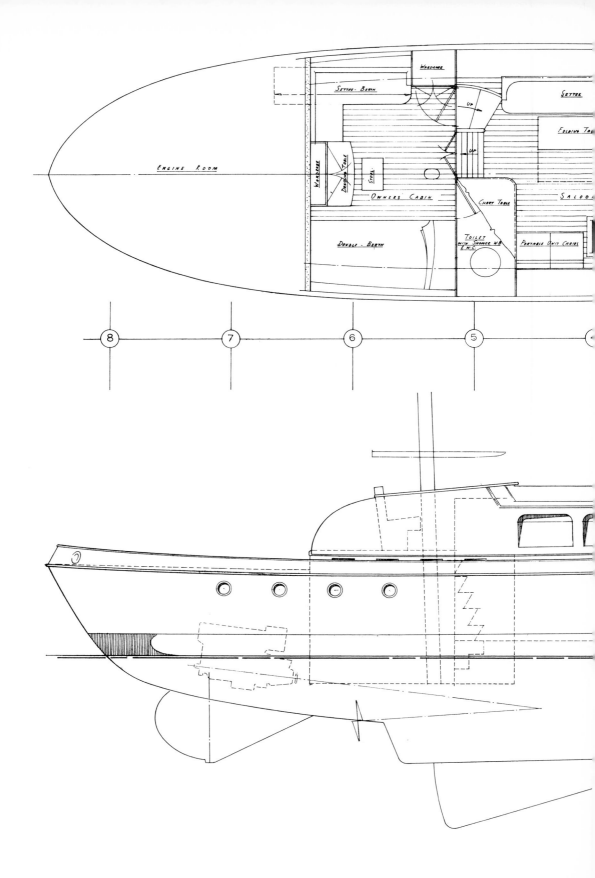

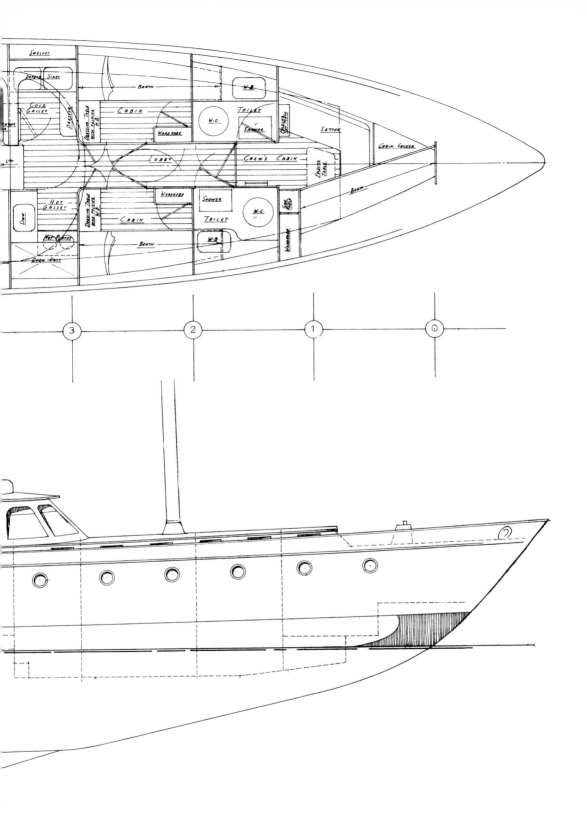

port opening into the forward cabin. This arrangement offers maximum privacy all around, and the deckhouse, with large windows on three sides, provides a common room full of light and air to compensate for the somewhat cramped sleeping quarters.

Merganser

DESIGNER *Colin Mudie, 5 Catherine House, 25–27 Catherine Place, London S.W.1, England*

LOA 52 ft

LWL 44 ft

BEAM 12 ft

DRAFT 4 ft 10 in. centerboard up, 8 ft centerboard down

DISPLACEMENT 50,400 lb

BALLAST 16,800 lb of iron

SAIL AREA 1,000 ft²

ENGINES Two 125-hp diesels

FUEL 400 gal

WATER 200 gal

CONSTRUCTION Laminated cold-molded wooden hull

(TEXT CONTINUED FROM PAGE 262)

length double cabin, it may be possible to have the after ends of the berths in caves that extend aft behind the main cabin settees and under any pilot berths there. A forward cabin bulkheaded off from the rest of the ship should have a head of its own, and if no other place for it can be found, it can be set in a small alcove that extends aft between the berths in the double cabin. What with one expedient or another, a double cabin in the central part of a boat need not take up more than 4 ft of over-all length, and the space between the berths will make up for any restriction in length.

Some yacht architects are men so devoted to their profession that they never sleep, a fact reflected in the berths they design. Far too many sailboat berths are simply appalling at sea, whatever their virtues at boat shows, and this failing is inexcusable since the requirements for a proper bunk are so simple. After all, people have not changed in their dimensions by more than a few inches either way in the past ten thousand years; and even in the dawn of history, nobody ever enjoyed falling out of bed in the middle of the night.

The very first thing a berth must offer is security. It is impossible to get any real rest when one feels about to be hurled rudely on the cabin sole. Any type of berth can be made adequately secure by providing a good leeboard, but it is not easy to alter the width of a berth once it has been built in, and the ability to wedge oneself in place is most valuable. I am a fairly large man (though not, I hope, quite the bloated capitalist yachtsman of the cartoons), but I find more berths to be too wide than too narrow. I think 26 to 27 in. wide at the head and tapering down somewhat at the foot is just about right; 30 in. is definitely too much for comfort at sea, and less than 24 in. is too little for most people for comfort in port. These figures apply only for berths with fixed bottoms and rigid leeboards. A pipe berth 22 in. at the head and 12 in. at the foot is acceptable, and a transom 20 in. wide is all right since it can be extended several inches by a slack canvas leeboard. Of course, the best kind of transom is one that pulls out; it can be narrow for sitting on, moderately wide with a canvas leeboard for sleeping at sea, and still wider in port. But some extension transoms slide in and out far too easily and need some kind of locking scheme if they are not to be bothersome.

A lot of first-class sack time has been spent in berths with canvas rather than wooden bottoms. Pipe and Root berths are old standbys in the forward cabin because they fold up out of the way when not in use, but they are also comfortable and are very secure in a seaway because their inboard sides can be lashed up high enough to retain the occupant no matter what. In fact, more than a few experienced sailors use a version of the pipe berth in the main cabin in place of an extension transom. This consists of a rigid frame with canvas laced to it and a curved bottom that, when hinged up, forms a seat back. Besides being comfortable, such a device permits bedding to be left in place. However, make sure that the curved bottom is deep enough for one to sink into the canvas without a protruding slat or pipe digging into one's ribs. Berths never used for seating—for instance, pilot berths or private cabin berths with seats inboard of them—can with advantage have canvas bottoms, but naturally the canvas must be firmly attached, and attention must be paid to suitably reinforcing the inboard panel to which the canvas is attached since crosspieces cannot be used. This panel will act as a leeboard and as a backrest for the seat beneath the berth, and flying bodies will whack against it now and then, so it should either be of heavier plywood than normal or else have supplementary framing secured to its back.

Leeboards are important. A wooden one should be 8 to 12 in. above the mattress, which makes it hard to get in and out of the berth if there is not much headroom or, if there is plenty of headroom, prevents one from sitting on the berth's edge. One solution is to have the entire board hinged. Another approach is to cut the leeboard down to mattress level for 18 in. or so in the middle and to use a triangular Dacron leeboard that secures overhead in the opening; if the opening is not too wide, the Dacron leeboard will seldom be needed. Dacron leeboards for transom berths should be nearly as long as the berth itself and stoutly made and attached, since quite fundamental loads may be placed upon them, and they should be readily detachable to permit getting out in a hurry. When not in use, the leeboard folds modestly out of sight under the mattress.

Sometimes an otherwise fine cabin arrangement is spoiled by the mast—for instance, when the mast position coincides with a doorway. In vessels of small or moderate size the solution is to step the mast on the cabin house, with plywood bulkheads or steel pillars or both to transmit the thrust to the keel. If the loading is properly taken care of, there is no objection to such a scheme from the point of view of hull structure; it is just a matter of reinforcing the cabin house to take stresses different from those it suffers from a normal mast. However, a mast stepped on deck is definitely less stiff than its twin whose base goes to the keel, and it must be better stayed and made with a correspondingly larger cross section. The effect of a "fixed end" on a column under compression is to enhance the rigidity of the part of the column nearest that end, while a "pin end" has no such effect. For this reason, it makes little sense to step a mast on the keel but to allow it to be free at the deck by not fitting wedges, as is sometimes done. The normal procedure of strengthening the deck and cabin house fore and aft of the mast permits the mast to be held firmly where it emerges without endangering the boat's structure; but the strengthening must be adequate, and plywood bulkheads or steel members running from one side of the boat to the other are best.

The main reason to keep track of details in advance is that it may be easy to provide for them in the design stage but impossible—that is, very expensive—after the boat is built. A case in point is providing for one or two open lockers or racks near the companionway to keep accessible yet out of the way and the weather such items as safety belts, flares, a Freon horn, a wrench or two, an oilcan, tape, and so on. Sometimes the companion ladder can be made a bit narrower to leave room for a series of such racks beside it, or a locker door can be placed so as to be convenient to the companionway instead of to the galley. A binocular rack and a fire extinguisher that can be reached from the deck are also handy in the companion if not provided on deck.

Life jackets for as many people as are likely ever to be aboard are necessary, and provision for their stowage belongs in the plans from the start to keep them from ending up in a hamper in the head or in the forepeak, where they cannot be gotten at quickly in an emergency. Life jackets are best kept below—where they can be put on in safety and will not get wet and perhaps waterlogged or rotten, as they might in a cockpit locker—and should be near the main companionway. While inflatable rubber life jackets occupy less space and can be worn deflated without being in the way, I believe that life jackets with fixed buoyancy in the form of expanded plastic foam or kapok sealed in polyethylene are more reliable in an extreme situation, but the bulk of eight or ten of the latter is not negligible.

Proper stowage space for foul-weather gear—oilskins, sou'westers, seaboots—makes a big difference below in bad weather. Ideally, a locker for this purpose should be near the companionway, since its contents are donned just before going on deck and shed just after coming below. Further, wet oilies bring salt as well as water below, and the less both of them are spread through the accommodation, the pleasanter it will be. Often an open space can be worked in aft of the companion ladder or beside it, and a few large hooks around this space will do nicely. A closed locker is not too good an idea—since the clothing will be wet when put away, and a door will get in the way in any case—but it may be all right if adequate ventilation is provided. A splendid touch is to have the oilie locker close to the engine muffler, which will be raised well above the waterline somewhere aft in any event, so that the locker will be dried out thoroughly each time the engine is run. In the old days when oilies were inflammable, this would have been a lunatic idea, but modern oilies are safe enough in this respect.

It is sometimes handy to have a little locker in some hidden spot that would be quite impossible to find without an X-ray machine. Even with considerable vigilance, suspicious characters may turn up aboard who are usually harmless but not always so, and concealment is always more effective than a mere lock for important papers, money, and other valuables.

It is the little things that usually make the difference between an adequate boat and one that inspires affection. There is, for instance, the matter of adequate handholds in the accommodation. Usually these are absent so as to keep the interior smooth and streamlined, though the advantage of a streamlined cabin is not entirely obvious. One of the first things an experienced sailor adds to a new boat is an overhead grab rail in just the right place to hang on to when making one's way back and forth in a seaway. (It is also useful to hang clothes on to dry.) Another place where a firm handhold is useful is in the head. Some kind of grip in the companionway is good—men have been thrown overboard in the brief interval between releasing their safety belts and getting down below, accidents that might not have happened in the presence of proper handholds. The navigator too appreciates a bar of some kind to steady himself when the boat lurches suddenly. Often these various grab rails can serve double duty—for instance, as anchors for Dacron leeboards. I myself prefer metal tubing set on little chocks so that I can get my fingers around it; a strip of wood on the side of the trunk cabin with only a groove along one edge is hard to get a secure hold on in a hurry. A vertical pillar in the main cabin is splendid if it can be worked in, for instance at one end of the table.

Bottom support for the cook is appreciated. Best of all is a horizontal bar that can be leaned against, perhaps a temporary one across the opening of a U-shaped galley. Sometimes a small seat can be worked in high enough to provide a perch with sink and stove within reach. If the chart table has no regular seat, the navigator too will benefit from a rail of some kind when the boat is on the wrong tack; if this is impossible, a small wooden strip in just the right place on the sole a bit back from the table will help keep him from slipping.

Large glass mirrors are a menace on any boat, particularly if they are mounted on locker or cabin doors. However, a mirror in a strategic position makes a small space seem larger, and few ladies are happy without one aboard somewhere. The solution is a plastic mirror made by silvering a suitable sheet of heavy Plexiglas. Silvering plastic is, I am told, a tricky process that only a few specialists can do, but all airplane mirrors are made this way, and I had no serious trouble finding a shop to make plastic mirrors for my boat. These mirrors reflect a little less light than good glass mirrors, though the difference is not at all apparent in a boat, the coatings tend to peel off at the edges (at least mine do), and they are expensive to have made—all in all, a reasonable price to pay for their total safety.

The tropical voyager will smile at the topic, but some means of heating the accommodation is often valuable. A coal- or charcoal-burning stove or fireplace has the substantial merits of safety and simplicity, and an open fire is a cheerful sight indeed on a cold night. But it is not always easy to find stowage space for a sufficient supply of fuel, and the heating apparatus may take a while to do its stuff. At the other pole, kerosene or diesel-oil hot-air heating plants are effective and quick on the trigger, and fuel presents no problems, but they are complicated gadgets that have been known to fail at just the wrong time. Somewhere in between are catalytic heaters, Sterno stoves, and the like, whose proper role is, I suspect, more as a supplement to a built-in heating system than as a replacement.

In a small cabin I am impressed with the heating ability of an ordinary kerosene lamp. While it will make nobody toasty, it can take the chill from the September air on the Maine coast. (It is imperative to have a smoke bell or its equivalent over the chimney, since the heat produced is concentrated there and may easily damage paint or woodwork above it.)

My own preference is for a solid-fuel stove, despite its deficiencies, because the very worst that can happen is merely that it is a bit of a bother to get a fire going in it. A little alcohol helps here, either in the form of alcohol-soaked sawdust cakes (which are sold for lighting fires in ordinary fireplaces) or as a liquid (which is poured over charcoal briquettes that are allowed to stand for a few minutes before being ignited). I package briquettes in small paper bags ashore, and they create no mess whatever on board. A variety of suitable stoves and fireplaces exist, but for some reason many of their makers prefer to hide their lights under bushels and one may never find the perfect stove even though it is made virtually next door. A case in point is the Pansy stove made by Pascall Atkey of Cowes: though it is a lovely little affair, light in weight and easy to install, many yachtsmen who would find it ideal have never heard of it. (An invaluable adjunct to a Pansy is a piece of steam hose in place of a smoke head. My own Pansy, installed in an after cabin, was a flop until the hose was used; it bends to leeward and encourages a proper draft.) In this connection, catalogs from Great Britain and Scandinavia may be useful, since it can be cool in that part of the world even in summer, and many different stoves are in use there. However, the familiar Tiny Tim stove and the Maiwald soapstone fireplace are hard to beat.

Ventilation is also essential for pleasant cruising—as much in inclement weather, when hatches and ports are kept shut, as on hot, sunny days. Every cabin deserves a waterproof ventilator whether or not it is also fitted with one or more opening ports. The latter have limited utility because they admit water as well as air, sometimes quite a bit of water. The Dorade ventilator (so named for the yawl *Dorade,* in which it was fitted by Rod and Olin Stephens) consists of a box fed by by a cowl whose pipe extends about halfway down. An adjacent pipe leads from just below the top of the box to the cabin underneath. The box has one or two scuppers on each side to drain away any water entering the cowl, while air can flow to or from the cabin with little impediment. This is a fine device and works well (too well according to my wife, who has one over her berth), but care must be taken to be sure that it is securely fastened; the whole system of box plus protruding vent must be able to take green water or a man's weight hurled against it. Often Dorade ventilators are permanently screened with a fine mesh, which gets clogged with dust and dirt until no air can get through; removable screens are better. A transparent plastic top on a Dorade box lets in light as well as air, which in certain locations is a welcome touch, especially so in the case of a flush deck.

Skylights are inefficient and leaky devices that add elegance to the exterior and a feeling of spaciousness to the interior of a yacht. A properly hinged hatch with a transparent top of Plexiglas lets in more light and air and has the advantage that things and people can pass through it. In a cabin that is not especially cramped, I think such a hatch is preferable to a skylight. On the other hand, if one has, say, a snug after cabin with not quite enough headroom, a skylight will enlarge it visually and provide the needed headroom without detracting from the appearance of the yacht on the outside. A skylight must be strongly constructed and integrated into the cabin-house or deck framing, not just screwed in place, and metal bars should protect the glass. A good trick is to stow a transparent- or translucent-bottomed plastic dinghy over the skylight. A canvas cover with transparent inserts is absolutely necessary for every skylight at sea—sooner or later water will find its way in otherwise. There is a contemporary tendency to condemn the skylight to oblivion because it is indifferent at performing its official functions and tends to leak besides, but it can at times mean the difference between a dismal cabin without headroom and a pleasant one in which a man can stand erect, and in such cases it is worth considering.

When a flush deck is used, no opportunity should be overlooked to admit light below. Prismatic deck lights admit a surprising amount of light, and several of them, strategically placed, add to the cheer below. They do a better job than circular deadlights of plate glass and do not affect privacy. However, they are still vastly less effective than windows set in the topsides themselves. Glass of considerable strength is made today, and there is no reason why such windows need compromise hull strength or integrity in any way if properly installed, although their framing may add a trifle to weight above the waterline. The 57-ft aluminum yawl *Ondine* has two windows in her hull on each side and has sailed a hundred thousand miles or so since her construction without a catastrophe. Smaller boats have also had windows in their hulls and been the better for them—in fact, several classes of fiberglass boats of all sizes from about 30 ft overall on up sport windows in their

[OVERLEAF] *A sail to windward in a good breeze aboard a fine, fast yacht like* CAPRICIA *is as glorious an experience as any to be found in this world. No one who has enjoyed a sail like this can ever again be content with puttering about in a slow, ugly tub. Seventy-two feet of varnished mahogany perfection,* CAPRICIA *is too large to be ideal as a short-handed cruiser, but she cannot be faulted on the other relevant grounds of beauty, speed, ability, and comfort. Olin Stephens, her designer, is at the helm in the photograph.* (Beken)

topsides. As in all aspects of yacht design, of course, careful choice of size and position will enhance the beauty of the boat, while a poor choice in this regard may make the vessel appear grotesque. But at its best, a hull window will add a discreet touch of visual interest, even glamour, to a flush-decker, and nobody aboard who has merely to raise himself on an elbow in his bunk to look outside will regret its presence.

Two or three decades ago, when paid hands were normally carried on cruising yachts of any size, the galley was invariably located forward of the main cabin, where it helped insulate the crew's quarters from the rest of the accommodation. Except in a fairly large boat—say, 60 ft long overall at least—this is a poor idea, since the motion forward of the mast when under way makes cooking there difficult and unpleasant. Further, when the cook is a nonprofessional, a galley aft means that he can carry out his most essential tasks without being isolated from the rest of the ship's company. Ventilation is better aft, especially in bad weather, and it is easier to pass up hot soup and sandwiches at midnight from an after galley without disturbing the watch below. The arguments for a galley aft of the main cabin in a cruising yacht are overwhelming. However, it is not necessarily desirable that the galley be sited adjacent to the companionway, though in small vessels there may be no alternative. Quarter berths can be valuable, the chart table has more claim to proximity to the cockpit, and so on. It is best to arrange things so that the flow of traffic bypasses the galley and, in particular, so that it is not necessary to sit in the sink in order to pull on seaboots if the cabin berths are occupied.

Too large a galley is bad, because the cook cannot then wedge himself in place while at work. A U-shaped galley with 6 to 8 ft^2 of floor space is ideal, but much good eating has had its origin in galleys of other shapes and sizes. Still, it is worth some effort to see that the galley is in a stable part of the ship and that the cook has help in keeping himself out of the stew.

A two-burner gimbaled stove is rock bottom on a cruiser, and the optimum is a stove with three or four burners and a good oven. Of course, a lot depends on the standard of cuisine that is contemplated, but there is no reason to handicap the cook from the start. I can think of few more welcome treats on a damp, cold day on passage than a freshly baked cake, nor can I think of many other things that give as much pleasure for as little effort if the proper equipment is at hand. Some elaborate stoves require considerable space, while others are more compact; the Hiller stove, for example, packs three burners and a small oven in a volume not much greater than that required by most two-burner stoves.

Kerosene—once, with coal, the standard galley fuel in yachts—is seldom specified any more for a number of reasons that outweigh its cheapness and universal availability: kerosene stoves are hard to light, tend to burn with a smoky flame, and are smelly, while accidental kerosene fires are not easy to extinguish. Alcohol stoves, long popular in America, are also gaining favor elsewhere. The merit of alcohol as a cooking fuel lies chiefly in its safety. However, alcohol stoves are inconvenient to use, since the burners must be preheated, and the heat they produce is less than that obtainable from other fuels. Alcohol is also expensive, though not prohibitively so, and is sometimes hard to get. But alcohol does not explode, and alcohol fires can be put out with water, splendid attributes for any fuel. To be sure, galley fires are not exactly unknown with alcohol stoves and are not always entirely humorous events, but at any rate the boat cannot be blown up as a result. And alcohol burns cleanly and leaves no smell behind, in contrast to kerosene.

Still, solid fuels are even safer than alcohol, but they are sensible only in boats destined for cruising in cold climates. Alcohol is simply more convenient, so the slight increase in hazard is acceptable. But alcohol stoves are not really adequate in large cruising boats that are lived aboard for extended periods, so it is a question of how much further hazard is acceptable in order to make the cook's life easier. Big vessels can use stoves that burn diesel oil, which are too heavy and bulky for most sailboats less than about 65 ft long overall. Sad to say, such stoves can usually be fitted with an internal hot-water boiler, which would make life that much more pleasant without adding to its complexity. However, diesel oil seems out of the question for most boats capable of being sailed by two people.

What an increasing number of yachtsmen have come to use is bottled gas, either propane or butane. Propane has the higher heat content, but in some parts of the world it is harder to obtain. Both are used in stoves almost identical with ordinary home gas stoves, and they furnish hot, clean flames that every woman appreciates. No preheating, no galley fires, no trouble in making a quick cup of coffee or roasting a turkey at sea with bottled gas—but every year it manages to blow up a certain number of boats. However, care and intelligence can reduce the danger of explosion to virtually nil without making gas cooking less efficient or convenient, so even the prudent man should not dismiss it out of hand.

In my first three boats, I installed alcohol stoves and had no serious trouble with them; that is, they tended to be a pain in the neck at times, but I always felt that they were basically benign affairs, and I could soothe my wife after the weekly conflagrations with the reminder that alcohol was the safest fuel to use. When I acquired my current boat, it had a bottled-gas installation, and my first impulse was to rip it out and put in another alcohol stove. However, this would have meant rebuilding the galley as well as buying a new stove, so that no money would be left for certain rather urgent repairs, and both my wife and I were curious about just how marvelous gas was anyway. So we agreed to leave the stove in temporarily— and it is still there, as are we.

In Europe, bottled gas is very widely used on yachts for refrigeration and cabin heating as well as for cooking. The normal practice there is to install the gas bottles below, not on deck. While twenty thousand miles of sailing with a bottled-gas stove has convinced me that it indeed has virtues that are worth the slight but nagging feeling of insecurity it induces, I don't think I could ever get used to having both the bottles in my lap and a gas-operated refrigerator with a pilot light. But thousands of European sailors have no such timidities, though they do seem to blow themselves up a bit more frequently than their American counterparts do.

I think there is no question that proper safety measures and an awareness of the problem can reduce the explosion hazard to an acceptable minimum in most boats that employ gasoline and/or bottled gas. What I find interesting is the relative degrees of danger that different observers attribute to these fuels. I know a number of sailors who blanch at the thought of bottled gas, though their alcohol stoves are no more than inches away from the gasoline engines that they regard with equanimity. My insurance company, on the other hand, gives me a reduced premium because I carry no gasoline, though it would provide no bonus at all for the absence of bottled gas. I personally agree with them in the sense that I believe propane to be less explosive than gasoline and a bottled-gas system to be much easier to make safe than a gasoline engine. If the bottles are secured on deck or in a locker that drains overboard, if the tubing runs unbroken from the regulator valve at the bottles to a proper valve at the stove that is always closed when the stove is not actually being used, if a leak detector is installed in the bilge under the galley with another bilge sensor under the entry of the gas tube, and if the bottle valves are always closed in bad weather at sea and when the boat is unoccupied, I see no reason not to enjoy the considerable advantages of gas cooking in a large boat. In a small boat, though, alcohol still seems the best choice.

Though most household "conveniences" are anything but convenient on a sailboat once the honeymoon is over and they have started to rust and develop short and open circuits, a distinct exception should be made in the case of a refrigerator. Tracking down ice and then lugging it aboard are among the least pleasant chores connected with cruising, but extended cruising without fresh food and cold beer is not much fun either. A proper refrigeration system means that a freezer is possible as well as a cold box; and if correctly installed, such a system can be entirely reliable. Absorption refrigerators that burn kerosene or bottled gas work well provided that the boat's motion and angle of heel are not excessive, but they also pose a certain hazard. A mechanical refrigerator that uses seawater in a heat exchanger to cool the refrigerant is both safe and efficient, although not cheap, and will work regardless of the boat's orientation. The compressor can be powered by an electric motor or by being belted directly to the propulsion engine. The former is the better scheme in a boat that has an independent generator, since in port one need not run the main engine just for the sake of the refrigerator. With only a single engine, one can install an oversize compressor and a large cold plate in the box to permit a single daily run of an hour or so that will do the trick. Nobody who has ever cruised extensively aboard a yacht with a refrigerator and freezer that worked would ever dream of trying to do without them, and it is not that difficult these days to have them built in.

An enclosed head is a necessity on any proper cruising yacht. The usual location is forward of the main cabin, though if there is a deckhouse as well, a good spot is between the deckhouse and the main cabin. A point to be kept in mind is the height of the washbasin: if the basin drains directly overboard, its bottom should be well above the design waterline, since the actual waterline in cruising trim may be several inches higher. I dislike sump tanks, which can give trouble at the wrong time; if a low sink is inevitable, I prefer a small pump on its drain, with no intermediate tank. An enclosed head should be large enough to turn around in but need not be much larger than that, since any advantages of more space in port are canceled out by reduced security at sea. Small bins or drawers are a convenience in the head; each member of the crew can keep his toilet articles there instead of having to dig for them elsewhere—a little thing, but worth keeping in mind.

A real shower is scarcely possible in sailboats less than 55 to 60 ft long overall, but a grating sole in the head compartment makes it possible to have a shower head mounted there. Just how good such a shower is in practice is debatable, but it is inexpensive if a pressure-water system is already fitted. With a hot-water system as well, I think a shower is a good idea, although otherwise I suspect that most people will prefer a washcloth and a basin of hot water.

In addition to a head in its own enclosed compartment, a cruising boat of any size should have another one somewhere else. This is partly as a convenience and partly as insurance. Several extremely compact yet robust heads are on the market that are too small for the throne room yet just the right size to fit into the triangle between the berths in the forward cabin, for example. If it can be managed, it is nice to have this head in a place where it can be used without disturbing the berths, but it is worth having even if it has to be housed under a removable piece of mattress or a pipe berth.

Marine toilets for some years have shown themselves to be sturdy, efficient, and reliable devices. I understand that a noted American yacht designer has been devoting part of his later years to a thorough study of the proper size, shape, and construction of the bucket head, but I feel sure that he is a few generations tardy in this endeavor. Even the most fervent exponent of simplicity would not offend his conscience by having a mechanical head. All books on boating stress that head inlets and outlets should have sea cocks and that the waste line should run above the waterline in a loop vented at the top, which is perfectly true, but I have never seen a sailboat head without such safety precautions. However, I have seen, and have had to fight with, heads so installed as to be impossible to disassemble easily when clogged or otherwise causing trouble. It is all very well to put up a big sign warning people not to throw bobby pins, carpet sweepings, and bath towels into the head, but these and a number of objects that delicacy keeps off the sign are still able—indeed, eager—to foul up the works; and in any case, accidents can always happen. I have even seen a head that must have been bolted in place at the very start of construction, before the hull was planked, because there was no way at all to gain access to the nuts underneath. Naturally, access to the head's mechanism was through the baseplate. So it can happen, and I suggest that one actually disassemble each head in a new boat at the beginning in order to be sure that it can be done.

Another precaution is to avoid a continuous metal pipe between head and sea cock that has a vent tube simply screwed into the pipe. Such pipes not only are the devil to clear if clogged but also tend to acquire deposits that narrow their internal diameters. This is not just a hypothetical danger: a deposit accumulating at the rate of $\frac{1}{16}$ in. per year, not an uncommon rate, means real trouble after a half-dozen years. The best scheme is to couple the head to an inverted vented metal U and the U to the sea cock with strong plastic or rubber hose. With this setup, deposits will be unlikely, and the entire discharge line can be disassembled readily if necessary.

Snooping around boatyards and marinas often turns up interesting ideas. The Nicholson-designed sloop ROCQUETTE *in the foreground has more than her share. Visible are the box at the base of the mast for rope falls and winch handles, abrasive strips glued on the plastic hatch cover, low-profile snagproof ventilators on the foredeck, internal trip wires on the aluminum spinnaker poles that emerge only a foot from either end, a small reel winch for the main boom downhaul, and Tufnol rollers on the shrouds that offer less windage than wooden ones and require no maintenance. The lifeline stanchions are set inboard from the rail to permit the genoa to be sheeted more effectively; less desirable for racing but better for cruising is to have the stanchions fastened to the rail as well as the deck for more strength. The high camber to the deck gives headroom below while making possible a flush deck in a yacht only 40 feet overall. In the background is an Alden* CHALLENGER *yawl.* (Beiser)

[X V I I]

Sailing in Style:

MINOTS LIGHT

LATE IN THE SPRING OF 1957, MY FAMILY and I set out from Mamaroneck, New York, for a passage to Maine, the first of our cruises to that enchanted coast. We were aboard the cutter *Nipinke,* which was designed by the late Ralph Winslow and built in 1935 by the Quincy Adams yard in Massachusetts. Only 28 ft long overall, *Nipinke* was on the small side, but she was pretty to look at and fun to sail—and all we could afford, anyway. On the way Down East, we stopped in at Padanaram, Massachusetts, and in the fleet of fine yachts moored there, one stood out immediately, the ketch *Minots Light.* I still recall sailing around her when we entered the harbor, and I would probably still be doing so if the club steward had not come out in his launch to show us to a guest mooring. I stared at *Minots Light* through binoculars the rest of the afternoon, and the more I looked, the more perfect she seemed. Somehow we managed to leave Padanaram the next day, but though the years went by and the larger sloop *Petrouchka* replaced *Nipinke,* I still remembered *Minots Light* fondly and dwelt longingly on her occasional mentions in the yachting press.

The Sunday after Thanksgiving of 1960, I happened to be at City Island to check that all was well with *Petrouchka,* which had been hauled out there, and I learned two interesting things. First, my old flame *Minots Light* was also at City Island for the winter, and, second, she had just then been put up for sale. As if by reflex, my hand went to my checkbook, and the deposit was in the broker's hands within ten minutes of my learning of her availability. I never made a wiser decision, and even today I tremble when I think of the half-dozen would-be buyers who turned up the following week. In due course a surveyor pronounced *Minots Light* fit, *Petrouchka* went on the market, and I went into hock up to my ears.

Minots Light was designed by John G. Alden & Co., Inc., as a development of *Malabar XIII,* the last of the *Malabar* series of John Alden's personal yachts. She was beautifully and soundly built in 1951 by Abeking and Rasmussen of Lemwerder, Germany, with a hull of welded steel, teak decks, deck structures of mahogany, spruce spars, stainless-steel rigging, Monel and stainless-steel tanks, a General Motors 3-71 diesel engine—everything of the best. Since she was built, a number of improvements have been made, both by the original owner and by me: added were ten winches of various kinds (including a powerful two-speed Nevins winch on the stern for sheeting the genoa—and even more useful in canal locks and for berthing in a crosswind), for a total of seventeen; a large freezer and separate refrigerator; a diesel auxiliary generator; all sorts

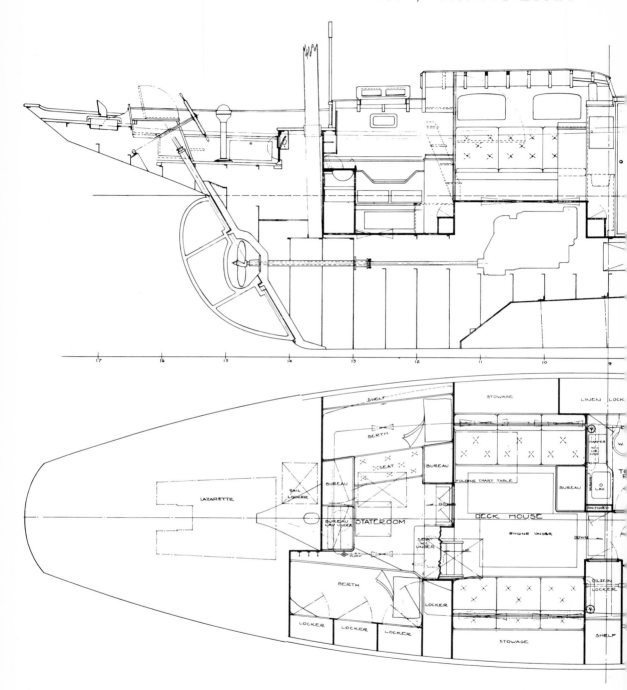

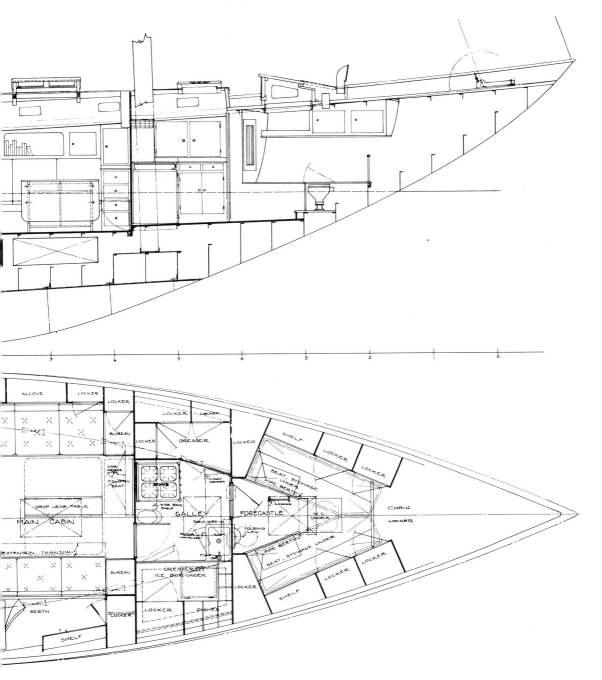

of electronic gear; a more practical main-cabin layout; an after pulpit; and so on and on. As a result of all of the care and money that has been lavished on her, *Minots Light* today comes very close to being the perfect cruising yacht. She is good looking (the more so since I have had her topsides painted black), fast under sail and power, easy to handle with a small crew, seaworthy and sea-kindly, inordinately comfortable at sea and in port—and I say all this after five years and twenty thousand miles of cruising on both sides of the Atlantic.

MINOTS LIGHT *on the slip ready for launching in the spring. Her hull is constructed of welded steel and is immensely strong.* (Beiser)

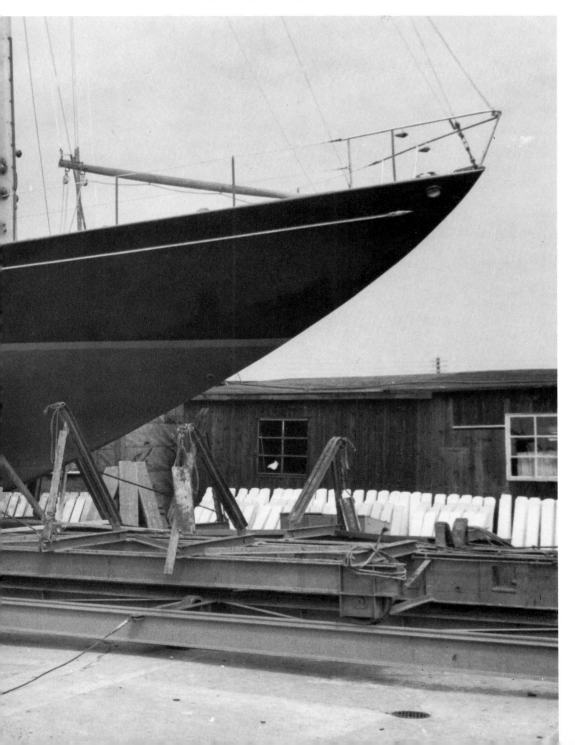

The great virtue of a ketch is that even the largest sail is moderate in size relative to the size of the vessel. A small crew can handle the 58-ft Alden ketch MINOTS LIGHT efficiently in all conditions; in these photographs, she is being sailed by the author, his wife, and a boy. The mainsail, mizzen, and furled forestaysail are of reddish-brown Terylene. (Byfield)

MINOTS LIGHT *in mid-Atlantic. The deck boxes on the starboard side of the cabin house hold docking lines, jib sheets, snatch blocks, an anchor davit, and other gear. An inflatable life raft stows between the deck boxes and the deckhouse, and the 9-ft molded-plywood dinghy is upright in chocks on the port side of the cabin house. The small deck box just aft of the mast holds a 360-ft anchor rode of 1-in. nylon; 200 ft of ½-in. chain stows down below and leads directly to the anchor winch, which is just forward of the ventilator in the foreground. The anchors normally are kept in chocks on either side of the forward companionway but were stowed in the bilge for the Atlantic passage. A Dacron dodger is laced to the lifelines and pulpit aft to help protect the cockpit.* (Beiser)

Why, then, in view of all this splendor, do I say that *Minots Light* merely "comes very close" to being the perfect cruiser? For one thing, there is no shelter for the helmsman in really unpleasant weather—a lack I hardly was aware of in American waters, but one that a North Sea gale and a hailstorm in the Bay of Biscay off La Coruña brought out very clearly. Such shelter is not easy to arrange in a ketch with a cockpit aft, but I am working on a removable folding hood with plastic inserts that I hope may do the trick. For another, the penalty of a big boat is deep draft, which bars putting in at many attractive harbors and canals. *Minots Light*'s draft of 7 ft 9 in. is not large for a boat of her size, but I would be much happier if it were 2 ft less (in which case a centerboard would be necessary, and whether

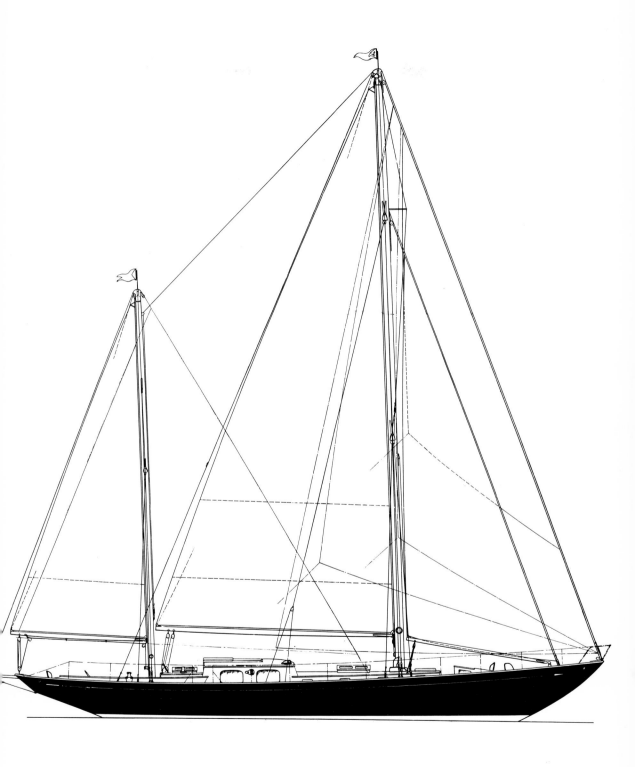

the new problems this would entail are worth the advantage of reduced draft I cannot say, but I would like to find out). The size and weight of the boat in themselves are no handicap, by the way; my wife and I have managed *Minots Light* by ourselves under a variety of conditions, and for all except long offshore passages, we take a crew of only one. In return, we have plenty of space and a sense of accomplishment, which are lacking when we race with a dozen on board. The third and last impediment to perfection is maintenance. With her perfect sheer, black topsides, gold cove stripe, teak decks, varnished-mahogany cabin sides, varnished-spruce spars, and reddish-brown sails (the only white on deck is found in the Dacron cordage), I like to think that *Minots Light* is as handsome a yacht as can be. But, except for the sails (and the sheer), all this beauty has to be kept up, and there are times when it is a nuisance. *Petrouchka* was all fiberglass with aluminum spars, and all she ever needed was a good scrubbing . . . but I have never seen a fiberglass boat that looked nearly as well as *Minots Light*. Because there are so many irreconcilabilities in the design and construction of a yacht, it is probably impossible to have a wholly perfect one, but *Minots Light* comes as close to the ideal as any that I know of.

MINOTS LIGHT *at anchor in Finland. The high cockpit sides furnish both comfort and protection. The curved box behind the wheel is a backrest for the helmsman, an alternative raised seat for small helmsmen, or a repository for binoculars, flashlight, and so on. Under the wheel is the automatic-pilot control box. The powerful Nevins winch on the counter is as useful in docking as it is for sheeting the genoa.* (Beiser)

MINOTS LIGHT

DESIGNER   *John G. Alden & Co., Inc., 131 State Street, Boston, Massachusetts*

LOA   58 ft 1 in.
LWL   42 ft 9 in.
BEAM   14 ft 3 in.
DRAFT   7 ft 9 in.
DISPLACEMENT   64,000 lb
SAIL AREA   1,518 ft²

ENGINE   General Motors 3-71 diesel (100 hp)
FUEL   185 gal
WATER   235 gal
CONSTRUCTION   Welded-steel hull; teak deck and mahogany deckworks; stainless-steel rigging; spruce spars

MISCELLANEOUS DATA

Performance: Under sail, highest verified speed, 10.4 knots for thirteen miles; average speed for cruising passage across Atlantic, 6.5 knots. Under power, maximum speed, 9 knots; usual cruising speed, 8 knots; most economical speed, 6.2 knots, when range is about eight hundred miles.

Rig: For shorthanded passages, usual rig is boomed forestaysail, jib topsail, main, mizzen, and, when wind permits, mizzen staysail. The running backstays are not needed except in strong winds. If the weather deteriorates, one or more sails are handed; reefing has never been necessary, and it is very seldom necessary to change headsails since the foretriangle is not large for the size of the boat. For day sailing and well-crewed passages, genoa and spinnaker are available and are both helpful and fun in light airs. (The forestay is set up with a lever and can be temporarily detached to facilitate tacking the genoa.)

Ground tackle: Three anchors are carried— a 35-lb Danforth, a 60-lb Danforth, and a 100-lb yachtsman's. The three cables consist of 200 ft of ½-in. chain, 360 ft of 1-in. nylon, and 150 ft of ¾-in. nylon. Normally the 60-lb Danforth is used with the chain. The light Danforth and the ¾-in. line are useful for temporary anchoring and for kedging off when aground. The yachtsman's anchor is rarely needed. A powerful and reliable Ideal electric windlass is indispensable, and a removable davit makes it possible for one man to get any of the anchors aboard without scarring the topsides paint.

Galley: The stove has four burners plus built-in oven and broiler; it is not gimbaled, but the boat is stiff enough for this seldom to be a handicap. Two 42-lb-capacity propane cylinders are carried in a deck box, and in normal cruising with two or three adults and three children, each one lasts about six weeks. Getting refills has never yet been a problem in the United States or in Europe, though in some countries only butane is available. A Sniffer, made by Johnson-Williams, was installed to detect gas leaks. The freezer holds about 110 lb of frozen meat, and to keep it frozen requires running either the main engine or the auxiliary generator for perhaps an hour a day unless shore current is available. The power requirement depends, of course, on the air and water temperatures at the time. The refrigerator has a capacity about that of an ordinary household unit. Enough fresh and frozen food can be carried for a crew of seven for an Atlantic passage, with another month's worth of canned and otherwise preserved food in reserve.

LIST OF DESIGNERS

John G. Alden & Company, Inc.   *Challenger, Lady Helene, Margaree,*
131 State Street   *Minots Light*
Boston, Massachusetts

Camper & Nicholsons, Ltd.   *Nicholson 32*
Southampton, England

William Garden   *Porpoise, Discovery*
3040 West Commodore Way
Seattle, Washington

Laurent Giles, & Partners, Ltd.   *Cardhu, Riwaru, Pazienza*
4 Quay Hill
Lymington, England

Cyrus Hamlin   *Wanderer*
Manset, Maine

Illingworth & Primrose   *Le Quarante Pieds, Melusine II, Outlaw*
36 North Street
Emsworth, England

Paul A. Kettenberg   *K-43, Thunderbird, K-50*
2810 Carleton Street
San Diego, California

Hugo van Kuyck   *Askoy II*
25 Rue des Capucines
Antwerp, Belgium

MacLear & Harris   *Seabreeze, Angantyr*
366 Madison Avenue
New York, New York

Colin Mudie
5 Catherine House
25–27 Catherine Place
London S.W.1, England

Mahanui, Merganser

Walter F. Rayner, Ltd.
22 Parkstone Road
Poole, England

Atlantic

Philip L. Rhodes
369 Lexington Avenue
New York, New York

Reliant, Gouden Draak

Arthur Robb
20D New Cavendish Street
London W.1, England

Bluebird of Thorne, Renown, Manukai

Sparkman & Stephens, Inc.
79 Madison Avenue
New York, New York

Alnair, Simba, The Clarion of Wight, Giralda

E. G. van de Stadt
Zuiddijk 412
Zaandam, Holland

Excalibur, Glass Slipper

Aage Utzon
Hellebaek, Denmark

Lene, Dandy

Bruno Veronese
Via Capo Santa Chiara 25
Genoa, Italy

Coppelia, Clio

INDEX

INDEX